"Mounting evidence indicates that refined carbohydrates and high glycemic index foods are contributing to the escalating epidemics of obesity and type 2 diabetes worldwide. This dietary pattern also appears to increase the risk of heart disease and stroke. The skyrocketing proportion of calories from added sugars and refined carbohydrates in westernized diets portends a future acceleration of these trends. *The Glucose Revolution* challenges traditional doctrines about optimal nutrition and the role of carbohydrates in health and disease. Brand-Miller and colleagues are to be congratulated for an eminently lucid and important book that explains the science behind the glycemic index and provides tools and strategies for modifying diet to incorporate this knowledge. I strongly recommend the book to both health professionals and the general public who could use this state-of-the-art information to improve health and well-being."

—JoAnn E. Manson, MD, DrPH, Professor of Medicine, Harvard Medical School, and Co-Director of Women's Health, Division of Preventive Medicine, Brigham and Women's Hospital

"Here is at last a book explaining the importance of taking into consideration the glycemic index of foods for overall health, athletic performance, and in reducing the risk of heart disease and diabetes. The book clearly explains that there are different kinds of carbohydrates that work in different ways and why a universal recommendation to "increase the carbohydrate content of your diet" is plainly simple and scientifically inaccurate. Everyone should put the glycemic index approach into practice."

—Artemis P. Simopoulos, MD,
senior author of *The Omega Diet* and
The Healing Diet and President, The Center for
Genetics, Nutrition and Health, Washington, DC,
on *The Glucose Revolution*

"*The Glucose Revolution* is nutrition science for the 21st century. Clearly written, it gives the scientific rationale for why all carbohydrates are not created equal. It is a practical guide for both professionals and patients. The food suggestions and recipes are exciting and tasty."

—Richard N. Podell, MD, MPH, Clinical
Professor, Department of Family Medicine,
UMDNJ-Robert Wood Johnson Medical School,
and co-author of *The G-Index Diet: The Missing
Link That Makes Permanent Weight Loss Possible*

"Although the jury is still out on the utility of the glycemic index, many of the curious will benefit from a careful reading of this book, and some will find that the glycemic index is particularly helpful for them. Everyone can enjoy the recipes, some of which are to die for!"

—Johanna Dwyer, DSc, RD, editor of
Nutrition Today, on *The Glucose Revolution*

"The glycemic index is a useful tool which may have a broad spectrum of applications, from the maintenance of fuel supply during exercise to the control of blood glucose levels in diabetics. Low glycemic index foods may prove to have beneficial health effects for all of us in the long term. *The Glucose Revolution* is a user-friendly, easy-to-read overview of all that you need to know about the glycemic index. This book represents a balanced account of the importance of the glycemic index based on sound scientific evidence."

—James Hill, PhD, Director,
Center for Human Nutrition, University of
Colorado Health Sciences Center

The New GLUCOSE REVOLUTION

The New GLUCOSE REVOLUTION

The Authoritative Guide to the Glycemic Index—The Dietary Solution for Permanent Weight Loss

Jennie Brand-Miller, PhD

Thomas M.S. Wolever, MD, PhD

Stephen Colagiuri, MD

Kaye Foster-Powell, M Nutr & Diet

RODALE

© 2005 by Jennie Brand-Miller, PhD; Thomas M.S. Wolever, MD, PhD; Stephen Colagiuri, PhD; and Kaye Foster-Powell

Printed in the United States of America
Rodale Inc. makes every effort to use acid-free ∞, recycled paper ♺.

Parts of this book have previously been published as *The New Glucose Revolution*, revised and expanded edition (Marlowe and Company, 2002); *The New Glucose Revolution Life Plan* (Marlowe and Company, 2004); and *The New Glucose Revolution Pocket Guide to Diabetes*, 2nd revised and expanded edition (Marlowe and Company, 2003).

ISBN–13 978–1–59486–691–3
ISBN–10 1–59486–691–0

2   4   6   8   10   9   7   5   3   1   hardcover

RODALE
LIVE YOUR WHOLE LIFE™

We inspire and enable people to improve their lives and the world around them
For more of our products visit **rodalestore.com** or call 800-848-4735

Contents

Part 3

The Glycemic Index and You

Part 4

The Glycemic Index Tables

Introduction

The right kind of carbohydrate can make an important contribution to the quality of your life: That was the essential message of the original edition of this book, and now, in *The New Glucose Revolution*, that message is more relevant to more people than ever before.

The New Glucose Revolution is about the glycemic index, which is simply a measure of carbohydrate quality—the degree to which the carbohydrates in different foods will raise blood-glucose levels. A knowledge and appreciation of the glycemic index will help you choose the right amount of carbohydrate and the right sort of carbohydrate for your health and well-being. The glycemic index—and its newer companion value, the glycemic load, which we discuss in this book—is relevant for everyone. People with diabetes, heart disease, the metabolic syndrome (Syndrome X), or an interest in controlling their weight will gain the most from putting into practice the findings and recommendations of *The New Glucose Revolution*. But it's also for those who want to do the best they can to prevent these problems in the first place, and to improve their overall health.

In 1996, we wrote *The Glucose Revolution*, the first book about the glycemic index (which we abbreviate as GI), the health breakthrough that revolutionized the way people approach their diet.

In the years since, researchers around the world, including us, have continued to investigate the glycemic index, and we've received thousands of letters and e-mails, with useful feedback from readers all over the world about our earlier books. Now, *The New Glucose Revolution* presents the most comprehensive, up-to-date information about the glycemic index and its application in the lives of everyone interested in their food choices.

———

The glycemic index (GI) is a physiologically based measure of carbohydrate quality—a comparison of carbohydrates (gram for gram) based on their immediate effect on blood-glucose levels.

- **Carbohydrates that break down quickly during digestion have high GI values. Their blood-glucose response is fast and high.**

- **Carbohydrates that break down slowly, releasing glucose gradually into the blood stream, have a low glycemic index.**

———

Most people have some notion of how blood "sugars" (in truth, glucose) rise and fall throughout the day. However, much of the information currently in print about food and blood glucose is wrong. *The New Glucose Revolution* tells you the true story about the connection between carbohydrate and blood glucose.

■ The blood-glucose response to a meal is primarily determined by its carbohydrate content.

■ Both the quantity and quality of carbohydrate in the food influence the rise in blood glucose.

■ Meals containing the same amount of carbohydrate can produce either high or low effects on blood glucose, depending on the type (or quality) of carbohydrate. In other words, its GI value.

Our research on the glycemic index began in the 1980s when health authorities all over the world began to stress the importance of high-carbohydrate diets. Until then dietary fat had grabbed all the public and scientific attention (and to some extent this is still true). But low-fat diets are by their very nature *automatically* high in carbohydrate. Nutrition scientists started asking questions: Are all carbohydrates the same? Are all starches good for health? Are all sugars bad? In particular, they began studies on the effects of carbohydrates on blood-glucose levels. They wanted to know which carbohydrate foods were associated with the least fluctuation in blood-glucose levels and the best overall health, including reduced risk of diabetes and heart disease.

An overwhelming amount of research on the glycemic index over the past twenty years shows that different carbohydrate foods have dramatically different effects on blood-glucose levels. These differences have important implications. We have played a significant role in validating and testing the glycemic index in the context of diabetes management, weight and appetite control, and sports. We know from our own experience and from letters from our readers that understanding the glycemic index of foods makes an enormous difference to people's lives. For some it means a new lease on life.

Scientists around the world, including our laboratories, have now tested the glycemic index of hundreds of foods, both singly and in mixed meals (meals that consist of a number of foods), and carried out long-term studies on its potential to improve diabetes control. Studies in the United States have shown that consuming low-glycemic-index foods is associated with a lower risk of both type 2 diabetes and coronary heart disease.

It is now obvious, not only to us, but to many expert committees and health authorities around the world, that the glycemic index of foods has implications for *everybody*. It is indeed a "Glucose Revolution" in that it has changed forever the way we think about carbohydrates.

The Glucose Revolution Helps People:

■ with type 1 diabetes

■ with type 2 diabetes

■ with gestational diabetes (diabetes during pregnancy)

■ who are overweight

■ who have a normal weight but too much fat around the middle (abdominal overweight)

■ whose blood-glucose levels are higher than desirable

■ who have been told they have pre-diabetes, "impaired glucose tolerance," or a "touch of diabetes"

■ with high levels of triglycerides and low levels of HDL-cholesterol

■ with the metabolic syndrome (Syndrome X or the insulin resistance syndrome)

■ who suffer from polycystic ovary syndrome

■ who want to prevent all of the above and live a healthier life!

In all these conditions, high blood glucose levels are
a key feature. High blood-glucose levels are undesirable
and have both short and long-term adverse effects.

The New Glucose Revolution gives people with diabetes a
new lease on life, freeing them from hard-to-follow, mis-
guided, and often counterproductive dietary restrictions.
Many people with diabetes find that, despite doing all the
right things, their blood-glucose levels remain too high. *The
New Glucose Revolution* provides the knowledge and know-
how to choose the right kind of carbohydrate for optimum
blood-glucose control.

The glycemic index is part of the solution to high blood glucose.

We also provide advice on choosing the best carbohydrates for weight reduction, the ones that give you control
over hunger pangs, those that minimize insulin levels
and help you burn fat. By preventing weight gain as we
age, we give our body the best chance of avoiding diseases
such as diabetes and heart disease. In this connection, we
discuss high-protein diets and Mediterranean diets. We
provide a clear scientific rationale for choosing between
all the different types of diets that are described in the popular press.

The New Glucose Revolution also helps answer your questions about diet in pregnancy and childhood, specifically diseases such as polycystic ovary syndrome (a form of infertility closely linked to insulin resistance) and celiac disease.

We argue more strongly than ever that the glycemic index is for *everybody, every day, every meal.* The scientific evidence that the glycemic index is important for health is now beyond dispute and goes much further than we ever imagined ourselves.

We give you all the details on the New Glucose Revolution, plus new recipes and more meal plans. We discuss the glycemic load, which helps you calculate the amount *and* type of carbohydrate you are consuming. We also include all the very latest findings, including:

- recent studies on the glycemic index

- information on the glycemic load

- current thinking about the importance of good fats in the diet

- new studies on heart disease and blood-glucose levels

- the latest studies on the glycemic index and diabetes, including type 1 diabetes in children

- recent studies on the glycemic index and weight reduction

- new studies on the glycemic index and cancer

- the latest on the glycemic index and polycystic ovary syndrome, weight gain in pregnancy, and gestational diabetes

- the lowdown on high-protein diets

- new GI values for recently tested foods, including high-protein bars, gluten-free foods, convenience meals, and many more

Lastly, we've included some real-life stories of how much the glycemic index has changed the lives of people who have adopted the low-GI approach.

Blood Sugar or Blood Glucose?

Blood sugar and blood glucose mean the same thing, although the latter is technically more correct. We will use the term blood glucose in this book.

How You Can Use This Book

We've arranged the chapters to make it easy for those who want to get straight to the point—exactly what you need to do to adopt a low-GI approach to eating. We recommend you read the introductory chapters as they will give you a complete overview and scientific update on the carbohydrate story. The facts we reveal about carbohydrate will surprise many people—and are facts that can make life a lot easier.

Part 1 contains the most recent information about what is considered a balanced diet and why—information based on scientific research, clinical trials, and large-scale studies in whole populations. It stresses what's wrong with today's diet and the proven value of diets high in fruits and vegetables. In this section, we explain the importance of being choosy about the types of carbohydrates *and* fats you eat, no matter what the proportions of protein, fat, or carbohydrate. Part 1 discusses high-protein diets and new concepts such as glycemic load and answers some of the most commonly asked questions about the glycemic index.

Part 2 is your guide to low-GI eating. We show you how you can include more of the right sort of carbohydrate in your diet, and give both hints for meal preparation and practical tips and food combinations to help you make the glycemic index work for you throughout the day. This section includes fifty imaginative and delicious recipes and meal ideas for breakfast, lunch, dinner, and in-between snacks, along with their GI rating and nutritional analysis.

In Part 3, there are separate chapters for specific applications of the glycemic index, including its use for weight control, type 1 diabetes, type 2 diabetes, heart disease, and the metabolic syndrome (Syndrome X), pregnancy and gestational diabetes, children, and sports performance.

If it's just the GI values you are after, you'll find them in the updated and much-improved tables in Part 4. We've grouped them according to types of food (breads, fruits, etc.) and included not only the glycemic index value and amount of carbohydrate per serving, but also their glycemic load per serving. We've added the foods that were often queried—meat, fish, cheese, broccoli, avocados, etc.—even though they don't contain carbohydrate and their glycemic load is zero. This is the most comprehensive list of GI values for different foods *ever* published. Finally, there's a complete list of scientific references on pages 556 to 560 to back up everything we say.

With *The New Glucose Revolution* you will discover that a new, healthier way of eating is both easy and delicious.

Dispelling Some Myths about Food

This book dispels many myths about food and carbohydrates. We now know from scientific research that the following popular beliefs about food and carbohydrate are not true.

MYTH 1 Starchy foods like bread and pasta are fattening.

FACT Most starchy foods are bulky and rich in carbohydrate. They fill you up and stave off hunger pangs—they are among the best foods you can eat to help you lose weight. Just watch your portion sizes.

MYTH 2 Sugar is the worst thing for people with diabetes.

FACT Sugar and sugary foods in normal portions have no greater effect on blood-glucose levels than many starchy foods. Overprocessed flours and grains, along with saturated fat, is of greater concern for people with diabetes.

MYTH 3 Sugar causes diabetes.

FACT Sugar has no unique role in causing diabetes. Foods that produce high blood-glucose levels may increase the risk of diabetes, but sugar has a more moderate effect than most starches, especially refined and highly processed ones.

MYTH 4 All starches are slowly digested in the intestine.

FACT Some starch, like that in most kinds of potatoes, is digested in a flash, causing a greater rise in blood glucose than many sugar-containing foods.

MYTH 5 Hunger pangs are inevitable if you want to lose weight.

FACT High-carbohydrate foods, especially those with a low GI value (e.g., rolled oats and pasta), will sustain the feeling of fullness almost to the next meal.

MYTH 6 Foods high in fat are more filling.

FACT Studies show that high-fat foods are among the least filling. It is extremely easy to "passively overconsume" foods like potato chips.

MYTH 7 Sugar is fattening.

FACT Sugar has no special fattening properties. It is no more likely to be turned into fat than any other carbohydrate. Sugar is often present in foods high in energy and fat (e.g., cakes and cookies), but it's the total energy (calories) rather than the sugar in those energy-dense foods that may contribute to new stores of body fat.

MYTH 8 Starches are best for optimum athletic performance.

FACT In many instances starchy foods (e.g., potatoes) are too bulky to eat in the quantities needed for active athletes. Sugars can help increase carbo-hydrate intake.

MYTH 9 Diets high in sugar are less nutritious.

FACT Studies have shown that diets high in sugar (from a range of sources, including dairy food and fruit) often have higher levels of micronutrients, including calcium, riboflavin, and vitamin C, than low-sugar diets.

MYTH 10 Sugar goes hand in hand with dietary fat.

FACT The reality is that high-sugar diets are usually low in fat and vice versa. Most sources of fat in the diet are not sweetened (e.g., potato chisps) and most sources of sugar contain no fat (e.g., soft drinks). Yes, there are many foods high in both fat and sugar (chocolate, ice cream, cakes, cookies, and pastries) but there are equally many that are delicious combinations of starch and fat (potato chips, french fries, some crackers).

———

Part

1

What Is the Glycemic Index?

All the latest research, new concepts,
and answers to your FAQs
about the glycemic index

1

What's Wrong with Today's Diet?

During the Paleolithic period, humans were hunter-gatherers, consuming the animals and plants that were part of their natural environment. How do we know this? Earlier humans left behind the remnants of their meals, the bones of animals, the shells of shellfish, the tools used to hunt and cut meat and extract the bone marrow. And they were fussy about which part of the ani- mal they ate. They preferred the hind legs of the largest animals and the females over the males because they contained more fat and were therefore juicier and more flavorful. They also enjoyed the organ meats—the liver, kidneys, brains—foods that are extremely rich sources of nutrients.

It is now clear that as humans evolved, they became more and more carnivorous, eating more animal food and less plant food. The latest studies of modern hunter-gatherers who lived 100–200 years ago show they obtained about two-thirds of their energy intake from animal foods, including fish and shellfish, and only one-third from plant foods. Some anthropologists believe hunting played a major role in allowing humans to evolve a large brain and high intelligence. Controversially, some believe we were responsible for the extinction of many of the giant animals that roamed the earth for thousands of years.

Since we wrote *The Glucose Revolution*, new studies have appeared on the nutrient composition of hunter-gatherer diets. It now appears that humans ate more protein and less carbohydrate than we do now. Their fat intake was roughly the same as now, but the type of fat was vastly different. Carbohydrate intakes were lower because the main plant foods were fruits and vegetables rather than cereals. Wheat, rice, and other cereal grains were largely absent until after the agricultural revolution, which began some 10,000 years ago. These findings have implications for current dietary recommendations. It doesn't mean that we all need to eat large amounts of meat to be healthy, but it does imply that the type and amount of protein, carbohydrate, and fat need to be carefully reconsidered.

The Agricultural Revolution

The agricultural revolution dramatically changed our diet. For the first time, we started eating large amounts of carbohydrate in the form of whole-grain cereals like wheat, rye, barley, oats, corn, and rice. Legumes (beans), starchy roots and tubers, and fruits and berries also contributed to the high carbohydrate intake. Back then, food preparation was a simple process: grinding food between stones and cooking it over the heat of an open fire. The result was that all the carbohydrates in food were digested and absorbed slowly and the blood-glucose rise was gradual and relatively small.

This diet was ideal because it provided slow-release energy that helped to delay hunger pangs and provided fuel for working muscles long after the meal was eaten. It was also easy on the insulin-producing cells in the pancreas.

As time passed, flours became more processed, and were ground more and more finely and bran was separated completely from white flour. With the advent of high-speed roller mills in the nineteenth century, it was possible to produce white flour so fine that it resembled talcum powder in appearance and texture. These fine white flours have always been highly prized because they make soft bread and delicious, airy cakes and pastries.

As incomes grew, the barley and oats, legumes and beans

commonly eaten by our ancestors were cast aside and fatty meat consumption increased. As a consequence, the composition of the average diet changed again: We began to eat more saturated fat, less fiber, and more easily digested carbohydrates. Something we didn't expect happened too. The blood-glucose rise after a meal was higher and more prolonged, stimulating the pancreas to produce more insulin (see below).

So, not only did we have higher blood-glucose levels after a meal, we had higher insulin responses as well. Insulin is a hormone that is needed for carbohydrate metabolism, but it has a profound effect on the development of many diseases. Medical experts now believe that high glucose and insulin levels are one of the key factors responsible for heart disease and hypertension. Insulin influences the way we metabolize foods, determining whether we burn fat or carbohydrate to meet our energy needs, and ultimately determining whether we store fat in our body.

The Pancreas Produces Insulin

The pancreas is a vital organ near the stomach. Its job is to produce the hormone insulin. Carbohydrate stimulates the secretion of insulin more than any other component of food. The slow absorption of the carbohydrate in our food means that the pancreas doesn't have to work so hard and produces less insulin. If the pancreas is overstimulated over a long period of time, it may become "exhausted," and type 2 diabetes may develop in genetically susceptible individuals. Even without diabetes, high insulin levels are undesirable because they increase the risk of heart disease.

————

Thus one of the most important ways in which our diet differs from that of our ancestors is the speed of carbohydrate digestion and the resulting effect on blood-glucose and insulin levels. Traditional diets all around the world contained slowly digested and absorbed carbohydrate—foods that we now know have a low GI value. In contrast, modern diets with their quickly digested carbohydrates are based on foods with a high GI value.

————

Food Provides More Than Just Nutrients

Food is part of our culture and way of life. Our food choices are determined by many factors, ranging from religious beliefs to the deliciously sensual role that food plays in our lives. For babies, food has a comforting role that goes well beyond meeting their immediate physical needs. For adults, food reflects status—we prepare special meals for special occasions and for special guests to show respect or friendship.

With so many factors influencing our food choices, we tend to overlook the very basic role food plays in the nourishment and growth of our bodies. With the busy lives many of us lead, it's easy to see food simply as a solution to overcoming hunger. In other circumstances, we focus on the social aspects of food and eat too much.

What's Wrong with Modern Diets

Today's Western diet is the product of industrialization based on many inventions—pasteurization, sterilization, refrigeration, freezing, roller drying, and spray drying, to name just a few. In the cereal-foods world, there's high-speed roller milling, high-temperature and high-pressure extrusion, puffing guns, short-time fermentation—you name it, they've invented it.

The benefits are many. We have a plentiful, relatively cheap, palatable (some would say too palatable), and reasonably safe food supply. Gone are the days of monotonous fare, gaps in the food supply, weevil-infested and tainted food. Long gone are widespread vitamin deficiencies such as scurvy and pellagra. Today's food manufacturers work hard to bring us irresistible and safe products that meet the demands of both gourmets and health-conscious consumers.

Many of the new foods are still based on our staple cereals—wheat, corn, oats—but the original grain has been ground down to produce fine flours with small particle size that produces fine-quality breads, cakes, cookies, crackers, pastries, breakfast cereals, and snack foods. Cereal chemists and bakers know that the finest-particle-size flour produces the most palatable and shelf-stable end product.

Unfortunately, this striving for excellence in one area has resulted in unforeseen problems in another. Our bodies quickly digest and absorb today's staple carbohydrate foods, including ordinary bread. The resulting effect on blood-glucose levels has created a problem of epidemic proportions.

All About Fat

One of the most undesirable aspects of the modern diet is the *type* of fat we eat. Food manufacturers, bakers, and chefs know we love to eat fat. We love its creaminess and feel in the mouth (what scientists call "mouth feel") and find it easy to consume in excess. It makes our meat more tender, our vegetables and salads more palatable, and our sweet foods even more desirable. We prefer potatoes as french fries or potato chips, our fish battered and fried, and our pastas in rich, creamy sauces.

With a wave of the fat wand, bland high-carbohydrate foods like rice and oats are magically transformed into highly palatable, calorically dense foods such as fried rice and high-fat granola. In fact, when you analyze it, much of our diet today is an undesirable but delicious combination of fat and quickly digested carbohydrate.

It's not just the amount of fat we eat, but the *type* of fat that can make us unhealthy. The problem is that most of the fat we now eat comes in the form of heart-unhealthy saturated fat.

Saturated fat is solid at room temperature and tends to clog up our arteries, unlike the unsaturated oils that are liquid in form. The fats used for baking and frying are usually saturated fats, such as hydrogenated vegetable oil or shortening. The fat in *fatty* meats and dairy products is saturated fat. But the fat in lean meat, fish, olive oil, canola oil, and oil made from other seeds, such as safflower and sunflower, is the heart-healthy unsaturated kind.

Hunter-gatherers, even though they ate a large amount of animal fat, did not eat vast quantities of saturated fat. This is because the fat of wild animals, including the fat in the brain and other organs, has much higher proportions of unsaturated fat.

In our desire to reduce saturated fat, all fats were lumped together as bad—the message "reduce fat" was easier than "reduce saturated fat." In many ways, we can now see that this simplified message was counterproductive. People avoided even the most essential of fats, the highly polyunsaturated, long-chain fats that are fundamental to human health. Secondly, we avoided fat because of its high energy content and propensity to be overeaten, only to replace it with large quantities of fast-release carbohydrates that have the same properties. We fooled ourselves into thinking that *any* low-fat diet, especially one formulated with the help of a sophisticated food industry, was automatically a healthy diet. *But it's not.* In chapter 4 of this book we explain how the right fats are actually good for you—and explain how to add these fats to your diet.

What Is a Balanced Diet?

It makes sense to balance our food intake with the rate our bodies use it. This way, we maintain a steady weight. These days, however, this balance is difficult to achieve. It is very easy to overeat. Refined foods, convenience foods, and fast foods frequently lack fiber and conceal fat so that even before we feel full, we have overdosed on calories. It is even easier not to exercise. It usually takes longer to walk somewhere than it does to drive (except, perhaps, during rush hour). With intake exceeding output on a regular basis, the result is weight gain.

We need to adapt our lifestyle to our supersized, high-calorie diet and fewer physical demands. Don't make the mistake of thinking that the best option is just to "diet" most of the time—i.e., reduce food intake to a low level that matches a low level of energy expenditure. That's a recipe for failure. It has become very important to find ways of increasing our energy output, to grab an opportunity for physical activity however and wherever we can, to increase our energy needs. It means using the stairs, taking a ten-minute walk at lunchtime, using the treadmill while you watch the news, reading on the exercise bike, working in the garden, walking to the stores, parking an extra distance from the office, or taking the dog for a walk each night. Whatever works for you, do it. Even housework burns calories. All of these seemingly small bursts of activity accumulate to increase our calorie burning. You don't have to take exercise very seriously, just do it regularly.

While you work on increasing your caloric output, *The New Glucose Revolution* can help you select the best foods to balance input and output. But what's a balanced diet? Is there just one healthy diet that all of us should be following, with a set proportion of fat, carbohydrate, and protein? In other words, does one size fit all? To be honest, we don't know, but it's highly likely that we can be flexible. After all, there were many different hunter-gatherer diets, some very high in protein and some very high in carbohydrate or fat. Nutritionists are beginning to appreciate that a healthy diet comes in many different forms that may differ greatly in terms of proportions of fat, protein, and carbohydrate.

But there are two fundamental principles in *all* the traditional healthy diets—any carbohydrates were slow-release and any fat was relatively unsaturated (even if the intake was high). So, our first message is to choose the type of diet that suits your lifestyle and cultural and ethnic origins best. This is the one you are most likely to stick to for life. But there are important principles to follow in all cases (see Dietary Guidelines for Americans, below).

Dietary Guidelines for Americans (2005 edition)

1. Consume a variety of foods within and among the basic food groups while staying within energy needs.
2. Control calorie intake to manage body weight.
3. Be physically active every day.
4. Increase daily intake of fruits and vegetables, whole grains, and nonfat or low-fat milk and milk products.
5. Choose fats wisely for good health.
6. Choose carbohydrates wisely for good health.
7. Choose and prepare foods with little salt.
8. If you drink alcohol, do so in moderation.
9. Keep food safe to eat.

SOURCE: U.S. Department of Agriculture, U.S. Department of Health and Human Services.

The following chapters tell you how you can eat a balanced and healthy diet that is tailored for you. No diet will work in the long term if it eliminates your favorite foods, whether these are bread or potatoes, ice cream or pasta. *The New Glucose Revolution* goes a *huge* step further than most nutrition books because the glycemic index of carbohydrates plays such an important, but still underrecognized, role in determining health and well-being.

2

Why We Need Carbohydrate

Nature's Primary Fuel

Carbohydrate is the most widely consumed substance in the world after water. In fact, carbohydrates hold a special place in human nutrition. Glucose, the simplest carbohydrate, is *essential* fuel for the brain, red blood cells, and a growing fetus, and the main source of energy for the muscles during strenuous exercise. Carbohydrate is a vital energy source, and you can't afford to leave it out. Carbohydrates, however, were not created equal—you must choose the right kind of carbohydrate for your lifestyle.

Our bodies run on fuel, just like a car runs on gasoline. The fuels our bodies burn are derived from a mixture of the protein, fat, carbohydrate, and alcohol that we consume. Every day we need to fill our fuel tanks with the right amount and the right kind of fuel for health, energy, and feeling our best. The actual proportions in our fuel mix will vary from hour to hour and are determined to a large extent by the last meal we ate.

What Is Carbohydrate?

Carbohydrate is a part of food. Starch is a carbohydrate; so too are sugars and certain types of fiber. Starches and sugars are nature's reserves created by energy from the sun, carbon dioxide, and water. The building block of starch is glucose.

The simplest form of carbohydrate is a single-sugar molecule called a **monosaccharide** (**mono** meaning one, **saccharide** meaning sweet). Glucose is a monosaccharide that occurs in food (as glucose itself and as the building block of starch) and is the most common source of fuel for the cells of the human body.

If 2 monosaccharides are joined together, the result is a **disaccharide** (**di** meaning two). Sucrose, or common table sugar, is a disaccharide, as is lactose, the sugar in milk.

As the number of monosaccharides in the chain increases, the carbohydrate becomes less sweet. Maltodextrins are **oligosaccharides** (**oligo** meaning a few) that are 5 or 6 glucose residues long and commonly used as a food ingredient. They taste only faintly sweet.

Starches are long chains of sugar molecules joined together like the beads in a string of pearls. They are called **polysaccharides** (**poly** meaning many). Starches are not sweet-tasting at all.

Dietary fibers are large carbohydrate molecules containing many different sorts of monosaccharides. They are different from starches and sugars in that they are not broken down by human digestive enzymes. Fiber reaches the large intestine without change. Once there, bacteria begin to ferment and break down the fibers.

Different fibers have different physical and chemical properties. Soluble fibers are those that can be dissolved in water. Some soluble fibers are very viscous when in solution and therefore slow the speed of digestion. On the other hand, other fibers, such as cellulose, are insoluble, meaning they are not soluble in water and do not directly affect the speed of digestion.

Sugars Found in Food

Monosaccharides (single-sugar molecules)	Disaccharides (two single-sugar molecules)
glucose	maltose = glucose + glucose
fructose	sucrose = glucose + fructose
galactose	lactose = glucose + galactose

There is a fuel "hierarchy," that is, an order of priority that the body follows for burning the fuels in food. Alcohol is at the top of the list because our bodies have no place to store unused alcohol. Protein comes second, followed by carbohydrate, while fat comes off last. In practice, the fuel mix is usually a combination of carbohydrate and fat in varying proportions. After meals the mix is predominantly carbohydrate and between meals it is mainly fat.

Our body's ability to burn all the fat we eat is vitally important to weight control. If fat burning is inhibited, fat stores gradually accumulate. The relative proportions of fat to carbohydrate in the fuel mix are therefore critical and are dictated *by the prevailing levels of insulin* in our blood. If insulin levels are low, as they are when we wake up in the morning, then the fuel mix is mainly fat. If our insulin levels are high, as they are when we consume a high-carbohydrate meal, then the fuel mix we burn is mainly carbohydrate. But if insulin is always high, as in insulin-resistant and over-weight people, then the cells are constantly forced to burn carbohydrate and have trouble burning the fat we eat and using it as a source of fuel. When this happens, fat stores mount up. Scientists now believe that subtle abnormalities in the ability to burn fat are behind most states of overweight and obesity.

Sources of Carbohydrate

Carbohydrate is the starchy part of foods like rice, bread, potatoes, and pasta. It is also the essential ingredient that makes foods taste sweet: the sugars in fruit and honey are carbohydrates, as are the refined sugars in soft drinks and sweets.

Carbohydrate comes mainly from plant foods, such as cereal grains, fruits, vegetables, and legumes (peas and beans). Milk products also contain carbohydrate in the form of milk sugar or lactose. Lactose is the first carbohydrate we encoun-ter as infants, and human milk contains more lactose than any other mammal milk. It accounts for almost half the energy available to the infant. Some foods contain a large amount of carbohydrate (such as cereals, potatoes, and legumes) while other foods are very dilute sources, such as carrots, broccoli. and salad vegetables.

Foods that are high in carbohydrate include:

Cereal grains including rice, wheat, oats, barley, rye and anything made from them (bread, pasta, noodles, flour, breakfast cereal).

Fruits such as apples, bananas, grapes, peaches, melons.

Starchy vegetables such as potatoes, yams, sweet corn, and sweet potato.

Top 20 Sources of Carbohydrate in the American Diet*

1. Potatoes (mashed or baked)
2. White bread
3. Cold breakfast cereal
4. Dark bread
5. Orange juice
6. Banana
7. White rice
8. Pizza
9. Pasta
10. Muffins
11. Fruit punch
12. Coca-Cola®
13. Apple
14. Skim milk
15. Pancake
16. Table sugar
17. Jam
18. Cranberry juice
19. French fries
20. Candy

SOURCE: Dr. Simin Liu, Harvard University School of Public Health.

*This data represents the findings of the Harvard Nurses' Health Study.

Legumes including baked beans, lentils, kidney beans, chickpeas, black beans, split peas, and cannellini beans.

Dairy products such as yogurt and ice cream.

Sources of Carbohydrate

Percentage of Carbohydrate (grams per 100 grams of food) in Food as Eaten			
apple	12%	peas	8%
baked beans	11%	pear	12%
banana	21%	plum	6%
barley	61%	potato	15%
bread	47%	raisins	75%
cornflakes	85%	rice	79%
flour	73%	split peas	45%
grapes	15%	sugar	100%
ice cream	22%	sweet corn	16%
milk	5%	sweet potato	17%
oats	61%	tapioca	85%
orange	8%	water cracker	71%
pasta	70%	wheat biscuit	62%

Digestion of Carbohydrates

To make use of the sugars and starches in foods, our bodies first have to break them down into a form that we can absorb and that our cells can use. This process is called digestion.

Digestion starts in the mouth where amylase, the starch-digesting enzyme in saliva, is incorporated into our food as we chew. Amylase chops up long-chain starch molecules into short-chain molecules such as maltose and maltodextrins. Its activity is halted by the acids secreted into the stomach, and most digestion continues only when the carbohydrate leaves the stomach and reaches the small intestine.

The rate at which food enters the small intestine from the stomach is called the rate of stomach (gastric) emptying. Some food components—such as viscous fiber, acidity, and highly osmotic solutions—help to slow down stomach emptying and therefore the overall speed of carbohydrate digestion.

In the small intestine, starch digestion continues. Huge amounts of amylase are secreted in pancreatic juice into the small intestine, so much so that the biochemists call it amylase "overkill." The speed of digestion now depends on the nature of the starch itself—how resistant it is in a physical and chemical sense to being attacked by enzymes. Many starches in food are rapidly digested, while others are more resistant and the process is slower.

Other food factors may influence the speed of digestion. If the mixture of food and enzymes is highly viscous or sticky, owing to the presence of viscous fiber, mixing slows down and the enzymes and starch take longer to make contact. The products of starch digestion will also take longer to move toward the wall of the intestine, where the last steps in digestion take place. At the intestinal wall, the short-chain starch products, together with the sugars in foods, are broken down by specific enzymes. The monosaccharides that finally result from starch and sugar digestion include glucose, fructose, and galactose. They are absorbed from the small intestine into the bloodstream, where they are available as a source of energy to the cells.

Brain Food

Except during starvation, carbohydrate is the only source of fuel that our brains can use. The brain is the most energy-demanding organ in the body—responsible for over half our obligatory energy requirements. Unlike muscle cells, which can burn either fat or carbohydrate, the brain does not have the metabolic machinery to burn fat. If you fast for twenty-four hours or decide not to eat carbohydrate, the brain relies initially on small stores of carbohydrate in the liver, but within hours these are depleted and the liver begins synthesizing glucose from non-carbohydrate sources (including your muscle tissue!). It has only a limited ability to do this, however, and it's now clear that any shortfall in glucose availability has consequences for brain function.

Recent medical literature shows that intellectual performance is improved following the intake of a glucose load or carbohydrate-rich food. Demanding mental tasks are most improved, while easy tasks are not affected. Furthermore, blood-glucose levels decline more during a period of intense cognitive processing. The tests included various measures of "intelligence," including word recall, maze learning, arithmetic, short-term memory, rapid information processing, and reasoning. The improved mental ability following a carbohydrate meal was demonstrated in all types of people—young people, university students, people with diabetes, healthy elderly people, and those with Alzheimer's disease. These new studies give us all the more reason to avoid a low carbohydrate intake.

At all times, our bodies need to maintain a minimum threshold level of glucose in the blood to serve the brain and central nervous system. If for some reason glucose levels fall below this threshold (a state called "hypoglycemia"), the consequences are severe, including trembling, dizziness, nausea, incoherent rambling speech, and lack of coordination. If not rectified quickly, coma and even death may ensue.

What's Wrong with a Low-Carbohydrate Diet?

There is little scientific evidence to back up or refute low-carbohydrate diets. One reason for the popularity of low-carbohydrate diets for weight loss is that initial loss is rapid. Within the first few days, the scales will show a weight loss of 4 to 7 pounds. That's an encouraging sign to anyone trying to lose weight. The trouble is that most of that weight loss isn't body fat, but muscle glycogen and water.

When carbohydrate is no longer being supplied in sufficient amounts by your diet, the body uses its small carbohydrate reserves (glycogen) to fuel muscle contraction. One gram of carbohydrate in the form of muscle and liver glycogen binds 4 grams of water. So when you use up your total reserves of 500 grams of glycogen within the first few days, you also lose 2 kilograms of water, for a total loss of 2.5 kilograms, none of it fat. Conversely, when you return to normal eating, the carbohydrate reserves will be rapidly replenished, along with the water.

People who have followed low-carbohydrate diets for any length of time observe that the rate of weight loss plateaus and they begin to feel rather tired and lethargic. That's not surprising, because the muscles have little left in the way of glycogen stores. Strenuous exercise requires both fat and carbohydrate in the fuel mix. So, in the long term, these low-carbohydrate diets may discourage people from the physical-exercise patterns that will help them keep their weight under control.

Our advice is that the best diet for weight control is one you can stick to for life—one that includes your favorite foods and that accommodates your cultural and ethnic heritage. This diet can vary somewhat in total carbohydrate, protein, and fat. At the present time, there is more scientific evidence supporting the use of bulky, higher-carbohydrate, low-GI, low-fat diets for weight loss. But the bottom line is that the type of carbohydrate and the type of fat are critical. Choosing low-GI foods will not only promote weight control, it will reduce postprandial glycemia, increase satiety, and provide bulk and a rich supply of micronutrients.

———————

> Only low-GI diets have the weight of
> scientific evidence in their favor.

To ensure that blood-glucose levels can be maintained between meals, our bodies draw on the glucose stored in the liver. The storage form of glucose is called glycogen, but supplies of this are strictly limited and must be replenished from meal to meal. If your diet is low in carbohydrate, your glycogen stores will be low, as well, and easily depleted.

Once the body has used up your glycogen stores (within twelve to twenty-four hours of beginning a fast), it will start breaking down muscle protein to synthesize glucose for the brain and nervous system. But remember, this process can't supply all of the brain's needs. When absolutely necessary, the brain will make use of ketones, a byproduct of the breakdown of fat. The level of ketones in the blood rises as the fast continues and you can smell the ketones on the breath (they smell a little like apple cider).

The brain is not at its best using ketones, however, and mental judgment has been shown to be impaired. In all likelihood, you'll have a headache and feel mentally sluggish. Since your muscle stores of glycogen will have been depleted, you'll also find strenuous exercise almost impossible and fatigue easily. All this leads us to an important question.

How Much Carbohydrate Do You Really Need?

As we have shown, there are good reasons to avoid a low-carbohydrate diet, but what then is the optimal level of carbohydrate in the diet? Should it be as high as 65 percent of total daily calories, as some nutritionists are recommending, or more moderate, about 45 percent of energy? New nutritional guidelines were published by the Institute of Medicine's Food and Nutrition Board in the fall of 2002. These recommendations clearly suggest that both levels or anything in between can work to meet the body's daily energy and nutritional needs while minimizing the risk for chronic disease. Understand and follow the level that works best for you within this range. It may be helpful to seek the guidance of a registered dietitian (see page 30).

If we look carefully at diets all around the world, it's clear that both high and moderate intakes of carbohydrate are commensurate with good health. We believe your carbohydrate intake can be *either*, as long as you give due consideration to the type of foods you eat.

Is a High-Carbohydrate Diet for You?

Is consuming 50 percent or more of energy as carbohydrate and less than 30 percent as fat (the remaining 15 percent or more should come from protein) realistic for you? That depends. If you have always been health conscious and avoided high-fat foods, or if you follow an Asian or Middle Eastern diet, then chances are you're already eating a high-carbohydrate diet.

Of course, the number of calories and hence the amount of carbohydrate varies with your weight and activity levels. If you are an active person with average energy requirements who is not trying to lose weight (i.e., with an average intake of 2,000 calories per day), you will require 275 grams of carbohydrate. If you are trying to lose weight and are consuming a low-calorie diet (i.e., a small eater on 1,200 calories per day), it means eating about 165 grams of carbohydrate a day. As an example of what these diets look like, see pages 38 to 42.

Is a Moderate Carbohydrate Intake for You?

Americans tend to eat too many calories from all food sources. This is because the typical American portions of carbohydrate and protein are oversized and should be reduced. A Mediterranean-type diet is higher in fat and provides only about 45 percent of energy as carbohydrate. In the past, most nutritionists would have frowned upon this, but that's no longer the case. As long as you carefully consider the types of fats and the types of carbohydrate, then this level of carbohydrate intake is perfectly commensurate with good health. At this level, you need to consume at least 125 grams of carbohydrate a day if you are a small eater and 225 grams if you are an average eater. Using bread as an example, this would mean eating between 9 and 15 slices each day.

━━━━━━━

What we emphasize is that the *type* or *source* of the carbohydrate and fat are as important as the amount. In the end the choice of how much carbohydrate you eat—moderate or high—is yours. The way of eating that you'll enjoy and tend to follow over the long term is the one that is closest to your usual diet and to your cultural and ethnic origins. We believe that, unlike with baseball caps, one size does not fit all. Our approach has built-in flexibility when it comes to the amount of carbohydrate you need to eat.

━━━━━━━

How to Find a Dietitian

For specific information about your own calorie and exact carbohydrate needs, you should consult a registered dietitian (RD). Look in the *Yellow Pages* under Dietitians or go to the American Dietetic Association's home page: www.eatright.org. Make sure that the

person you choose has the letters RD after his or her name.

———

Most of the world's population eats a high-carbohydrate diet based on staples such as rice, corn, millet, and wheat-based foods like bread or noodles. In some African and Asian countries, carbohydrate may form as much as 70 to 80 percent of a person's caloric intake (this is probably too high for optimum health). In contrast, people in industrialized nations such as the United States and Australia eat only half of these carbohydrate calories. Our diets typically contain about 40 to 45 percent carbohydrate and 33 to 40 percent fat.

The Carbohydrate–Fat Seesaw

Carbohydrate and fat are not only the two primary fuels for the body's tissues, they are also the two main components of food, displaying a reciprocal relationship to each other. The reason protein isn't one of the body's primary fuels is because it usually contributes less than 20 percent of the energy in food, while fats and carbohydrates make up the other 80 percent or more. In a high-carbohydrate diet, at least 50 percent of the total energy comes from carbohydrate and less than 30 percent from fat. In a high-fat diet, typically 40 percent of energy comes from fat and only 40 percent from carbohydrate.

This reciprocal or seesaw relationship means that carbo-hydrate displaces fat from our diet. When we make an effort to eat more carbohydrates, fat intake decreases, and vice versa. Foods high in carbohydrates are often bulky and filling—think fruits and vegetables—and rich in micronutrients. The problem with fats, on the other hand, is that they are highly palatable—a lot of the flavor in food is actually dissolved in the fat—think chocolate and cheese. Fats are also very con-centrated sources of energy, and gram for gram, pure fat con-tains more than double the energy of pure carbohydrate or protein.

Today's health recommendations are as much about the *type* of fat and the *nature* of the carbohydrate as about the total amounts of each.

The upshot of this is that many foods that are high in fat are exceptionally palatable, low in bulk, high in energy, and very easy to overconsume. If your diet is dominated by these foods and you're not very active, it's all too easy to put on excess weight. Saturated fat also plays a role in the develop-ment of heart disease. This is why many nutritionists have promoted high-carbohydrate diets in which 50 to 60 percent of daily caloric intake comes from carbohydrate.

There have been, however, unforeseen consequences to this universal low-fat, high-carbohydrate approach. For one, many people succeeded in reducing total fat intake to 30 per-

cent or less but still had an undesirably high intake of saturated fat. Consumers also demanded more palatable low-fat
foods, and they ended up eating foods that were just as energy
dense and easy to overeat as the original high-fat product—
think of low-fat yogurts and ice creams. Nutritionists have
had to rethink and fine-tune the health message.

Simple Versus Complex Carbohydrate

So far, we've emphasized the *amount* of carbohydrate in the
diet. What about the type or *nature* of the carbohydrate?

Traditionally, the nature of carbohydrates was described
by their chemical structure: simple or complex. Sugars were
simple and starches were complex, simply because sugars
were small molecules and starches were big. By virtue of their
large size, it was automatically assumed that complex carbohydrates such as starches would be slowly digested and
absorbed and would cause only a small and gradual rise in
blood-glucose levels. Simple sugars, on the other hand, were
assumed to be digested and absorbed quickly, producing a
rapid rise in blood glucose.

A few simplistic experiments on raw starches and pure
sugars supported these assumptions, and for fifty years
they were taught to every medical and biochemistry student
as "fact."

We now know that the whole concept of "simple" versus "complex" carbohydrate does not tell us anything about how the carbohydrates in food change blood-glucose levels in the body. Twenty years of scientific research have shown that the assumptions about the speed of digestion were all wrong.

The rise in blood glucose after meals could not be predicted simply on the basis of a simple versus complex chemical structure. An- other system of describing the nature of carbohydrates and classifying them according to their effects on blood glucose was needed: the glycemic index.

The Nature of Carbohydrate: The Glycemic Index

Surprisingly, scientists did not study the actual blood-glucose responses to common foods until the early 1980s. Prior to that, they'd tested solutions of pure sugars and raw starches and had drawn conclusions that did not apply to real foods in real meals.

Since 1981, hundreds of different foods have been tested as single foods and in mixed meals with both healthy people and people with diabetes. Professors David Jenkins and Tom Wolever at the University of Toronto were the first to introduce the term "glycemic index" to compare the ability of different carbohydrates to raise blood-glucose levels.

The glycemic index is simply a numerical way of describing how the carbohydrates in individual foods affect blood-glucose levels. Foods with a high glycemic index value contain carbohydrates that cause a dramatic rise in blood-glucose levels, while foods with a low glycemic index value contain carbohydrates with much less impact.

> **The glycemic index describes the *type* of carbohydrate in foods. It indicates their ability to raise your *blood-glucose* levels.**

This research has turned some widely held beliefs upside down (it truly is a revolution) and in the process, quite understandably, caused a lot of controversy.

The first surprise was that the starch in foods like bread, potatoes, and many types of rice is digested and absorbed very quickly—not slowly, as had always been assumed.

Second, scientists found that the sugar in foods (like fruit, candy and ice cream) did not produce more rapid or prolonged rises in blood glucose, as had always been thought. The truth was that most of the sugars in foods, regardless of the source, actually produced quite moderate blood-glucose responses, lower than most starches.

We need to forget the old distinctions that have been made between starchy foods and sugary foods, or simple versus complex carbohydrates. They have no useful application at all when it comes to blood-glucose levels. Even an experienced scientist with a detailed knowledge of a food's chemical composition finds it difficult to predict a food's glycemic index value.

> Forget about the words *simple* and *complex*
> carbohydrate. Think in terms of *low* and *high*
> GI values.

Eating Carbohydrates

To ensure that you are eating enough carbohydrate and the right kind, you should eat:

- fruits at every meal

- vegetables with lunch and dinner and even as snacks

- at least one low-GI food at each meal

- at least the minimum quantity of carbohydrate foods suggested for small eaters (see pages 39 to 42)

- lots of fiber (foods with low energy density or fewer calories per gram)

You will find that when you are choosy about your carbohydrate, your insulin levels will be lower and you will automatically burn more fat. You may not feel this change as it is happening, but you will see the results—you'll lose weight—over time! Eating high-fiber foods will also help fill you up and prevent you overeating.

If you are looking for ways to improve your own diet, there are two important things to remember.

1. Identify the sources of carbohydrate in your diet and reduce high-GI foods. Don't go to extremes; there is room for your favorite high-GI foods.

2. Identify the sources of fat and look at ways you can reduce saturated fat. Choose monounsaturated and polyunsaturated fats, such as olive oil and sunflower oil, instead of saturated fats like butter and shortening. Again, don't go overboard—the body needs some fat, and there's room for your favorite fatty foods on occasion. Just remember to watch your portions.

How Could You Change Your Diet?

Some of the most common foods people tell us they have started eating to achieve a low-GI diet are:

- grainy breads
- low-GI breakfast cereals
- more fruit
- yogurt
- lots of pasta, beans, and vegetables

The Right Kind of Carbohydrate Diet

Both high and moderate carbohydrate intake can be healthy—the choice is simply up to you. Both types of diets, however, need to emphasize low-GI carbohydrates and healthy fats.

A High-Carbohydrate Diet

Here we show you an example of what's involved in eating a high-carbohydrate diet (65 percent of total daily energy from carbohydrate) for small or average eaters.

For Small Eaters

Even the smallest eater needs these carbohydrate foods every day:

- around 4 slices of bread or the equivalent (crackers, rolls, English muffins)
- at least 2 pieces of fresh fruit or the equivalent (juice, dried fruit, or fruit canned in its own juice)
- about 1 cup of starchy cooked vegetables (corn, legumes, potato, sweet potato)
- about 1 cup of cooked cereal or grain food (breakfast cereal, cooked rice or pasta, or other grains)
- at least 2 cups of fat-free or low-fat milk or the equivalent (yogurt, ice cream), including milk in your tea or coffee and with your cereal

Small Eaters May:

- be small-framed females
- have small appetites
- do very little physical activity
- be trying to lose weight

If this amount of food sounds right for you, try it as a minimum amount of carbohydrate. This supplies 190 grams of carbohydrate, suitable for a 1,200-calorie diet. Listen to your appetite if it demands more, and if necessary add a small low-GI snack.

For Average Eaters

Average eaters need to eat:

- around 8 slices of bread or the equivalent (crackers, rolls, muffins)

- about 4 pieces of fresh fruit or the equivalent (juice, dried fruit, or fruit canned in its own juice)

- 1 cup of starchy cooked vegetables (corn, legumes, potato, sweet potato)

- at least 2 cups of cereal or grain food (breakfast cereal, cooked rice or pasta, or other grains)

- 2 cups of low-fat milk or the equivalent (yogurt, ice cream)

Average Eaters May:

- do regular physical activity (but not strenuous exercise)
- be adults of average frame size

This provides 250 grams of carbohydrate, which is suitable for a 1,800-calorie diet.

Overconsumption of food is highly unlikely on the high-fiber, high-carbohydrate, low-fat diet described above. So, base your diet on high-fiber carbohydrate foods like whole-grain breads, cereals, fruit, vegetables, and legumes, and let your appetite dictate how much you need to eat.

A Moderate-Carbohydrate Diet

If you think you'd prefer a more moderate carbohydrate intake (45 percent of total daily energy) and more fat, then here's an example of how much carbohydrate food small and average eaters would need each day.

For Small Eaters

For a balanced intake of nutrients on a moderate-carbohydrate diet, even a small eater needs these carbohydrate foods every day:

- around 4 slices of bread or the equivalent (crackers, rolls, English muffins)

- at least 2 pieces of fresh fruit or the equivalent (juice, dried fruit or fruit canned in its own juice)

- about ½ cup of cooked starchy vegetables (corn, legumes, potato, sweet potato)

- about ½ cup of cereal or grain food (breakfast cereal, cooked rice or pasta, or other grains)

- 2 cups of low-fat milk or the equivalent (yogurt, ice cream)

These carbohydrate foods supply 135 grams of carbohydrate, which is about 45 percent of total daily energy from carbohydrate in a 1,200-calorie diet.

For Average Eaters

Even on a moderate carbohydrate diet, the average eater needs to eat:

- around 6 slices of bread or the equivalent (crackers, rolls, muffins)

- about 2 pieces of fresh fruit or the equivalent (juice, dried fruit, or fruit canned in its own juice)

- about ½ cup of high-carbohydrate vegetables (corn, legumes, potato, sweet potato)

- at least 1½ cups of cereal or grain food (breakfast cereal, cooked rice or pasta, or other grain)

■ 2½ cups of low-fat milk or the equivalent (yogurt, ice
   cream)

This provides 200 grams of carbohydrate, which is 45
percent of total daily energy in a 1,800-calorie diet.

―――――――――

To work out the percentage of calories supplied by
carbohydrate, multiply the grams of carbohydrate by 4
(the number of calories supplied per gram of carbohydrate) and then divide by the total number of calories.

Thus: (225 × 4 × 100)/1800 = 50 percent (approximately).

―――――――――

3

All About the
Glycemic Index

The glycemic index was first developed in 1981 by Dr. David Jenkins, a professor of nutrition at the University of Toronto, Canada, to help determine which foods were best for people with diabetes. At that time, the diet for people with diabetes was based on a system of carbohydrate exchanges. Each exchange, or portion of food, contained the same amount of carbohydrate. The exchange system assumed that all starchy foods produced the same effect on blood-glucose levels even though some earlier studies had already proven this was not correct. Jenkins was one of the first researchers to challenge the use of exchanges and investigate how real foods behave in the bodies of real people.

Jenkins's approach attracted a great deal of attention because it was so logical and systematic. He and his colleagues tested a large number of common foods, with some surprising results. An exchange of ice cream, for example, despite its sugar content, had less effect on blood glucose than an exchange of ordinary white bread. Over the next fifteen years, medical researchers and scientists around the world, including the authors of this book, tested the effect of many foods on blood-glucose levels and helped develop this new concept of classifying carbohydrates based on the glycemic index.

So what exactly is the glycemic index? The glycemic index of foods is a ranking of carbohydrate exchanges in foods according to their immediate impact on blood-glucose levels. To make a fair comparison, all foods are compared with a reference food such as pure glucose in equivalent carbohydrate amounts.

Today we know the glycemic index values of hundreds of different food items that have been tested following the standardized method. The detailed tables in Part 4 give the glycemic index values of a range of common foods, including many tested by Dr. Jennie Brand-Miller and her colleagues at the University of Sydney and Dr. Thomas M.S. Wolever and his colleagues at the University of Toronto.

For some years the glycemic index was a very controversial topic. There were avid proponents and opponents of this new approach to classifying carbohydrate. The two sides almost came to blows at conferences aimed at reaching a consensus.

Initially, there was some justified criticism. In the early days there was no evidence that the glycemic index values of single foods could influence the resulting blood-glucose levels of the entire meals in which they were consumed or that low-GI foods could bring long-term benefits. There were no studies of the glycemic index's reproducibility or the consistency of GI values from one country to another, and many of the early studies used healthy volunteers; there was no evidence that the results could be applied to people with diabetes.

Now, however, the evidence is in. We know that the glycemic index is reproducible and a clinically proven tool in its application to diabetes, appetite, and coronary health. To date, studies in the United Kingdom, France, Italy, Sweden, Australia, and Canada have proven without doubt the value of the glycemic index. Notably, the United States remains officially opposed. However, The Harvard School of Public Health and the Children's Hospital in Boston recommend the glycemic index even for healthy people.

The Glycemic Index Measures the Rate of Digestion

Foods containing carbohydrates that break down quickly during digestion have the highest glycemic index values. The blood-glucose response is fast and high. In other words, the glucose (or sugar) in the bloodstream increases rapidly. Conversely, foods that contain carbohydrates that break down slowly, releasing glucose gradually into the bloodstream, have a low glycemic index value.

An analogy is the popular fable of the tortoise and the hare. The hare, just like high-GI foods, speeds away but loses the race to the tortoise with his slow and steady pace. Similarly, the slow and steady low-GI foods produce a smooth blood-glucose curve without wild fluctuations. The graph on page 48 shows the effect of slow and fast carbohydrates on blood-glucose levels.

For most people, the foods with low glycemic index values have advantages over those with high glycemic index values. But there are some athletes who can benefit from the use of high-GI foods during and after competition. This is covered in chapter 14. High-GI foods are also useful in the treatment of hypoglycemia (covered in chapter 11).

The glycemic index is a clinically proven tool in its applications to diabetes, appetite control, and coronary health.

The substance that produces one of the greatest effects on blood-glucose levels is pure glucose itself. Glycemic index testing has shown that *most* foods have less effect on blood-glucose levels than glucose. The glycemic index value of pure glucose is set at 100, and every other food is ranked on a scale from 0 to 100 according to the actual effect on blood-glucose levels. (Note: There are a few foods that have GI values of more than 100, e.g., jasmine rice. While this seems extraordinary, there's a simple explanation. Glucose is a highly concentrated solution that tends to be held up briefly in the stomach. On the other hand, jasmine rice contains starch that leaves the stomach without delay and is then digested at lightning speed.)

How Scientists Measure the Glycemic Index

1. An amount of food containing a standard amount of carbohydrate (usually 25 or 50 grams) is given to a volunteer to eat. For example, to test cooked spaghetti, the volunteer will be given 200 grams of spaghetti (about 7 ounces or 1¾ cups), which supplies 50 grams of carbohydrate (determined from food-composition tables).

2. Over the next 2 hours (or 3 hours if the volunteer has diabetes), we take a sample of their blood every 15 minutes during the first hour and thereafter every 30 minutes. The blood-glucose level of these blood samples is measured in the laboratory and recorded.

3. The blood-glucose level is plotted on a graph and the area under the curve is calculated using a computer program (Figure 1).

Figure 1. Measuring the glycemic index value of a food.

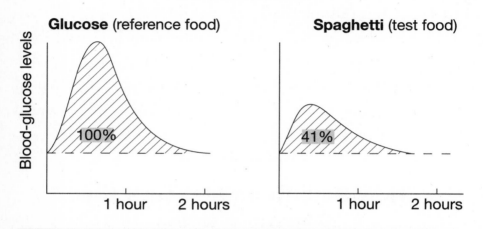

The test food and the reference food must contain the same amount of carbohydrate. The usual dose is 50 grams, but sometimes 25 grams is used when the portion size would otherwise be too large. Even smaller doses such as 15 grams have been used. The GI result is much the same whatever the dose because the glycemic index is simply a relative measure of carbohydrate quality.

4. The volunteer's response to spaghetti (or whatever food is being tested) is compared with his or her blood-glucose response to 50 grams of pure glucose (the reference food).

5. The reference food is tested on 2 or 3 separate occasions and an average value is calculated. This is done to reduce the effect of day-to-day variation in blood-glucose responses.

6. The average GI value found in 8–10 people is the GI value of that food.

High, Intermediate, or Low GI Value . . .
         High-GI   70 or higher
Intermediate-GI   56–69
      Low-GI   0–55

The glycemic index value of a food cannot be predicted from its composition or the glycemic index values of related foods. To test the glycemic index, you need real people and real foods. We describe how the GI value of a food is measured on page 47. There is no easy, inexpensive substitute test. Standardized methods are always followed so that results from one group of people can be directly compared with those of another group.

Glucose or White Bread?

In the past, some scientists used a 50-gram carbohydrate portion of white bread as the reference food because it was more typical of what we actually eat. On this scale, where the GI value of white bread is set at 100, some foods will have a GI value of over 100 because their effect on blood-glucose levels is higher than that of bread.

The use of two standards has caused some confusion, so the glucose = 100 scale is now recommended. It is possible to convert from the bread scale to the glucose scale using the factor 0.7 (70/100). This factor is derived from the fact that the GI value of white bread is 70 on the glucose = 100 scale.

To avoid confusion throughout this book, we refer to all foods according to a standard where glucose equals 100.

───────────

In total, eight to ten people need to be tested, and the GI value of the food is the average value of the group. We know this average figure is reproducible and that a different group of volunteers will produce a similar result. Results obtained in a group of people with diabetes are comparable to those without diabetes.

The higher the GI value, the higher the blood-glucose levels after consumption of the food. Foods with a high GI value usually reach a higher peak, i.e., the "glycemic spike" is higher, but sometimes blood-glucose levels remain moderately high over the whole two hours—white bread is a good example of this.

Rice Krispies™ (GI value of 87) and baked potatoes (GI value of 85) have very high GI values, meaning their effect on blood-glucose levels is almost as high as that of an equal amount of pure glucose (yes, you read it correctly). Figure 2 shows the blood-glucose response to white bread compared with pure glucose. Foods with a low GI value (such as lentils at 29) show a flatter blood-glucose response when eaten, as shown in Figure 3. The peak blood-glucose level is lower and the return to baseline levels is slower than with a high-GI food.

Figure 2. The effect of pure glucose (50 grams) and white bread (50-grams-carbohydrate portion) on blood-glucose levels.

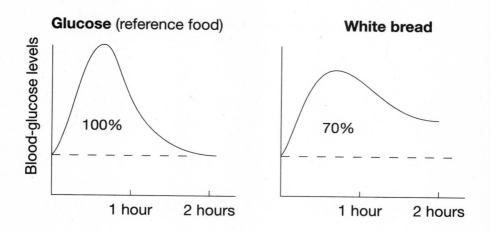

Figure 3. The effect of pure glucose (50 grams) and lentils (50-grams-carbohydrate portion) on blood-glucose levels.

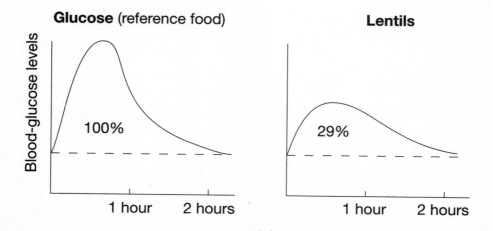

Why the Glycemic Index Is So Important

The slow digestion and gradual rise and fall in blood-glucose responses after eating a low-GI food helps control blood-glucose levels in people with diabetes or glucose intolerance. This effect may benefit healthy people as well, because it reduces the secretion of the hormone insulin over the course of the day. (This is discussed in greater detail in chapters 1 and 10.) Slower digestion helps to delay hunger pangs and thereby promote weight loss in overweight people.

Lower glucose levels over the course of the day also improve coronary health by reducing the oxidative stress associated with glycemic spikes. Keeping blood-glucose levels on an even keel helps ensure that the blood vessels remain elastic and supple, reducing the formation of fatty streaks and plaques that cause "hardening" of the arteries (atherosclerosis).

Lastly, good blood-glucose control means there's less tendency to form a blood clot, the final event that precipitates a heart attack.

These facts are not an exaggeration. They are not just preliminary findings. They are the confirmed results of many studies published in prestigious scientific journals around the world.

Can the Glycemic Index Be Applied to Real Meals?

Normally, real meals consist of a variety of foods. We can still apply the glycemic index to these real meals, even though the GI values are originally derived from testing single foods in isolation. Scientists have found that it is possible to predict the blood-glucose rise for a meal based on several foods with different GI values. The total carbohydrate content of the meal and the contribution of each food to the total carbohydrate must be known. Data like this can be found in food-composition tables.

For example, say you have a breakfast based on orange juice, Corn Flakes™ with milk and a slice of toast with a little margarine. In the following table, you can see how the GI value of the total meal has been calculated. This may look complicated. In practice, people don't need to make these sorts of calculations at all, but dietitians and nutrition researchers sometimes have to. Many studies have shown a very close relationship between the predicted blood-glucose response (based on published GI values of the relative effects of different foods and meals) and the actual observed blood-glucose response.

For more on calculating the GI value of a meal, menu, or recipe, see page 136.

How We Calculate the Overall Glycemic Index value of a Meal

FOOD	CARB. (G)	% TOTAL CARB.	GI VALUE	CONTRIBUTION TO MEAL GI VALUE
Orange juice (4 oz)	13	23	46	23% × 46 = 11
Kellogg's Corn Flakes™ (1 oz)	24	43	84	43% × 84 = 36
Milk (4 oz)	6	11	27	11% × 27 = 3
1 slice of toast (1 oz)	13	23	70	23% × 70 = 16
Total	56			Meal GI = 66*

* All calculations have been rounded off to the nearest whole number. These calculations provide a reasonably accurate assessment of the GI value of mixed meals, as long as the single components have been tested in the physical state in which they are finally eaten. However, in recipes that incorporate ingredients such as raw wheat flour and sugar that are subsequently cooked (e.g., cakes and cookies), the final GI value is not predictable.

A New Development: The Glycemic Load

When we eat a meal containing carbohydrate, our blood glucose rises and falls. The extent to which it rises and remains high is critically important to health and depends on two things: the amount of carbohydrate in the meal and the nature of that carbohydrate (its GI value). Both are equally important determinants of changes in blood-glucose levels. Unfortunately, the amount of carbohydrate still gets the lion's share of the attention.

It's easy to determine the amount of carbohydrate in a food by looking at the food label or consulting food-composition tables. (See sample food label below.) What you can't yet

Nutrition Facts		
Serving Size 1/2 cup (130g)		
Servings Per Container 3		
Amount Per Serving		
Calories 90	Calories from Fat 0	
		% Daily Value*
Total Fat 0g		**0%**
Saturated Fat 0g		**0%**
Cholesterol 0 mg		**0%**
Sodium 140 mg		**4%**
Total Carbohydrate 16g		**5%**
Dietary Fiber 6g		**22%**
Sugars 3g		
Protein 5g		
Vitamin A 0%	•	Vitamin C 2%
Calcium 2%	•	Iron 8%
*Percent Daily Values are based on a 2,000 calorie diet.		

determine from the food label or table of food composition is the GI value of the carbohydrate. That's where the GI tables in the back of this book come in. They allow you to look up the GI values of nearly 600 individual foods. It's the largest, most comprehensive and reliable list of GI values in the world.

Because both the amount and type of carbohydrate are needed to predict blood-glucose responses to a meal, we need a way to combine and describe the two. Researchers at Harvard University did this by coming up with the term "glycemic load." The glycemic load helps us predict what the effect of a particular carbohydrate food will be on our blood-glucose level after consuming that food. The glycemic load is greatest for those foods containing the most carbohydrate (like rice or spaghetti), especially when eaten in large quantities. The glycemic load is calculated simply by multiplying the GI value of a food by the amount of carbohydrate per serving and dividing by 100.

Glycemic load =
(GI value × carbohydrate per serving) ÷ 100

Compare the glycemic load of the following foods to see how the serving size as well as the GI value are significant in determing the glycemic response, i.e., how much of an impact the particular food, eaten in the particular quantity, will have on the resulting blood-glucose level.

Rice: 1 cup cooked instant rice has a GI value of 87 (see GI list at back of this book) and contains 37 grams of carbohydrate (from food-values reference tables)

Glycemic load: (87 × 37) ÷ 100 = 32

Spaghetti: 1 cup cooked has a GI value of 41 (average) and contains 52 grams carbohydrate

Glycemic load: (41 × 52) ÷ 100 = 21

Don't get carried away with glycemic load. The glycemic load doesn't distinguish "slow carbs" from "low carbs." It is much better to make food choices based on the GI rather than the GL because you want to see at least moderate amounts of carbohydrates in your meal. If you choose only on the basis of glycemic load, you could easily find yourself eating a lot of unwanted fat and excess protein. Low GI carbohydrates give you much more than just control of blood glucose—you'll feel fuller for longer, thanks to prolonged absorption, and you'll reduce your insulin levels at the same time.

What Determines a Food's Glycemic Index Value?

Scientists have been studying what gives one food a high GI value and another one a low GI value. There is a wealth of information, which can easily confuse. We have summarized the results of their research in the following table, which looks at the factors that influence the GI value of a food.

The key message is that the physical state of the starch in a food is by far the most important factor influencing its GI value. That's why the advances in food processing over the past 200 years have had such a profound effect on the overall GI values of the carbohydrates we eat.

Factors that Influence the GI Value of a Food

FACTOR	MECHANISM	EXAMPLES OF FOOD WHERE THE EFFECT IS SEEN
Starch gelatinization	The less gelatinized (swollen) the starch, the slower the rate of digestion	Al dente spaghetti, oatmeal, cookies have less gelatinized starch.
Physical entrapment	The fibrous coat around beans and seeds and plant cell walls acts as a physical barrier, slowing down access of enzymes to the starch inside.	Pumpernickel and grainy bread, legumes and barley

FACTOR	MECHANISM	EXAMPLES OF FOOD WHERE THE EFFECT IS SEEN
High amylose to amylopectin ratio*	The more amylose a food contains, the less water the starch will absorb and the slower its rate of digestion.	Basmati rice and legumes contain more amylose than other cereals.
Particle size	The smaller the particle size, the easier it is for water and enzymes to penetrate.	Finely milled flours have high GI values. Stone-ground flours have larger particles and lower GIs.
Viscosity of fiber	Viscous, soluble fibers increase the viscosity of the intestinal contents and this slows down the interaction between the starch and the enzymes. Finely milled whole-wheat and rye flours have *fast* rates of digestion and absorption because the fiber is not viscous.	Rolled oats, beans, lentils, apples, Metamucil®

(continues)

FACTOR	MECHANISM	EXAMPLES OF FOOD WHERE THE EFFECT IS SEEN
Sugar	The digestion of sugar produces only half as many glucose molecules as the same amount of starch (the other half is fructose). The presence of sugar also restricts gelatinization of the starch by binding water and reducing the amount of "available" water.	Social Tea™ biscuits, oatmeal cookies, and some breakfast cereals (Kellogg's Frosted Flakes™ or Smacks™) that are high in sugar, have relatively low GI values.
Acidity	Acids in foods slow down stomach emptying, thereby slowing the rate at which the starch can be digested.	Vinegar, lemon juice, lime juice, some salad dressings, pickled vegetables, sourdough bread
Fat	Fat slows down the rate of stomach emptying, thereby slowing the digestion of the starch.	Potato chips have a lower GI value than boiled white potatoes.

*Amylose and amylopectin are two different types of starch. Both are found in foods, but the ratio varies (see pages 64–65).

The Effect of Starch Gelatinization on the Glycemic Index

The starch in raw food is stored in hard, compact granules that make it difficult to digest. This is why potatoes might give you a stomach-ache if you ate them raw. Most starchy foods need to be cooked for this reason. During cooking, water and heat expand the starch granules to different degrees; some granules actually burst and free the individual starch molecules. This is what happens when you make a gravy by heating flour and water until the starch granules burst and the gravy thickens.

If most of the starch granules have swollen and burst during cooking, the starch is said to be fully gelatinized. Figure 4 (below) shows the difference between raw and cooked starch in potatoes.

Figure 4. The difference between raw (compact granules, left) and cooked (swollen granules, right) starch in potatoes.

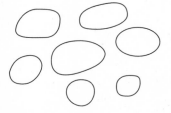

The swollen granules and free starch molecules are very easy to digest because the starch-digesting enzymes in the small intestine have a greater surface area to attack. The quick action of the enzymes results in a rapid, high blood-glucose rise after consumption of the food (remember that starch is nothing more than a string of glucose molecules). A food containing starch that is fully gelatinized will therefore have a very high GI value.

In foods such as cookies, the presence of sugar and fat and very little water makes starch gelatinization more difficult, and only about half of the granules will be fully gelatinized. For this reason, cookies tend to have intermediate GI values.

The Effect of Particle Size on the Glycemic Index

Another factor that influences starch gelatinization, and the GI value, is the particle size of the food. The grinding or milling of cereals reduces the particle size and makes it easier for water to be absorbed and enzymes to attack. That is why cereal foods made from fine flours tend to have a high GI value. The larger the particle size, the lower the GI value, as shown in Figure 5 (on page 63).

One of the most significant alterations to our food supply came with the introduction of steel roller mills in the mid-nineteenth century. Not only did they make it easier to remove the fiber from cereal grains, but also the particle size of the starch became smaller than ever before. Prior to the nineteenth century, stone grinding produced quite coarse flours that resulted in slower rates of digestion and absorption.

Figure 5. The larger the particle size, the lower the GI value.

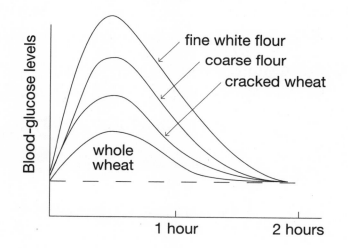

When starch is consumed in "nature's packaging"— whole intact grains that have been softened by soaking and cooking—the food will have a low GI value. For example, cooked barley has a GI value of only 25. Most cooked legumes have a GI value of between 30 and 40. Cooked whole wheat has a GI value of 41.

The Effect of Amylose and Amylopectin on the Glycemic Index

There are two sorts of starch in food—amylose and amylopectin—and researchers have discovered that the ratio of one to the other has a powerful effect on a food's GI value.

Amylose is a straight-chain molecule, like a string of beads. These tend to line up in rows and form tight compact clumps that are harder to gelatinize and therefore digest (see Figure 6, below).

Figure 6. Amylose is a straight-chain molecule that is harder to digest than amylopectin, which has many branching points.

Amylose slowly digested

individual glucose molecules

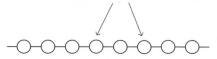

Amylopectin quickly digested

branch point

individual glucose molecules

On the other hand, amylopectin is a string of glucose molecules with lots of branching points, such as you see in some types of seaweed. Amylopectin molecules are therefore larger and more open and the starch is easier to gelatinize and digest.

Thus foods that have little amylose and plenty of amylopectin in their starch have higher GI values—for example, jasmine rice and wheat flour. Foods with a higher ratio of amylose to amylopectin have lower GI values—for example, Basmati rice (a long-grain fragrant rice) and legumes such as black beans, lentils, and soy beans.

The only whole (intact) grain food with a high GI value is low-amylose rice, such as Calrose or sticky rice (GI value of 83). These varieties of rice have starch that is very easily gelatinized during cooking and therefore easily broken down by digestive enzymes. This may help explain why we sometimes feel hungry not long after rice-based meals. However, some varieties of rice (Basmati and Uncle Ben's® Converted® long-grain white rice) have lower GI values because they have a higher amylose content than normal rice. Their GI values are in the range of 38–58.

The Effect of Sugar on the Glycemic Index

Table sugar or refined sugar (sucrose) has a GI value of only 60–65. This is because it is a disaccharide (double sugar) composed of one glucose molecule coupled to one fructose molecule. Fructose is absorbed and taken directly to the liver where it is immediately oxidized (burned as the source of energy). The blood-glucose response to pure fructose is very small (GI value of 19). Consequently, when we consume sucrose, only half of what we've eaten is actually glucose; the other half is fructose. This explains why the blood-glucose response to 50 grams of sucrose is approximately half that of 50 grams of corn syrup or maltodextrins (where the molecules are all glucose).

Why Does Pasta Have a Low GI Value?

We formerly thought that pasta had a low GI value because the main ingredient was semolina (cracked wheat) and not finely ground wheat flour. Research has now shown, however, that even pasta made with flour has a low GI value, and that the reason for the slow digestion rate is the physical entrapment of ungelatinized starch granules in a sponge-like network of protein (gluten) molecules in the pasta dough. Pasta is unique in this regard. Pastas of any shape and size have a fairly low GI value (30 to 60). Overcooked pasta is very

**soft and swollen in size and will have a higher GI value
than pasta cooked al dente. Asian noodles such as
hokkein, udon, and rice vermicelli also have low to intermediate GI values.**

———

Many foods containing large amounts of refined sugar
have a GI value of close to 60. This is the average of glucose
(GI value of 100) and fructose (GI value of 19). It is lower
than that of ordinary white bread, with a GI value averaging
around 70. Kellogg's Cocoa Puffs™, which contains 39 percent sugar, has a GI value of 77, lower than that of Rice
Krispies™ (GI value of 87), which contains little sugar.

So, contrary to popular opinion, most foods containing
simple sugars do not raise blood-glucose levels any more than
most complex starchy foods like bread.

Sugars that naturally occur in food include lactose,
sucrose, glucose, and fructose in variable proportions,
depending on the food. The overall blood-glucose response
to a food is very hard to predict on theoretical grounds
because stomach emptying is slowed by increasing concentration of the sugars, whatever their structure.

Some fruits, for example, have a low GI value (grapefruit
has one of only 25) while others are relatively high (watermelon has a GI value of 72). It seems the higher the acidity

of the fruit, the lower the GI value. Consequently, it is not possible to lump all fruits together and say that they will have a low GI value because they are high in fiber. They are not all equal. See the tables in Part 4 to compare fruits.

Many foods containing sugars are a mixture of refined and naturally occurring sugars—sweetened yogurt, for example. The overall effect on the blood-glucose response is too hard to predict. This is why we need to test the glycemic index of sugary foods in real people before we make generalizations about their GI values.

The Effect of Fiber on the Glycemic Index

The effect of fiber on the GI value of a food depends on the type of fiber and its viscosity. Finely ground wheat fiber, such as in whole-wheat bread, has no effect whatsoever on the rate of starch digestion and subsequent blood-glucose response. Similarly, any product made with whole-wheat flour will have a GI value similar to that of its white counterpart. Breakfast cereals made with whole-wheat flours will also tend to have high GI values, unless there are other confounding factors. Puffed Wheat (GI value of 80), which is made from well-cooked whole-wheat grains, has a high GI value, *despite* its high fiber content.

If the fiber is still intact it can act as a physical barrier to digestion, and then the GI value will be lower. This is one of the reasons why All-Bran® has a low GI value. It is also one of the reasons why whole (intact) grains usually have low GI values.

Viscous fiber thickens the mixture of food entering the digestive tract. This slows the passage of food and restricts the movement of enzymes, thereby slowing digestion. The end result is a lower blood-glucose response. Legumes contain high levels of viscous fiber, as do oats and psyllium (found in some breakfast cereals and dietary-fiber supplements such as Metamucil®). These foods all have low GI values.

The Effect of Acid on the Glycemic Index

Within the last few years, several reports in the scientific literature have indicated that a realistic amount of vinegar or lemon juice in the form of a salad dressing consumed with a mixed meal has significant blood-glucose-lowering effects.

As little as 4 teaspoons of vinegar in a vinaigrette dressing (4 teaspoons vinegar and 2 teaspoons oil) taken with an average meal lowered blood glucose by as much as 30 percent.

These findings have important implications for people with diabetes or individuals at risk of diabetes, coronary heart disease, or the metabolic syndrome (see chapters 10, 11, and 12).

The effect appears to be related to the acidity, because other organic acids (such as lactic acid and propionic acid) also have a blood-glucose-lowering effect, but the degree of reduction varies with the type of acid. Our findings show that lemon juice is just as powerful. Vinegar or lemon juice may also be used in marinades or sauces.

Essentially, the acidity in food puts the brake on stomach emptying, slowing the delivery of food to the small intestine. Digestion of the carbohydrate in the food is therefore slowed and the final result is that blood-glucose levels are significantly lower. Good news for people with diabetes!

> **A side salad with your meal, especially a**
> **high-GI meal, will help to keep blood-glucose**
> **levels under control.**

Sourdough breads, in which lactic acid and propionic acid are produced by the natural fermentation of starch and sugars by the yeast starter culture, also can reduce levels of blood glucose and insulin by 22 percent compared to normal bread. In addition, there was higher satiety associated with breads having decreased rates of digestion and absorption. Thus there is significant potential to lower blood glucose and insulin and increase satiety with sourdough bread formulations.

The Glycemic Index Was Never Meant to Be Used in Isolation!

At first glance it might appear that some high-fat foods such as chocolate seem a good choice simply because they have a low GI value. Thisis absolutely not the case. A food's GI value was never meant to offer the only criterion by which it is judged as fit to eat. Large amounts of fat (and protein) in food tend to slow the rate of stomach emptying and therefore the rate at which foods are digested in the small intestine. High-fat foods will therefore tend to have lower GI values than their low-fat equivalents. For example, potato chips have a lower GI value (54) than potatoes baked without fat (85). Many cookies have a lower GI value (55–65) than bread (70). In these instances, a lower GI value doesn't mean an automatically better choice from a nutritional standpoint. Saturated fat in these foods will have adverse effects on coronary health, far greater than the benefit of lower blood-glucose levels. These foods should be treated as "indulgences," or for special occasions.

This is not to say that all fats in foods should be avoided. One of the reasons why legumes have such a low GI value is their relatively high fat content compared to cereal grains. But just as there are differences in the nature of carbohydrates in foods, there are differences in the quality of fats. We need to be choosy about fats too. Healthy fats, such as the omega-3 polyunsaturated fats, are not only good for us, they help to lower the blood-glucose response to meals.

Glycemic Index Values and Glycemic Load* of Some Popular Foods
(Glucose = 100)

	GI	GL
BREAKFAST CEREALS		
Kellogg's All-Bran®	30	4
Kellogg's Cocoa Puffs™	77	20
Kellogg's Corn Flakes™	92	24
Kellogg's Mini Wheats™	58	12
Kellogg's Nutrigrain™	66	10
Old-fashioned oatmeal	42	9
Kellogg's Rice Krispies™	82	22
Kellogg's Special K™	69	14
Kellogg's Raisin Bran™	61	12
GRAINS/PASTAS		
Buckwheat	54	16
Bulgur	48	12
Rice		
Basmati	58	22
Brown	50	16

	GI	GL
Instant	87	36
Uncle Ben's® Converted®, white	39	14
Noodles—instant	47	19
Pasta		
egg fettuccine (avg)	40	18
spaghetti (avg)	38	18
vermicelli	35	16
tortellini, Stouffer's™	50	1
BREAD		
Bagel	72	25
Croissant*	67	17
Crumpet	69	13
"Grainy" breads (avg)	49	6
Pita bread	57	10
Pumpernickel (avg)	50	6
Rye bread (avg)	58	8
White bread (avg)	70	10
Whole-wheat bread (avg)	77	9
CRACKERS/CRISPBREAD		
Kavli™	71	12
Puffed crispbread	81	15
Ryvita®	69	11
Water cracker	78	14
COOKIES		
Oatmeal	55	12
Milk Arrowroot™	69	12

(continues)

	GI	GL
Shortbread (commercial)*	64	10
CAKES		
Chocolate, frosted, Betty Crocker®	38	20
Oatbran muffin	69	24
Sponge cake	46	17
Waffles	76	10
VEGETABLES		
Beets, canned	64	5
Carrots (avg)	47	3
Parsnip	97	12
Peas (green, avg)	48	3
Potato		
baked (avg)	**85**	**26**
boiled	**88**	**16**
french fries	**75**	**22**
microwaved	**82**	**27**
Potato new	57	12
Pumpkin	75	3
Sweet corn	60	11
Sweet potato (avg)	61	17
Rutabaga	72	7
Yam (avg)	37	13
LEGUMES		
Baked beans (avg)	48	7
Broad beans	79	9
Butter beans	31	6

	GI	GL
Chickpeas (avg)	28	8
Cannellini beans (avg)	38	12
Kidney beans (avg)	28	7
Lentils (avg)	29	5
Soy beans (avg)	18	1
FRUIT		
Apple (avg)	38	6
Apricot (dried)	31	9
Banana (avg)	51	13
Cherries	22	3
Grapefruit	25	3
Grapes (avg)	46	8
Kiwi fruit (avg)	53	6
Mango	51	8
Orange (avg)	48	5
Papaya	59	10
Peach (avg)		
canned (natural juice)	38	4
fresh (avg)	42	5
Pear (avg)	38	4
Pineapple	59	7
Plum	39	5
Raisins	64	28
Cantaloupe	65	4
Watermelon	72	4

(continues)

	GI	GL
DAIRY FOODS		
Milk		
full fat	27	3
skim	32	4
chocolate flavored	42	13
condensed	61	33
Custard	43	7
Ice cream		
regular (avg)	61	8
low fat	50	3
Yogurt, low fat	33	10
BEVERAGES		
Apple juice	40	12
Coca-Cola®	63	16
Lemonade	66	13
Fanta®	68	23
Orange juice (avg)	52	12
SNACK FOODS		
Tortilla chips* (avg)	63	17
Fish sticks	38	7
Peanuts* (avg)	14	1
Popcorn	72	8
Potato chips*	57	10
CONVENIENCE FOODS		
Macaroni & cheese	64	32

	GI	GL
Soup		
lentil	44	9
split pea	60	16
tomato	38	6
Sushi (avg)	52	19
Pizza, cheese	60	16
SWEETS		
Chocolate*	44	13
Jelly beans (avg)	78	22
Life Savers	70	21
Mars Bar®*	68	27
Kudo whole-grain chocolate-chip bar	62	20
SUGARS		
Honey (avg)	55	10
Fructose (avg)	19	2
Glucose	100	10
Lactose (avg)	46	5
Sucrose (avg)	68	7
SPORTS BARS		
Clif® bar (cookies & cream)	101	34
PowerBar® (chocolate)	83	35
METRx® bar (vanilla)	74	37

4

Fats: Facts and Fallacies

You can't turn on the television or open a newspaper these days without reading something about fat. The problem is, much of the information we're getting is either too scientific or too confusing. What's the bottom line? Is fat healthy or unhealthy?

The short answer: It depends. It's true that the type of fat you eat determines, to a large degree, whether you'll suffer a heart attack or stroke. What's more, the right type of fat in your diet (even if it's a low-fat diet) may reduce your risk of certain types of cancer, depression, many autoimmune diseases such as arthritis, and may generally promote health and longevity. Indeed, there's good evidence that the type of fat an infant receives in its first few weeks of life may increase intelligence and learning ability!

One of the main findings of the past decade is that not all fats are bad for your heart; in fact, we all need to eat some fat for optimal health. In our quest for a non-fattening diet, though, we've unwittingly thrown out the baby with the bath water. Many of us decided that all fats were bad and that a healthy diet contained as little fat as possible. Not true! In reality, it's possible to replace the harmful fats with the beneficial ones, which allows you to consume as much as 35 to 40 percent of your calories as fat. For many people, higher-fat diets taste better, and they're easier to stick with, since a diet higher in heart-healthy fats more closely matches our early eating habits, ingrained since childhood.

Some Facts about Fats

Fatty acids are described as saturated, monounsaturated or polyunsaturated, which is determined by their molecular structure. The most important thing to remember about dietary fats is this: Saturated fats are heart-unhealthy, while unsaturated fats (mono- and polyunsaturated) are heart-healthy.

The "Good" Fats

As we mentioned earlier, you may be surprised to learn that some fats are good for you. For example, monounsaturated fats, or MUFAs, such as those in olive and canola oils, can reduce the risk of cardiovascular disease by reducing triglycerides in the blood and increasing levels of good HDL cholesterol.

Fats in a Nutshell

ALL FATS and oils contain differing amounts of the following:

■ Monounsaturated fats, or MUFAs;

■ Polyunsaturated fats, or PUFAs; and

■ Saturated fat.

(This is especially important if you have diabetes or a family history of heart disease.) Research has shown that a low HDL level is one of the best predictors of increased risk of heart attack.

The best types of fat to consume are those that contain a high proportion of monounsaturated (MUFAs), polyunsatu-

MUFAs	PUFAs	Saturated fats
Heart healthy	Heart healthy	Heart un-healthy
Lower LDL	Lower LDL	Increase LDL
Protect HDL	Lower HDL	
Food sources	**Food sources**	**Food sources**
Olive oil, canola oil, avocados, peanut butter, almonds, pistachios	Salmon, sardines, mackerel, bluefish, canola oil, walnuts, flaxseed, white albacore tuna	Full-fat dairy products,fatty cuts of meat, poultry skin

rated (PUFAs), and omega-3 fatty acids. In practice, this means you should prepare meals with lean meat, seafood, olive oil, canola oil, and peanut oil, because they all contain a lot of monounsaturated fatty acids. You can also include nuts, avocados, and polyunsaturated oils such as safflower oil and sunflower oil. These foods and oils should take the place of saturated fats, such as you find in fatty meat, fried foods, high fat dairy products, and most bakery products.

Polyunsaturated fats (PUFAs) include omega-3 and omega-6 fatty acids; both are essential in your diet. Research suggests that we should be eating more omega-3s than omega-6s, but we're not—in fact, though we need both types of fatty acids in our diet, many experts believe that we're eating too much of the omega-6s. We'll describe these two omega fats in greater detail later in this chapter.

Polyunsaturated margarines and seed oils, such as safflower, sunflower, and soybean oils, are the major sources of omega-6 fatty acids in most of our diets. Fish and other seafood are the main source of omega-3 fatty acids, as is canola oil.

Essential Fatty Acids

Not only are some types of fat good for you, but also your body actually requires some types of fats—called essential fatty acids—which you can only get through your diet. We used to think a very small amount of these fatty acids would suffice, but we were wrong: We appear to need much larger amounts of them because they play a fundamental role in the development of our cell membranes, and we also need them to grow and develop normally.

The human brain requires two of the most important essential fatty acids, eicosapentanoic acid (EPA) and docosahexanoic acid (DHA). Both of these essential fatty acids are omega-3s, which we'll discuss in more detail later in this chapter. Without EPA and DHA our body tissues can suffer, causing a high tissue turnover rate. The earliest sign of this high turnover rate would be scaly dermatitis (skin irritation), and we die if the deficiency exists for longer than a few months. But that's not all: We also appear to need essential fatty acids to achieve the best of mental health and to reach our full intellectual potential. Science has proven that depression is linked to a lack of these special fatty acids in our diet.

The best sources of EPA and DHA are seafood, especially "fatty" fish, such as salmon, mackerel, sardines and herring (which, in truth, are actually no fattier than lean meat, but do contain more fat than most other fish). Our absolute dependency on these fatty acids may go all the way back to our evolutionary ancestors, who ate large amounts of fish and shellfish.

Dairy Foods: A Mixed Blessing

THOUGH DAIRY foods are a rich, readily absorbed source of calcium, they can be high in saturated fat. To meet calcium requirements, experts recommend that adults eat two to three servings of dairy products every day. Good low-fat dairy choices include skim or 1 percent milk and nonfat or low-fat yogurts.

———

If you're lactose intolerant, try calcium-fortified orange and grapefruit juices, lactose reduced milk, high-calcium soy milk, salmon (canned, with bones), high-calcium tofu, calcium-fortified breakfast cereal and dried figs—all great-tasting nondairy sources of calcium.

———

Many experts believe that infants don't get enough EPA and DHA in infant formulas and therefore recommend supplements. Breast milk is a good source of these special fatty acids, and Japanese women, whose normal diet includes lots of fish, produce milk with the highest essential fatty acid levels of all.

The "Bad" Fats

Most people have heard that saturated fat isn't good for us, and there's no argument from anybody on this point. Solid at room temperature, saturated fat comes in the form of fatty marbling in meat, the cream in milk and other high fat dairy products, and in some of the tropical oils such as palm oil, widely used as shortening for frying and for making cakes, pies, cookies and crackers. Many studies from all around the world have clearly shown that saturated fat increases our risk of coronary heart disease. But don't make the mistake of thinking animal foods are all bad just because some contain saturated fat. In fact, humans evolved on a steady diet of animal foods and we are dependent on them to get many of the nutrients we need. In our evolutionary past, however, animal foods were not as high a source of saturated fat as they are now. Game meat, even today, is lower in fat and has relatively less saturated fat compared with that of domesticated animals.

When animals are confined so that they can't move around naturally and are over-fed a diet of grains, they gain excess body fat in and around the muscles. Grain-fed meat is typically what we find in America today: It's highly marbled (that is, it has fat within the muscle tissue that's impossible to avoid eating) and, to most Americans, this means high quality, good-tasting meat. Though it may taste good, it's extremely high in saturated fat, and may increase your risk of heart disease, obesity and certain cancers. Fats from other animals (including pigs and chickens) are less saturated and contain some polyunsaturated fatty acids. Fats from deer and other game animals are lower still in saturated fats and often contain significant amounts of polyunsaturated fatty acids.

Recently, researchers have found that trans-fatty acids

(also known as trans fats or partially hydrogenated vegetable oil) are just as bad for our health as saturated fats. In fact, the fda has ruled that, as of 2006, food manufacturers must list the amount of trans fats included in one serving of all products. Trans-fatty acids are produced during the manufacture of margarines and behave like saturated fat in the products (increasing its firmness), as well as in our bodies (increasing the risk of heart attack). Foods high in trans fats include fried fast foods, some margarines, crackers, cookies, and snack cakes.

Is Vegetable Oil a Friendly Fat?

WE USED to think—thanks to many of the television commercials in the 1960s and '70s—that all vegetable oils are good for us. While it's true that all vegetable oils are cholesterol free, their fatty acids can be highly saturated, promoting high blood cholesterol. Coconut and palm oils, for example, are highly saturated vegetable fats. Most other plant oils, on the other hand, contain little saturated fat; for example, avocado, peanut, and other nut oils are largely monounsaturated, making them heart-healthy.

For the Love of Cheese

HAVING A hard time finding a tasty low-fat cheese? Try these tips for making the most of your higher-fat cheese choices.

- Consider eating a little of a strong-flavored cheese rather than a lot of something bland and tasteless.
- Shave some fresh Parmesan on your pasta. It's delicious and super high in calcium.
- Enjoy full-fat cheeses in small amounts. This includes regular types of cheddar, American, Swiss, Brie, Colby, cream cheese, Gouda and Havarti.
- Try grating hard cheeses to make them go further.
- Serve your favorite soft cheeses with low-fat crackers, and fresh and dried fruit.
- Try some mozzarella cheese—whole milk or part skim—it may contain less fat than some reduced-fat cheeses. Use it in recipes and sandwiches.
- Feel free to use lower-fat cheeses, such as cottage cheese, ricotta and feta daily.

Our Recommended Intakes

Health experts advise us to increase our carbohydrate intake to about 55 percent of our total calories and to choose low-GI versions of the high carbohydrate foods. The remaining calories in our diet (45 percent of it) should be split between protein and fat. Chances are that you're eating at least 15 percent of your energy as protein—most people eat this amount without even trying. This still leaves plenty of room for some fat: In fact, most experts consider a diet "low fat" if no more than 30 percent of total calories come from fat. It's not necessary to eat less fat than this, especially when you consume heart-healthy monounsaturated fats (MUFAs), which have important health effects. It's important not to throw out the healthy fats with the unhealthy ones—and that's exactly what many people have been doing in their quest for the ultimate low-fat diet.

Which Oil for What?

Try using a variety of different oils, depending on the dish:

- For stir fries, add a distinctive flavor with canola-based flavored oils or peanut or sesame oil. You can also drizzle a little sesame oil over the top of the stir-fry for added flavor.

- For salad dressings you can add a nutty flavor with walnut or macadamia oil, or use some sesame oil for an oriental salad.

- For Mediterranean cooking, including salads, use extra virgin olive oil for its distinctive flavor.

■ For everyday cooking, including roasting and frying, choose a neutral-flavored oil with a high smoke point, such as sunflower or canola. Looking for a pleasant nutty flavor in baked goods? Try corn oil.

The Omega Story

Omega-3 fats, one of the most important good-for-you fats, are polyunsaturated fatty acids found in several plants and plant oils, including canola, peanut, flaxseed, and soy. They're found in even greater quantities in fatty fish and seafood.

Several studies have shown that if you eat fish regularly you could reduce your risk of coronary heart disease. In fact, studies have found that eating just one serving of fish a week could reduce your risk of a fatal heart attack by 40 percent! (Eating fish more often than once a week doesn't seem to increase this protective effect.) The likely protective components of fish are the long-chain marine omega-3 polyunsaturated fatty acids called eicosapentanoic acid (EPA) and docosahexanoic acid (DHA). The omega-3 fatty acid derived from plants, alpha-linolenic acid or ALA (one source of which is canola oil), may also decrease the risk of heart attack, but the effect is not as strong as with the fatty acids from fish. Many experts believe that many of our diets are relatively deficient in omega-3 fatty acids.

How Omega-3s Help

Omega-3 fatty acids are essential for normal growth and development, and may play an important role in the prevention and treatment of heart disease, hypertension, arthritis, and cancer. Scientists are still trying to work out how omega-3 fatty acids help to prevent heart attacks. To be sure, consuming more omega-3 fats reduces several risk factors, for example:

■ At high doses, marine omega-3 fatty acids have been shown to lower triglyceride levels in the blood, and high triglyceride levels are a recognized risk factor for heart disease.

■ Omega-3s may also slightly raise levels of HDL—the good cholesterol—in the blood. (These effects are specific to marine sources of omega-3 fats; experts don't see the same effects with the plant omega-3 fatty acids.)

■ Some studies suggest that marine omega-3 fatty acids reduce blood clotting. Although we want blood to clot quickly when we're bleeding, if it tends to coagulate excessively, clots could form inside our blood vessels, a condition called thrombosis. One of the common precipitating events of a heart attack is when blood clots form in the heart's arteries, which can completely cut the blood supply to a vital part of the heart muscle. The heart then loses its ability to pump blood to the brain, causing death. Clots in less important arteries can mean that you survive the attack but the risk of having another is high.

■ Omega-3 fats may also reduce your susceptibility to an irregular heartbeat, known as heart arrhythmia or ventricular fibrillation, which is one of the main causes of sudden death after an acute heart attack. Studies have shown that omega-3 fatty acids help to restore regular beating in isolated heart cells.

■ High intakes of omega-3 fatty acids can also reduce high blood pressure (also called hypertension). However, scientists only find this effect when people consume large amounts of fish oil supplements, not the quantities that you might consume just from eating fish.

Omega-3 Fats And Your Health

Arthritis Relief

In clinical trials, marine omega-3 fatty acids consistently reduce the pain and morning stiffness that's associated with rheumatoid arthritis. Certain substances in the blood, called eicosanoids and cytokines, initiate the immune response and its consequent inflammation. Scientists believe that omega-3 fatty acids decrease these reactions.

Brain Development

Omega-3 fatty acids help nerve growth in fetuses and young infants. Some experts believe that infants are not able to synthesize enough docosahexanoic acid (DHA) for optimal growth from the precursor compound alpha-linolenic acid (ALA). Breast milk, however, is naturally rich in DHA, and DHA levels in the brains of breast-fed babies are higher than those in formula fed babies.

Formulas enriched with DHA have been found to improve visual acuity and neuromental development in premature infants compared with conventional formula, but the long-term implications of adding DHA to formula are unknown, so some infant formula manufacturers are unwilling to risk the safety of the formula by adding it. This is yet another reason why we should feed all babies human milk whenever possible.

Pregnant and lactating women can increase their intake of omega-3s by eating more fish; they will pass the benefit onto their infants either through the placenta or in their breast milk.

(continues)

Cancer Risk

Many studies show an association between high fish consumption and reduced risk of colon and breast cancer. In addition, animal experiments have shown that high doses of fish oils inhibit the development of chemically-induced mammary (breast) and colorectal cancers. Experts say, however, that the current evidence is insufficient to prove that eating fish decreases cancer risk.

Does the Ratio of Omega-3 to Omega-6 Fatty Acids Matter?

Experts disagree about the importance of the ratio of omega-3 to omega-6 fats in our diets. Some believe the ratio is too low: that we eat too few omega-3s and too many omega-6s from safflower and sunflower oils and their margarines. Many researchers agree that the ratio of omega-6s to omega-3s should be 1:4 or 1:1 at the most. That is, you should consume about four times more omega-3s than omega-6s, but certainly no more omega-6s than omega-3s.

Concerns with Omega-3 Fats

One of the concerns scientists have with omega-3 fatty acids is that they oxidize, or turn rancid. Oxidized fats have been implicated in causing arteriosclerosis, or hardening of the arteries. In fact, all polyunsaturated fats (PUFAs) are susceptible to oxidation, so we should consume them with adequate amounts of antioxidants such as vitamin E. Fortunately, both PUFAs and vitamin E tend to occur together in the same foods, including: polyunsaturated plant oils such as margarines, salad dressings, green and leafy vegetables, wheat germ, whole-grain products, liver, egg yolks, nuts and seeds.

In their natural state, all PUFAs are rich sources of vitamin E, but sometimes food processing can inadvertently reduce antioxidant (such as vitamin E) concentrations, which is one reason why we should avoid foods and oils that have been stored for long periods of time—even in the freezer—or under inappropriately high temperatures. Oils are usually packaged in dark containers to protect against light, which increases chances of rancidity.

Omega Fats in a Nutshell

Omega-6 (Linoleic Acid)

Our bodies can't make linoleic acid, so we must get it from the foods we eat. We need this fatty acid for cell membrane integrity, blood pressure regulation, blood clot formation, regulation of blood lipids, and immune response to injury and infection.

Good food sources: Leafy vegetables, seeds, nuts, grains, vegetable oils (corn, safflower, soybean, cottonseed, sesame, sunflower)

(continues)

Omega-3 (Linoleic Acid)

Like linoleic acid, linolenic acid is also essential to our bodies, is not produced by our bodies and, therefore, must come from food. Omega-3s aid in brain development, bring arthritis pain relief, and may lower cancer risk.

Good food sources: Fats and oils (canola, soybean, walnut, wheat germ, some margarines), nuts and seeds (butternuts, walnuts, soybean kernels), soybeans

EPA (Eicosapentanoic Acid) and DHA (Docosahexanoic Acid)

Since our bodies only make small amounts of EPA and DHA, we must rely on getting these fatty acids from our diets, especially from fish and seafood. EPA helps nerve growth in fetuses and young infants and DHA has been found to improve visual acuity and neuromental development in premature infants.

Good food sources: Human milk, shellfish, mackerel, tuna, salmon, bluefish, mullet, sturgeon, anchovy, herring, trout, sardines

There's more than enough evidence to suggest that marine omega-3 fatty acids can be good for your health—especially for people with coronary heart disease. Plant and marine sources of omega-3s have distinct physiological effects, so they cannot replace each other. Try to eat fish at least once a week, and include a plant source of omega-3s, such as canola oil, in your diet. (Olive oil is not a rich source of omega-3 fatty acids.) To increase the plant omega-3 fatty acids further, aim to eat green leafy vegetables every day.

The Best Fish Sources of Omega-3 Fats

BOTH CANNED and fresh fish are rich sources of omega-3 fats. The following lists show some of the richest varieties:

Canned Fish	
Salmon (including pink and red)	Mackerel
Sardines	White albacore tuna
Fresh fish	
Atlantic and Pacific salmon (fresh or smoked)	Sea mullet
	Southern bluefin tuna
Mackerel (Atlantic, Pacific, Spanish)	Swordfish
Shellfish	
Eastern and Pacific oysters	
Squid (calamari)	

5

The Most Frequently Asked Questions—Answered

Everybody can benefit from adopting the low-GI approach to eating. It is the way nature intended us to eat. All the nutrients in nature's original packaging are in a slow-energy-release form. Since the Industrial Revolution, however, we have taken natural carbohydrate foods and manufactured them into fast-release or instant food as part of our quest for a more palatable and convenient and less perishable food supply. Unfortunately, the effect of all those instant foods is catching up with us in the form of diseases of affluence such as obesity, heart disease, and diabetes. They also make us feel hungry and sluggish at times.

There is, however, no need to turn our backs on progress. We have sufficient knowledge of food and nutrition to let the pendulum swing back just enough to suit our needs. But we need the facts. We need answers. In this section we answer the most frequently asked questions about carbohydrates, diet, and the glycemic index.

Q. Can you tell me the GI values of beef, chicken, fish, eggs, nuts, and avocados? Why don't these foods appear in GI lists?

A. These foods contain no carbohydrate, or so little that their GI values can't be tested according to the standard methodology. Bear in mind that the glycemic index is a measure of carbohydrate quality, not quantity. Essentially, these types of foods, eaten alone, won't have much effect on your blood-glucose levels. But because we're constantly asked about them, we've included these foods in the tables and given them a GI value of [0]. And the glycemic load of these foods is 0.

Q. Can you tell me the GI values of alcoholic beverages?

A. Alcoholic beverages contain very little carbohydrate. In fact, most wines and liquors contain virtually none. A 12-ounce can of beer contains about 11 grams of carbohydrate (just 4 grams in a can of light beer), while a can of regular soda has between 35 and 40 grams of carbohydrate. For this reason, a beer will raise glucose levels a little. If you drink beer in large volumes (not a good idea, really) then you could expect it to have a significant effect on blood glucose. The tables contain alcoholic beverages with an assigned GI value of [0].

Q. Does the GI value increase with the serving size? If I eat twice as much, does the GI value double?

A. The GI value *always* remains the same, even if you double the amount of carbohydrate in your meal. This is because the glycemic index is a relative ranking of foods containing the *same amount* of carbohydrate (whether it's 15 grams or 50 grams). But if you double the amount of food you eat, you should expect to see a higher blood-glucose response, i.e., your glucose levels will reach a higher peak and take longer to return to baseline compared with a normal serving.

The rise and fall in blood glucose after eating is determined by both the quantity and quality of the carbohydrate. Even if you eat twice as much, the blood-glucose level won't quite double, because the body tries to limit the rise as much as it can. The area under the curve might be 50 percent greater, instead of 100 percent.

Q. If my blood-glucose level is determined by both the quantity and quality of the carbohydrate in a meal, how can I predict what I'll see? How can I compare two meals containing different foods with different amounts of carbohydrate and varying GI values?

A. To do this, we calculate the glycemic load of each meal.

Let's say one meal contains a 5-ounce apple, which contains 15 grams of carbohydrate and has a GI value of 40. The glycemic load is $(15 \times 40) \div 100 = 6$. Let's say the other meal contains a 5-ounce potato, which contains 20 grams of carbohydrate and has a GI value of 90. The glycemic load is $(20 \times 90) \div 100 = 18$. So the glycemic load is about three times higher with a potato than an apple (18 versus 6). While the glycemic response might not be three times higher, the demand for insulin will be.

Q. What is the effect of extra protein and fat on the glycemic index and blood-glucose response?

A. Eaten alone, protein and fat have little effect on blood-glucose levels. So a steak or a piece of cheese won't produce a rise in blood glucose. It's the carbohydrates in foods that are primarily responsible for the rise and fall in glucose after meals. Adding fat and protein to a meal doesn't affect the nature of the carbohydrate and thus does not affect its GI value. But that's not to say that protein and fat won't affect the blood-glucose response when eaten together *with* carbohydrate. Both tend to cause a delay in stomach emptying, thereby slowing the rate at which carbohydrate can be digested and absorbed. So a high-fat meal will have a lower glycemic effect than a low-fat meal, even if they both contain the same amount and type of carbohydrate. However, you can still count on the fact that a high-GI carbohydrate food will produce a higher response than a low-GI food, even if there's extra fat and protein added to the meal.

Q. If additional fat and protein cause lower glycemic responses, shouldn't we advocate higher-protein or higher-fat diets for people with diabetes?

A. The difficulty with both suggestions is that *very* high-fat or high-protein diets have been associated with insulin resistance. This means that, over the long term, the consumption of any carbohydrate accompanying the fat or protein will tend to greatly increase blood-glucose and insulin levels and cause deterioration in overall blood-glucose control.

More moderate increases in protein and fat (particularly monounsaturated fat) may be possible, but there is relatively little research to guide us. Diets high in monounsaturated fat may improve blood lipids, but they have not been shown to improve overall glycemic control as judged by glycated hemoglobin levels (one of the best measures of diabetes control).

Q. Does the glycemic index predict the glycemic effect of a normal serving of food?

A. Generally (although there are some exceptions), the ranking of foods from high to low turns out to be roughly the same when compared per serving, per 200 calories, or per 100 grams of food. Critics of the GI approach often argue that foods contain different amounts of carbohydrate (both per serving and per 100 grams), while the glycemic index is based on a comparison of the same amount of carbohydrate.

Q. Can you use the glycemic index to predict the effect of a meal containing a mixture of foods with very different GI values?

A. Yes, the glycemic index can predict the relative effects of different mixed meals containing foods with very different GI values. More than fifteen studies have looked at the GI values of mixed meals. Twelve of these studies showed an excellent correlation between what was expected and what was actually found. You can predict the GI value of a mixed meal by making a few simple calculations (see page 54). If half the carbohydrate in the mixed meal comes from a food with a GI value of 30 (e.g., black beans) and the other half comes from a rice with a GI value of 80, then the mixed meal will have a GI of (50% × 30) + (50% × 80) = 55. This is a good example, showing that you don't have to avoid all high-GI foods to eat a low-GI diet. Inclusion of one low-GI food per meal might be all that's needed.

Q. What about low-carbohydrate diets? If carbohydrates increase my blood-glucose level, wouldn't a low-carbohydrate intake make sense?

A. The difficulty with this proposition is that there is hardly a shred of scientific evidence that very low carbohydrate intake benefits anyone. Some popular diets are based on the concept of avoiding carbohydrate foods—even fruits and vegetables are restricted, while meat and dairy foods laden with saturated fat, cholesterol, and calories form the basis of the diet. This is a recipe for sudden heart attack—there's a wealth of evidence that diets high in saturated fat are unhealthy.

Low-carbohydrate diets come in many forms, however. Some are not so extreme as that described above. The Zone diet recommends less carbohydrate (about 40 percent instead of 55 percent) and more protein (30 percent instead of 15 percent) but keeps fats to no more than 30 percent. It includes advice about quality of carbohydrate (low versus high GI value) and type of fat (unsaturated versus saturated). To keep within the recommended limits, many specially prepared and packaged foods are often necessary. If you enjoy this way of eating, then there's nothing really wrong with it. But over time you may find yourself yearning for high-carbohydrate foods like bread and potatoes.

One recent study from the Netherlands gave support to a moderate increase in protein (from 15 to 25 percent) and a moderate decrease in carbohydrate (from 55 to 45 percent). Fat intake was the same in both the control group and the high-protein group—30 percent of energy. Volunteers in the study were permitted to eat as much food as they wished but all were trying to lose weight. At the end of the twelve-week study, both weight loss and body-fat loss were greater on the high protein diet. The investigators suggested that the higher protein intake had increased the metabolic rate and also increased satiety. It is well known that protein stimulates more thermogenesis (heat production) than any other nutrient and is also the most satiating nutrient. There was no advice about the glycemic index on either diet.

> **You don't have to avoid all high- GI foods to eat a low-GI diet. Inclusion of one low-GI food per meal may be all that's needed.**

Q. The glycemic index has been criticized because of variability in blood-glucose responses between people and in the same person from day to day. How much variation should we expect? How much is acceptable?

A. When we measure the GI value of a food in a group of individuals, not everyone produces the same GI value (see Figure 7, page 105). For example, if we test apples (average GI value of 40), then one individual might give 20 and another 60. This variation is a natural biological variation that has been traced back to day-to-day variability in glucose tolerance. One of the reasons we test the reference food three times in any one person is to obtain a reliable indication of their normal glucose tolerance. If we tested apples three times, we would also find that each person moved closer to the average result for the whole group. The bottom line is that foods classed as having high, medium, or low GI values will show the same ranking in different individuals (as shown in Figure 7, on page 105).

This natural variability in blood-glucose response has been a major source of criticism of the glycemic index. But it is illogical to criticize the glycemic index on these grounds because the variability applies to all dietary approaches, whether it be carbohydrate exchanges, carbohydrate counting, or a lower-carbohydrate diet. You can rely on the published GI value as a reliable ranking of foods, reflecting how you as an individual will respond to different foods most of the time.

Q. I've read that dairy products cause an increase in insulin secretion. Their GI value is around 30–50 but their insulin index is three times higher.

A. Scientists don't know the reason why dairy products do this. Our guess is that milk proteins are "insulinogenic" because they are meant to stimulate the growth of young mammals. Insulin is an anabolic hormone designed to drive nutrients into cells—not just glucose but also fatty acids and amino acids, the building blocks of new tissue. Milk may contain a unique combination of amino acids that together are more insulin stimulating than any alone. This disparity between glucose and insulin response is not unique to dairy products. We've found that certain sweets and baked products also do this. Chocolate may also contain insulinogenic amino acids.

Figure 7. Three foods with high (●), intermediate (△), and low (■) GI values will follow the same ranking in different individuals.

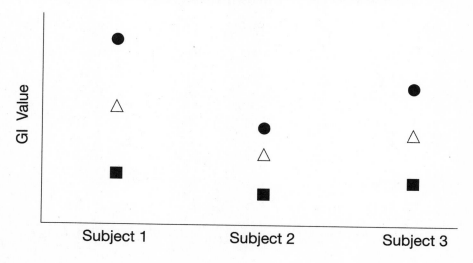

Q. Isn't the insulin response more important? Wouldn't it be better to have an insulin index of foods, rather than a glycemic index?

A. While it's clear that the insulin demand exerted by foods is important for long-term health, it doesn't necessarily follow that we need an insulin index of foods instead of a glycemic index. When both have been tested together, the glycemic index is extremely good at predicting the food's insulin index. In other words, a low-GI food has a low insulin index value and a high-GI food has a high insulin index value. Furthermore, the level of glucose in the blood is directly related to adverse reactions such as protein glycosylation (linkages between glucose and protein) and oxidative molecules.

There are some instances, however, where a food has a low GI value but a high insulin index value. This applies to dairy foods and to some highly palatable, energy-dense "indulgence foods." Some foods (such as meat, fish, and eggs) that contain no carbohydrate, just protein and fat (and essentially have a GI value of zero), still stimulate significant rises in blood insulin.

At the present time, we don't know how to interpret this type of response (low glycemia, high insulinemia) for long-term health. It may be a good outcome because the rise in insulin has contributed to the low level of glycemia. On the other hand, it may be not-so-good, because the increased demand for insulin contributes to beta-cell "exhaustion" and the development of type 2 diabetes. Until studies are carried out to answer these types of questions, the glycemic index remains a proven tool for predicting the effects of food on health.

Q. Why do most varieties of rice have such a high GI value?

A. Most varieties of rice have a high GI value—a GI value over 70 is typical. Imported varieties from Thailand are also high, and even brown rice usually has a high GI value. The reason can be traced back to the state of gelatinization of the starch in the cooked grains.

Despite the "whole-grain" nature of rice, complete gelatinization takes place during cooking. This is because millions of microscopic cracks and fissures in the grains allow water to penetrate right to the middle of the grain during cooking, allowing the starch granules to swell and the starch to hydrate. Some varieties of white rice, such as Basmati, have substantially lower GI values. This is because they have more amylose starch, which resists gelatinization. If you are a big rice eater, we recommend choosing Basmati or Uncle Ben's® converted®, or alternatively rice noodles (rice vermicelli has a low GI value). If you are fond of sushi, you are also in luck. The vinegar used in making sushi as well as nori (seaweed) helps to lower the GI value of sushi to only 48.

Q. Why do GI values sometimes change? For example, one bread used to have a GI value of 19, but now it is 36.

A. These changes worry a lot of people! But you should not be overly concerned. In the case of the bread above, the manufacturer changed the formulation because consumers were concerned that there was too much fat in the bread. Reducing the fat increased the GI value, but both types of bread were still classified as low GI. Both were the best choices for people who wanted to lower their blood-glucose level.

The issue is, however, important from a food-labeling perspective. Manufacturers need to have their products retested if they make significant changes to the formulation of a product, or source ingredients from different suppliers.

Another example of a change in a GI value was the case of a breakfast cereal that increased from 54 to 73. This was a substantial change, taking it from a low-GI to a high-GI food. In this instance, it turned out that the first value had been obtained incorrectly, using a 50-gram carbohydrate portion that inadvertently included the fiber. Since this particular food was a very high-fiber product, fiber accounted for over a quarter of the weight. When the product was retested using the larger corrected weight (i.e., a 50-gram portion of "available" carbohydrate), the GI value was, of course, much higher.

This was a good lesson for all laboratories involved in GI testing. Reliable food composition data are needed and, in some instances, direct testing of carbohydrate content is required.

Q. Why has the GI value of carrots changed from 92 to 47?

A. When carrots were first tested in 1981, the result was 92, but only five people were included in the study and the variation among them was huge. This was in the early days of GI testing and the reference food was tested only once. When carrots were assessed more recently, ten people were included, the reference food was tested twice, and a mean value of 32 was obtained with narrow variation. It was clear that this result was more accurate and the other value should be ignored.

Unfortunately, one of the most repeated criticisms of the GI approach was the fact that carrots were being excluded from diets simply because of their high GI value. This is a good example of the need for reliable, standardized methodology for GI testing. It is also another case for *not* using the GI in isolation.

Q. Does the area under the curve give a true picture of the blood-glucose response? What about the shape of the curve and the size of the glycemic spike?

A. The area under the curve may not be perfect, but it is thought to give the best summary measure of the overall degree of hyperglycemia experienced after eating. In research studies, the postprandial (after-eating) area under the curve has correlated strongly with measures such as glycated hemoglobin (HbA1c) that are related to risk of complications. In fact, recent studies have surprised even the experts, because the findings show that postprandial glycemia influences overall control much more than fasting or pre-meal blood-glucose levels. Glycemic spikes appear to be important too, but there is a close relationship between the area under the curve and the peak response. If one is high, the other is high and if one is low, the other is low.

Q. If testing were continued long enough, wouldn't you expect the areas under the curve to become equal, even for very high and very low-GI foods?

A. Many people make the assumption that since the amount of carbohydrate in the foods is the same, then the areas under the curve will finally be the same. This is not the case, however, because the body is not only absorbing glucose from the gut into the bloodstream, it is also extracting glucose from the blood. Just as gentle rain can be utilized better by the garden than a sudden deluge, the body can metabolize slowly digested food better than quickly digested carbohydrate. Fast-release carbohydrate causes "flooding" of the system and the body cannot extract the glucose from the blood fast enough. Just as water levels rise quickly after torrential rain, so do glucose levels in the blood. But the same amount of rain falling over a longer period can be absorbed into the ground and water levels do not rise.

Q. My doctor has recommended *Sugar Busters!* Their advice is the opposite to yours and I'm a little perplexed.

A. *Sugar Busters!* uses the glycemic index in their advice. The big difference is how they view sugar— they see it as a high-GI food and recommend strict avoidance. Americans eat approximately 16 percent of their daily calories (62 lbs/year for women, 89 lbs/year for men) from added high-GI sugars such as high-fructose corn syrup, dextrose, invert sugar, barley malt, and honey. These sweeteners are found primarily in soft drinks, candy, sweet baked goods, ice cream, and sweetened fruit drinks. So their advice is warranted in the United States because of the overabundant use of very high-GI sweeteners (corn syrups).

Q. Is there a difference between naturally occurring sugars and refined sugar?

A. Naturally occurring sugars are those found in foods like milk, dairy products, and fruits and vegetables, including their juices. Refined sugar means added sugar, table sugar, honey, maple syrup, or corn syrup. Both sources include varying amounts of sucrose, glucose, fructose, and lactose. Some nutritionists made a distinction between them because natural sugars are usually accompanied by micronutrients like vitamin C.

The rate of digestion and absorption of naturally occurring sugars is no different, on average, from that of refined sugars. There is, however, wide variation within both food groups, depending on the food. The GI value of fruits varies from 22 for cherries to 72 for watermelon. Similarly, among the foods containing refined sugar, some have a low GI value and some a high one. The GI value of sweetened yogurt is only 33, while a Mars Bar™ has a GI value of 62 (lower than bread).

People who eat three or four servings of fruit a day (particularly apples and oranges) have overall the lowest-GI diet and the best blood-glucose control.

Q. Why do nutritionists still recommend starchy foods over sugary foods?

A. Sugar has an image problem stemming largely from research with rodents using unrealistic amounts of pure sugar. It's also seen as a source of "empty calories" (energy without vitamins or minerals) and concentrated energy. But much of the criticism doesn't stand up in the cold, hard light of scientific fact.

Most starchy foods have the same energy density as sugary foods, and even a soft drink has the same calorie content per gram as an apple. Starchy foods, such as whole-grain cereals, can be excellent sources of vitamins, minerals, and fiber, but some pure forms of starch and modified starches are added to foods that are "empty calories." So there is really no big distinction between sugars and starches in either nutritional terms or in terms of the glycemic index. Our advice is to use sugar to your advantage, as a means of increasing the palatability of nutritious foods (such as brown sugar in oatmeal or honey in tea, or jam on bread).

Q. A high-fat food may have a low GI value. Doesn't this give a falsely favorable impression of that food?

A. Yes it does, especially if the fat is saturated fat. The GI value of potato chips or french fries is lower than that of baked potatoes. The GI value of corn chips is lower than that of sweet corn. Large amounts of fat in food tend to slow the rate of stomach emptying and therefore the rate at which foods are digested. Yet the saturated fat in these foods will contribute to a greatly increased risk of heart disease.

If we were to weigh the health benefits of a high-GI but low-fat food (e.g., mashed potatoes) versus one high in saturated fat with a low GI value (e.g., some cookies), then the prize goes to the potatoes. The glycemic index was never meant to be the sole determinant when choosing what food to eat. It is essential to base your food choices on the overall nutrient content of a food, including fiber, fat, and salt.

It is more important to look at the type of fat in foods than to avoid it altogether. Foods that contain heart-healthy fats, such as avocados, nuts, and legumes, are excellent foods. Foods that contain saturated fats, even if their GI value is low, such as full-fat dairy products, cakes, and cookies, are not as healthy. We'd all be better off if they were saved for special occasions.

Q. Why do many high-fiber foods still have a high GI value?

A. Dietary fiber is not one chemical constituent like fat and protein. It is composed of many different sorts of molecules. Fiber can be divided into soluble and insoluble types.

Soluble fiber is often viscous (thick and jelly-like) in solution and remains viscous even in the small intestine. For this reason it will slow down digestion, making it harder for enzymes to digest the food. Foods with more-soluble fiber, like apples, oats, and legumes, therefore have low GI values.

Insoluble fiber, on the other hand, is not viscous and doesn't slow digestion, especially if it's finely milled. Whole grain bread and white bread have similar GI values. Brown pasta and brown rice have similar values to their white counterparts. In some instances, insoluble fiber is present in a form that acts as a physical barrier delaying access of the enzymes and water to the starch. This applies to intact grains of wheat, rye, and barley and to products like All-Bran™.

Q. Do low-GI foods need to be eaten at every meal in order for people to see a benefit?

A. No, because the effect of a low-GI food carries over to the next meal, reducing its glycemic impact. This applies to breakfast eaten after a low-GI dinner the previous evening. It also applies to lunch eaten after a low-GI breakfast. This unexpected beneficial effect of low-GI meals is called the "second meal" effect. Don't take this too far, however. On the whole, we recommend that you aim for at least one low-GI food per meal.

Q. Most breads and potatoes have high GI values (70 to 80). Does this mean I have to avoid my favorite foods?

A. Potatoes and bread, despite their high GI values, can play a major role in a high-carbohydrate and low-fat diet, even if your goal is to reduce the overall GI value. Only about half the carbohydrate needs to be exchanged from high GI to low GI to derive health benefits. So, there is still room for bread and potatoes. Of course, some types of bread and potatoes have a lower GI value than others, and these should be preferred if the goal is to lower the GI value as much as possible.

Q. Opponents of the low-GI approach say that low-GI diets are too restrictive, narrowing the range of foods that can be eaten. Is there any truth in this?

A. It is a myth that you have to narrow the range of foods you eat on a low-GI diet. In fact, some people have told us the opposite. They have found that the advent of the glycemic index has expanded their range of foods because they have been encouraged to try foods they have never eaten before (e.g., Indian dals, Asian noodles, lentil soups). They also say that there is considerable relief that they now have "permission" to consume foods containing sugar such as jams and ice cream. In children with diabetes, studies have shown that those following flexible low-GI diets ate the same number of different carbohydrate foods per day (i.e., there was no hint of restricted food choices), they ate the same amount of fat, protein, and fiber, and they had the same refined-sugar intake as children instructed to follow a conventional carbohydrate-exchange diet.

The myth that all low-GI foods are high in fiber and not very palatable also needs dispelling. It may be true that legumes or All-Bran™ may not be everyone's favorite foods, but pasta, oats, fruit, and many favorite Mediterranean recipes using low-GI cracked wheat and chickpeas have become popular choices. To dispel such myths, we have included many mouthwatering recipes using legumes and lentils in Part 2.

Q. What is resistant starch? What effect does it have on the GI value of a food?

A. Resistant starch is the starch that completely resists digestion in the small intestine. It cannot contribute to the glycemic effect of the food because it is not absorbed. In testing the GI value of a food, resistant starch should not be included in the 50-gram-carbohydrate serving. By definition, this portion should include only available or glycemic carbohydrate.

Resistant starch is not viscous like some forms of soluble fiber that delay absorption in the small intestine and flatten the blood-glucose curve. Hence the mere presence of resistant starch in the food will not affect the GI value of a food. Bananas and potato salad both have high amounts of resistant starch, but the GI values of these two foods are very different. The difficulty that arises in GI testing is that the carbohydrate content of a food is often estimated by subtracting the sum of the fat, protein, fiber, water, and ash from 100 (the ash represents the minerals in foods—the residue left after burning off all the fat, protein, and carbohydrate in a very hot oven). Unfortunately, this will include resistant starch in the carbohydrate value. Measuring resistant starch separately is complex and time-consuming. Thankfully, most foods contain only small amounts of resistant starch and the argument is largely academic.

Q. I have recently been diagnosed with celiac disease (gluten sensitivity) on top of diabetes. It's extremely hard to find both low-GI and wheat-free foods. Any suggestions?

A. This may not be as hard as you think. If you like Asian food—Indian dals, stir-fries with rice, sushi, noodles—you're in luck, because they all have low GI values. Choose vermicelli noodles prepared from rice or mung beans and low-GI rices such as Basmati. Use sweet potato instead of potato and all manner of vegetables without any regard for their GI values. Choose fruits for their low GI values. If you can tolerate dairy products, then take advantage of their universal low GI values. If lactose intolerance is a problem, try yogurts with active cultures and lactose-free milks. Even ice cream can be enjoyed if you ingest a few drops of lactase enzyme (Lactaid®) first. See gluten-free foods in the GI tables for more information.

Q. Will the GI values be appearing on food labels?

A. Food manufacturers are showing increasing interest in having the GI values of their products measured. Some are already including the GI value of foods on food labels. As more and more research highlights the benefits of low-GI foods, consumers and die-

titians are writing and telephoning food companies and diabetes organizations asking for GI data. The symbol above is an international symbol registered in several countries (including the United States and Australia) to indicate that a food has been *properly* GI tested (in real people, not a test tube) and also makes a positive contribution to nutrition. You can find out more about the program at www.gisymbol.com.au.

As consumers, you have a right to information about the nutrients and physiological effects of foods. You have a right to know the GI value of a food and to know it has been tested using appropriate standardized methodology.

Q. Wouldn't it be better to use the glycemic load instead of the glycemic index to compare foods?

A. The glycemic load is the product of the GI value and the amount of carbohydrate per serving of food. You'll find this value in the tables in Part 4 of the book. It provides a measure of the degree of glycemia and insulin demand produced by a normal serving of the food. The glycemic load of a whole day's food intake or whole diet can be calculated from diet records and food-frequency questionnaires.

Some nutritionists have argued that this is an improvement on the glycemic index because it provides an estimate of both quantity and quality of carbohydrate (the glycemic index gives us just quality) in a diet.

In large-scale studies from Harvard University, however, the risk of disease was predicted by both the GI values of the overall diet as well as the glycemic load. The use of the glycemic load strengthened the relationships, suggesting that the more frequent the consumption of high-carbohydrate, high-GI foods, the more adverse the health outcome.

The controversy surrounding the use of the glycemic load concept stems from its implication that the less carbohydrate consumed, even in low-GI forms, the lower the risk of developing type 2 diabetes or heart disease. But this is not the correct interpretation of the data. Carbohydrate content alone showed absolutely no relationship to disease risk. The low risk of disease associated with the lowest glycemic load was driven by the consumption of low-GI foods, not by low-carbohydrate intake. So our message here is: *Don't* aim for a very low-carbohydrate diet. This type of diet might have a low glycemic load, but it could also have a high saturated-fat content and high energy density. Use the glycemic index to compare foods of similar nature (bread with bread, breakfast cereal with breakfast cereal). Use the glycemic load when you note a high GI value but low carbohydrate content per serving (e.g., pumpkin).

There is more information about using the glycemic load on pages 430–431.

Part

2

Your Guide to Low-GI Eating

Simple tips to help you change to a low-GI diet and 50 delicious recipes to help you enjoy low-GI foods

6

Making the Change
to a Low-GI Diet

Low-gi diets are easy to teach and easy to learn. The basic technique is to swap high-GI carbohydrates in your diet with low-GI foods. This could mean eating muesli at breakfast instead of cornflakes, whole-grain bread instead of white, or fruit in place of cookies, for example. In our experience helping people modify the GI values of their diet, we've identified some other key points that are crucial in putting the glycemic index into practice. Remember:

▶ The glycemic index relates only to carbohydrate-rich foods

The foods we eat contain three main nutrients—protein, carbohydrate, and fat. Some foods, such as meat, are high in protein, while bread is high in carbohydrate and butter is high in fat. It is necessary for us to consume a variety of foods, in varying proportions, to provide all three nutrients, but the glycemic index applies only to high-carbohydrate foods. It is impossible for us to measure a GI value for foods that contain negligible carbohydrate. These foods include meats, fish, chicken, eggs, cheese, nuts, oils, cream, butter, and most vegetables. There are other nutritional aspects you could consider in choosing these foods. For example, the amount and type of fats they contain is significant and varied.

▶ The glycemic index is not intended to be used in isolation

The GI value of a food does not make it good or bad for us. High-GI foods such as potatoes and bread still make a valuable nutritional contribution to our diet. And low-GI foods such as sausage that are high in saturated fat are no better for us because of their low GI values. The nutritional benefits of different foods are many and varied, and it is advisable for you to base your food choices on the overall nutritional content of a food, particularly considering the saturated fat, salt, fiber, and GI value.

▶ There is no need to eat only low-GI foods

While most of us will benefit from eating carbohydrates with a low GI value at each meal, this doesn't mean consuming it at the exclusion of all other carbohydrates. When we eat a combination of low- and high-GI carbohydrate foods, like baked beans on toast, fruit and sandwiches, lentils and rice, potatoes and corn, the final GI value of the meal is intermediate. The high GI value of foods like potato is moderated by including a low-GI carbohydrate at the same meal. For example, if your main meal contains potato with a GI value of 90, then choose a low-GI dessert such as low-fat yogurt with a GI value of 33. Let's assume that half the carbohydrate comes from the potato and half from the yogurt. The GI value for the meal then becomes (50% × 90) + (50% × 33) = 62.

▶ Consider both the GI value of the food and the amount of carbohydrate it contains, i.e., the glycemic load

For some foods, the normal serving size contains so little carbohydrate that the GI value of that carbohydrate is insignificant. This is generally the case for vegetables like carrots (47), peas (48), and pumpkin (75) which provide about 6 grams of carbohydrate per serving. Small amounts of jam (51) or honey (55) also have little glycemic impact. You can calculate the glycemic load by multiplying the GI value of the food by the amount of carbohydrate in that particular food for a particular serving size and then dividing by 100. (See pages 56 and 136 for more information.) We have included the glycemic load of foods in the tables in Part 4. Take a look there at how a food's glycemic load differs from its GI value.

Two GI Food Pyramids, Two Simple Steps to a Low-GI Diet

1. Begin with a healthy, balanced diet based on a variety of foods.

The first step in developing a healthy, low-GI diet is to begin with a meal plan based on good nutrition principles. It should be low in saturated fat, have a moderate to high carbohydrate content, be high in fiber, and contain a sufficient variety of foods to meet vitamin and mineral requirements.

To guide your daily food choices, we've created two GI food pyramids, one for moderate carbohydrate eaters and one for high carbohydrate eaters. The recommended servings of each food group are shown within each pyramid. If you are a big bread and cereal eater, the GI pyramid for high carbohydrate eaters will suit you best. Either way, the information on the next page, which illustrates basic sample serving sizes, applies to both pyramids.

More detailed information on the different nutritional needs of adults, pregnant and breastfeeding women, children and adolescents is available from the U.S. Department of Agriculture's Center for Nutrition Policy and Promotion at www.usda.gov/cnpp.

How Much Is a Serving?

■ **Indulgences**

1 oz butter, margarine, oil

2 oz cream, mayonnaise

1½ oz chocolate

2 oz cake

1½ oz potato chips

Alcohol: 12-ounce can beer, 5-oz glass wine,
   1½ oz liquor

■ **Fish and Seafood, Lean Meat, Poultry and Eggs**

2–3 oz cooked fish

2–3 oz cooked lean meat or poultry

1 egg

■ **Low-fat Dairy Products**

8 oz low-fat milk or yogurt

1½ oz reduced-fat cheese

■ **Bread, Breakfast Cereals, Grains, etc.**

1 slice bread

1 oz cereal

½ cup cooked rice, pasta or noodles

■ **Vegetables and Salads**

½ cup cooked vegetables

1 cup raw salad vegetables

■ **Beans, Legumes and Nuts**

1 cup cooked dried beans, peas or lentils

1 oz nuts

■ **Fruits and Juices**

1 medium piece of fruit

1 cup of small fruit pieces

½ cup juice

The Glycemic Index Pyramid for HIGH Carbohydrate Eaters

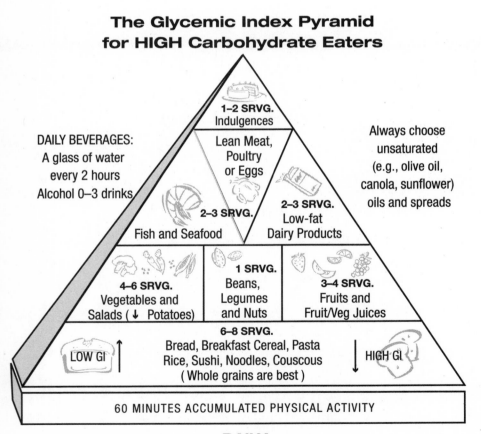

1–2 SRVG.
Indulgences

Lean Meat, Poultry or Eggs

DAILY BEVERAGES:
A glass of water
every 2 hours
Alcohol 0–3 drinks

Always choose
unsaturated
(e.g., olive oil,
canola, sunflower)
oils and spreads

2–3 SRVG.
Fish and Seafood

2–3 SRVG.
Low-fat
Dairy Products

4–6 SRVG.
Vegetables and
Salads (↓ Potatoes)

1 SRVG.
Beans,
Legumes
and Nuts

3–4 SRVG.
Fruits and
Fruit/Veg Juices

6–8 SRVG.
Bread, Breakfast Cereal, Pasta
Rice, Sushi, Noodles, Couscous
(Whole grains are best)

LOW GI ↑

↓ HIGH GI

60 MINUTES ACCUMULATED PHYSICAL ACTIVITY

DAILY

The Glycemic Index Pyramid
for MODERATE Carbohydrate Eaters

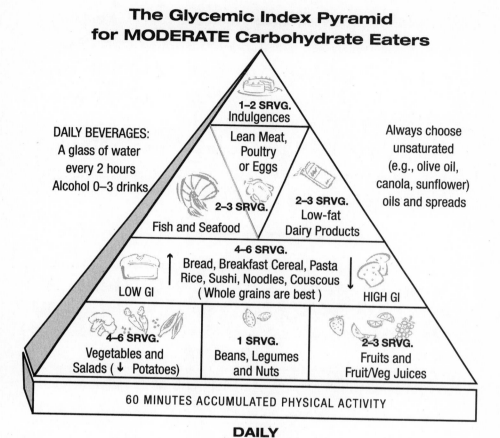

DAILY BEVERAGES:
A glass of water
every 2 hours
Alcohol 0–3 drinks

1–2 SRVG.
Indulgences

Lean Meat,
Poultry
or Eggs

2–3 SRVG.
Fish and Seafood

2–3 SRVG.
Low-fat
Dairy Products

Always choose
unsaturated
(e.g., olive oil,
canola, sunflower)
oils and spreads

4–6 SRVG.
Bread, Breakfast Cereal, Pasta
Rice, Sushi, Noodles, Couscous
(Whole grains are best)

LOW GI

HIGH GI

4–6 SRVG.
Vegetables and
Salads (↓ Potatoes)

1 SRVG.
Beans, Legumes
and Nuts

2–3 SRVG.
Fruits and
Fruit/Veg Juices

60 MINUTES ACCUMULATED PHYSICAL ACTIVITY

DAILY

2. Substitute low-GI alternatives for carbohydrate foods with high-GI values.

The next step toward a low-GI diet is to look at the type of carbohydrate foods you eat. Focus on those that you eat the most of as these have the greatest glycemic impact. Consider the high-carbohydrate foods you consume at each meal and replace at least one of these with one low-GI food (e.g., replace potato with sweet potato, replace a high-GI breakfast cereal with oatmeal, use noodles or Basmati rice instead of instant rice). Changing half the total carbohydrate from high-GI to low-GI foods will result in a significant reduction in the overall GI value of your diet.

Compare the following menus to see how the GI values of a diet can be lowered by making a few simple changes in carbohydrate choices.

High-GI Menu	Low-GI Menu
GI value: 74	**GI value: 51**
Breakfast	**Breakfast**
1 cup cornflakes with milk	¾ cup All-Bran™ with low-fat milk
2 slices whole wheat toast with margarine	2 slices of whole-grain pumpernickel bread with margarine
Snack	**Snack**
5 vanilla wafers	2 small oatmeal cookies
Lunch	**Lunch**
A whole-wheat roll with ham and a salad	A sourdough roll with ham and a salad

High-GI Menu	Low-GI Menu
An apple	Soft-serve vanilla yogurt with strawberries
Snack	**Snack**
4 slices crackerbread with cottage cheese and chives	A banana
Main Meal	**Main Meal**
Roast chicken	Roast chicken
1 large baked potato	1 small baked potato
Baked pumpkin	1 piece of baked sweet potato
Peas	Peas
A 2-inch-square sponge cake with chocolate icing	2 scoops of low-fat ice cream and ½ cup of unsweetened canned peaches
Energy value	**Energy value**
1,800 calories	1,800 calories
Carbohydrate: 50% of energy Fat: 30% of energy	Carbohydrate: 50% of energy Fat: 30% of energy

These menus are identical in all but the carbohydrate foods they contain. Careful selection of low-GI carbohydrate foods and smaller amounts of high-GI carbohydrates in the menu on the right bring about a 40 percent reduction in the overall GI value.

Lowering the GI Values of Your Diet

Bread Include more grainy varieties and sourdough. If you are making your own bread, substitute about 50 percent of the flour with whole or cracked grains such as stoneground 100% whole wheat, barley flakes, oat bran, or flaxseed.

Breakfast cereals Many processed cereals have high GI values. Check the tables in Part 4 for low-GI varieties and use these more often.

Casseroles Try substituting kidney beans, pinto beans, or lentils for a portion of the meat. Boosts the fiber and drops the fat too!

Flour Bakery products such as muffins, cakes, cookies, doughnuts, and pastries are made with highly refined flour, which is quickly digested and absorbed. With your own cooking, try to increase the soluble-fiber content by partially substituting flour with oat bran, rice bran, or rolled oats, and increase the bulkiness of the product with dried fruits, nuts, muesli, All-Bran™, or unprocessed bran.

Fruit Most fruits have a low GI value. Tropical fruits, such as mango, papaya, pineapple, and cantaloupe, tend to have higher values than temperate fruits such as apples and oranges. But all fruits are good for you.

Potatoes Their glycemic impact is lessened by eating smaller portions and varying your diet with alternatives such as sweet potato or lima beans. Tiny new white potatoes have a lower GI value than normal varieties.

Rice Try Basmati or Uncle Ben's® Converted® long-grain rice, or pearled barley, quick-cooking wheat, buckwheat, bulgur, couscous, or noodles.

Beef patty or meat loaf Add cooked lentils, canned beans, or rolled oats in combination with the ground beef.

Soups These are a great way to incorporate legumes into your diet. Add lentils, barley, split peas, cannellini beans, and pasta—make a minestrone! Soup can be a very filling meal.

Sugar Enjoy sugar in moderation. It has an intermediate GI value. For a low-GI alternative, try apple juice, apple-sauce, or dried fruit to sweeten dishes. Honey, particularly pure floral honeys, also has a lower GI value.

How Do We Calculate the GI Value
of a Meal, Menu, or Recipe?

It is difficult to calculate the precise GI value of a combination of foods unless you have access to food-composition tables or a nutrient-analysis computer program, and it is seldom necessary. This is, however, one of the questions most frequently asked by our readers, so here's how it's done.

First of all, the GI value of a meal is not the sum of the GI values of each food in the meal, nor is it simply an average of their GI values. The GI of a meal, menu, or recipe consisting of a variety of carbohydrate foods is a weighted average of the GI values of each food. The weighting is based on the proportion of the total carbohydrate contributed by each food.

For example, let's say we have a snack of peaches (42) and ice cream (61). Depending on the amounts of each food, we could calculate the total content of these carbohydrates from food-composition tables. Let's say the meal contains 60 grams of carbohydrate, with 20 grams provided by the peaches and 40 grams by the ice cream.

To estimate the GI value of this dish we multiply the GI value of peaches by their proportion of the total carbohydrate:

$$42 \times 20/60 = 14$$

and multiply the GI value of ice cream by its proportion of the total carbohydrate:

$$61 \times 40/60 = 41$$

We then add these two figures to give a GI value for this dish of 55.

We have estimated a GI value rating for the recipes in this book. Because food processing, including heating, mashing, fermenting, acidifying, etc., changes the nature of the carbohydrate, a calculation of the precise GI value of the recipes is not possible.

A Sensible Approach to Changing the Way You Eat

Some people can change their diet easily, but for the majority of us, change of any kind is difficult. Unlike altering bad habits such as smoking, changing our diet is seldom just a matter of giving up certain foods. A healthy diet contains a wide variety of foods, but we need to eat them in appropriate proportions. The decisions behind what we eat are many and complex, and often some professional assistance is necessary to make changes. Helping people improve their diet is something dietitians do every day, so seek one out if you need some help. (See "How to Find a Dietitian" on page 30.) Keep these four guidelines in mind if you are considering changes to your diet:

1. Aim to make changes gradually.

Major changes to diet, for example following a fad diet from a magazine article or current best-seller, are usually short-lived. Identify one aspect of your diet that you want to work on (for example, eating more vegetables) and make that your focus.

2. Attempt the easiest changes first.

Nothing inspires like success, so increase your chances by attacking the easiest changes first. For example, plan to eat one fruit snack each day.

3. Break big goals into a number of smaller, more achievable goals.

A big goal may be wanting to lose weight. This is unlikely to happen quickly, but it is attainable through gradual, consistent change. Smaller goals could be to exercise for thirty minutes every day and to reduce the saturated-fat content of your diet. Even smaller goals (which are the way to begin) could be to do a fifteen-minute walk twice a week and limit takeout to only once a week.

4. Accept lapses in your habits.

Lapses are not failures but are natural stages in the progression to new habits. Remember, it usually takes about three months for a new change to become a habit.

Putting the Glycemic Index to Work in Your Day

Breakfast: Sustaining You Through the Day

Too many Americans skip breakfast. This is an alarming phenomenon given the evidence that people who do eat breakfast are calmer, happier, and more sociable. Studies prove that eating breakfast improves mood, mental alertness, concentration, and memory. Nutritionists know that having breakfast helps people lose weight and can lower cholesterol levels. We also know it helps stabilize blood-glucose levels.

Missing breakfast can cause symptoms of fatigue, dehydration, and loss of energy. Eating a high-GI breakfast is not the answer, though, as it can also leave you hungry by mid-morning. Many breakfast cereals and breads have a high GI value, which means while they pick you up initially, they won't last long. When the energy runs out and your blood glucose starts to drop, you feel hungry again. Try some low-GI choices at breakfast and see how much easier it is to make it through to lunchtime.

Three-quarters of people who skip breakfast say they have "no time to eat," so we've included lots of quick, healthy, low-GI breakfast ideas. Whether you prefer a liquid breakfast on the go, a hearty hot breakfast or simply a low-fat granola bar and an apple on the way to work, we guarantee you'll find something to sustain you through the day.

Low-GI Breakfast Basics

1. Start with some fruit or juice.

Fruit contributes fiber and, more importantly, vitamin C, which helps your body absorb the nutrient iron.

Lowest-GI Fresh Fruits and Juices

Apples	38	Kiwi fruit	58
Apple juice	40	Mango	51
Bananas	52	Oranges	42
Carrot juice	43	Peaches	42
Cherries	22	Pears	38
Grapefruit	25	Pineapple juice	46
Grapefruit juice	48	Plums	39
Grapes	46	Tomato juice	38

Did You Know?

Skipping breakfast is not a good way to cut back your food intake. Breakfast-skippers tend to make up for the missed food by eating more snacks during the day and more food overall.

2. Try a low GI breakfast cereal.

Cereals are important as a source of fiber and vitamin B. When choosing processed breakfast cereals, look for those with a high fiber content.

Low-GI Breakfast Cereals

Kellogg's Bran Buds™ with Psyllium	45
Old-fashioned oatmeal (made with water)	49 (avg)
Quaker Oats™ oat bran	50
Kellogg's All-Bran™ with Extra Fiber	51
Hot Apple and Cinnamon Cereal (Con Agra)	37

We know the GI values for about ninety different cereals eaten throughout the world and more are being tested all the time. See the tables in Part 4 for more comprehensive values.

3. Add milk or yogurt.

Low-fat milk or yogurt will make a valuable contribution to your daily calcium intake and both have a low GI value. Lower-fat varieties have just as much, or more, calcium as regular types.

4. Add bread or toast if you are still hungry.

Lowest-GI breads

Whole-grain pumpernickel	51
Sourdough	52
100% stone-ground whole wheat	53
Whole wheat pita	57
Sourdough rye	57

Ten Luscious Low-GI Breakfasts

1. Toast pumpernickel, spread lightly with margarine and accompany with a hot chocolate drink made with low-fat milk.

2. Lightly toast some sourdough English muffins. Spread with natural peanut butter and spreadable fruit jam.

3. Add unsweetened canned peaches or applesauce to creamy oatmeal (made with fat-free or low-fat milk), sprinkle cinnamon and drizzle with a teaspoon of honey.

4. Pan-fry or toast ham and melted cheese (part skim) sandwich made with 100 percent stone-ground whole-wheat bread.

5. Top a bowl of vanilla-flavored, low-fat yogurt with a sliced peach and chopped strawberries, then scatter the top with low-fat granola.

6. Combine an 8-ounce container of low-fat fruit yogurt with 2 tablespoons of chopped almonds, 1 diced banana or pear and 1 cup of Bran Buds™. Divide between 2 bowls and serve.

7. Spread a generous layer of Nutella® or natural peanut butter on Ryvita® dark rye whole-grain crackers and team it with a mug of low-fat latte.

8. Beat together 2 eggs, ¼ cup of skim milk, and a teaspoon of pure vanilla extract. Dip 4 thick slices of sourdough bread into the egg mixture, then cook over medium heat in a greased, nonstick frying pan for 2 to 3 minutes each side, until golden. Serve topped with pan-fried pear or apple slices and a sprinkling of cinnamon.

9. Toast pita bread and top with fresh lite ricotta and a dollop of blackberry all-fruit preserves.

10. Make a big bowl of steaming oatmeal, then stir in some frozen blueberries or raspberries. Top with a dollop of low-fat natural yogurt and a sprinkling of brown sugar.

Refueling with a Low-GI Lunch

Although lunch is often a meal grabbed on the run, it is important to refuel after the four or five hours since breakfast. Lunch needn't be a big meal. In fact, if you find yourself feeling sleepy after lunch, it may help to eat a lighter meal of protein, vegetables, and a small portion of carbohydrate. (A cup of coffee helps too!)

Low-GI Lunch Basics

1. Carbohydrate-rich foods with a low GI value, such as whole-grain bread, pasta, or noodles, grains or legumes.
2. Proteins like fish, lean meat, chicken, cheese, or egg.
3. Vegetables to bulk it out and fill you up. A large salad with a variety of vegetables would be ideal.
4. Round it off with fruit.

Lunching Out

Buying lunch and want to know how to get a low-GI choice? The following list provides examples of low-GI foods you can buy for lunch. Many of the traditional dishes on ethnic-restaurant menus will have a low GI value because they are based on legumes.

Sushi	48	Stuffed grape leaves	30
Moroccan couscous (with chickpeas)	58	Ravioli	39
Rice noodle soup	40	Tabbouleh	30
Tortilla with beans and tomato sauce	39	Lentils and rice	24
Thai noodles with vegetables	40	Pasta marinara	40
Lentil soup	44	Hummus	6

Ten Light and Lively Low-GI Lunch Ideas

Just a note: You may think some of these recipes are too time-consuming. (Of course nothing is quicker than ordering in or stopping at 7-Eleven!) But if you want to improve the wholesomeness of your lunches and feel your best throughout the afternoon, here are some great ideas. Make extra for multiple servings.

1. Take a piece of pita bread, spread it with hummus, top with thinly sliced lean roast beef and tabbouleh and roll up.

2. Make a lentil and sweet potato soup by browning an

onion with 2 cloves of crushed garlic. Add 1 lb. sweet potato chunks, ½ cup of split red lentils and 3½ cups of vegetable stock. Simmer for 25 minutes, adding 1 coarsely grated zucchini after 20 minutes.

3. Slice a sweet potato into very thin slices. Cut a zucchini in half lengthways and cut a red onion into 6 segments. Place vegetables in a freezer bag with a clove of crushed garlic, add a tablespoon of olive oil, and shake to coat. Spread out on a baking sheet and roast in a hot oven 20–30 minutes until tender. Toss the roasted vegetables with boiled pasta, along with chopped parsley, oregano, or basil, and a drizzle of olive oil.

4. Divide a small package (8 oz) of tortilla chips (preferably a salt-reduced, low-fat variety from the health-food section) among 4 ovenproof plates. Top with a 16-ounce can of Mexican or chili-flavored kidney beans and sprinkle with reduced-fat cheddar or Monterey Jack cheese. Put under a hot grill for 2 to 3 minutes, then top with dollops of mashed avocado.

5. Take a small (3 oz) can of tuna in spring water and ¼ cup of drained cannellini beans. Mix in a bowl with half a diced cucumber, 1 diced tomato, a handful of baby spinach (or other greens), and chopped parsley. Dress with an equal mix of olive oil and lemon juice and a sprinkle of black pepper.

6. Spread 1 slice of 100 percent whole-wheat bread with whole-grain mustard. Add chopped sun-dried tomatoes, grilled eggplant, and a slice of mozzarella cheese. Melt the cheese under a grill, then add salad greens and another slice of bread. Cut in half and serve.

7. Try canned salmon, thinly sliced green apple, and red onion with, snow-pea sprouts on sourdough bread.

8. Sauté 2 sliced green onions with a teaspoon each of crushed garlic and ginger until soft (do not brown). Add 2 to 3 sliced mushrooms, 1 teaspoon of minced jalapeño, 1 tablespoon of soy sauce and 1 teaspoon sesame oil and cook until the mushrooms soften. Add 1 cup of vegetable stock, bring to a boil, then stir in a packet of Japanese noodles, diced cooked chicken or tofu, and a handful of shredded spinach.

9. Cook ½ a cup of split red lentils in boiling water until tender (about 10 minutes). Drain. When cool, mash with 2 tablespoons mayonnaise, 2 chopped green onions and a clove of crushed garlic. Season with black pepper. Use on your favorite bread as a sandwich filling with salad greens.

10. Make a vegetarian chickpea burger by combining a can of drained chickpeas with fresh whole-wheat bread crumbs, parsley, garlic, and an egg in a food processor. Shape into patties and pan fry. Serve with char-grilled

vegetables on a whole-wheat bun. You can also select from the fresh and frozen veggie burgers in your supermarket.

Low-GI Main Meals: Choosing the Best

What to make for dinner is the perennial question. When organizing the ingredients in your mind for a main meal, think of them in the following order.

1. Choose the carbohydrate.

Which will it be? Potato, rice, pasta, noodles, grains, legumes or a combination? Could you add some bread or corn? It isn't just a matter of choosing the food with the lowest GI value. It is best to include a wide variety of foods in your diet to optimize your nutrient intake. Compare the nutritional properties of the following carbohydrate foods and see why variety is important.

2. Add vegetables—and lots of them.

Fresh, frozen, canned—whatever you have, the more the better. The main meal tends to be the prime time for eating vegetables, so if they aren't on your dinner plate, chances are you aren't eating enough of them.

3. Include protein for nutrients, flavor and fill-up value.

Protein may come in many forms, but we urge you to make sure it's low in saturated fat.

Here are some ideas: slivers of flank steak in a stir-fry, a fillet of fresh fish, strips of lean boiled ham, a dollop of lite ricotta cheese, a tender skinless chicken breast, slices of salmon, a couple of eggs, a handful of nuts, a sprinkle of cheese, or use the protein found in your grains and legumes.

Choosing Your Main Meal Carbohydrate

Potatoes Baked and mashed potatoes have high GI values (see the tables in Part 4). New white potatoes (canned or fresh) and sweet potatoes are lower value GI choices. Despite their high GI value, potatoes are a healthy food providing a fat-free source of carbohydrate along with significant amounts of vitamin C, potassium, and fiber. Their glycemic impact is lessened by eating moderate quantities and eating other low-GI carbohydrates at the same meal.

Rice White rice is bland in flavor, making it an ideal accompaniment to a wide variety of foods. Milling of rice removes the bran and germ, resulting in a considerable loss of nutrients. Because of this, brown rice is a much better source of B vitamins, minerals, and fiber. Vary your diet to include both brown and white rice. The lower-GI rices are Basmati (58) and Uncle Ben's® Converted® long grain (50).

Sweet potato Orange sweet potato (44), a great source of beta-carotene (the plant precursor of vitamin A), is also rich in vitamin C and makes a colorful addition to any dinner. It is a good source of fiber.

Sweet corn Corn on the cob, or loose kernel corn, is generally a popular vegetable with children and is high in fiber. Corn (54) is also a source of B vitamins.

Legumes Chickpeas, lentils, and beans are all high in protein and so are a nutritious alternative to meat. Their content of niacin, potassium, phosphorus, iron, and zinc is also high, while their fiber content is higher than for the other carbohydrate foods listed here. GI values vary—check the tables in Part 4.

Pasta Pasta is higher in protein than rice or potato and is often eaten as a meal without including meat. It is very satisfying and quick to prepare with the addition of vegetables, or a vegetable sauce and a sprinkling of Parmesan. The GI value varies from 37 to 55.

Cracked wheat Bulgur is parboiled whole or cracked grains of wheat. Because the whole grain is virtually intact, bulgur (48) provides lots of fiber, thiamin, niacin, vitamin E and minerals.

4. Think twice about the fat you add.

Check that you are using a healthy oil, such as olive, canola, mustard seed, soybean, or another mono- or polyunsaturated type. Don't overdo it—use only the amount you need.

Ten Low-GI Main Meals in Minutes

1. Quick Thai Noodle Curry

Stir-fry some strips of onion, red pepper, baby corn, and snow peas (or any stir-fry vegetable mix) in a large pan or wok. Add a tablespoon of red curry paste. Prepare instant Asian noodles according to directions. Add the noodles to the vegetables with enough stock to make a sauce. Stir in a tablespoon of light coconut milk, heat through, and it's ready to serve.

Tip: Canned coconut milk or cream (which is high in saturated fat) can be poured into ice-cube trays, frozen, and then kept in a plastic bag, making it easy to add just a table-spoon to a dish. Alternatively, coconut-milk powder can be kept in the pantry and mixed as needed, or look for low-fat, lite varieties.

2. Speedy Spaghetti

Bring a large pot of water to a boil, add some spaghetti, and cook according to the directions on the packet. Meanwhile, open a jar of chunky tomato marinara sauce and heat. Make a green salad with lettuce, spring onions, and cucumber, or a bag of mixed lettuce. Serve the spaghetti, topped with the pasta sauce, a good sprinkle of Parmesan cheese and the green salad with vinaigrette alongside. Fresh or frozen vegetables can be added to the sauce to increase its nutrient value (for example, mushrooms, onion, eggplant, zucchini, etc.).

3. Fast Fish and Tiny Taters

Take a boneless fillet of fresh fish. Dust it with seasoned flour. Heat a nonstick pan with a thin film of cooking spray or oil and pop the fish in to fry. Wash a handful of tiny new potatoes and microwave or steam them until tender. Squeeze lemon juice over the fish, once you have cooked both sides, and sprinkle with pepper. Serve immediately with the potatoes and a salad or cooked mixed vegetables.

4. Quick Pita Pizza

Spread a round of pita bread with pesto or tomato sauce. Top with sliced tomato, mushrooms, roasted peppers, black olives, chopped scallions, oregano, and a sprinkle of Parmesan cheese. Heat through under the grill or in a hot oven.

5. Asian Noodle and Vegetable Stir-Fry

Stir-fry two strips of diced bacon (all fat removed) or ham. Add a packet of Asian stir-fry frozen-vegetable mix, cooking according to the directions on the bag. Mix in some fresh egg noodles, or prepare instant noodles a few minutes before the end of cooking time, and heat through before serving.

Tip: Look for the packets of frozen stir-fry vegetable mixes that have noodles and a sauce packet included.

6. Time-saving Tortellini

Boil a packet of spinach-and-cheese (or your favorite filling) tortellini according to packet directions. Heat some bottled tomato sauce and serve this on top of the tortellini with a sprinkle of Parmesan cheese. Add a large salad and vinaigrette alongside.

7. Racy Rice and Lentils

Put some Basmati rice on to cook. Heat a heavy-based frying pan with a little oil. Add a finely diced onion, crushed garlic, and a couple of teaspoons of dried red-pepper flakes. Sauté until the onion is soft. Meanwhile dice a tomato. Open a can of lentils and add to onion with the tomato. Add ground cumin, salt, and pepper to season, heat through, and serve alongside the rice.

8. Easy Chicken Pasta

Cook 4 ounces of shell pasta. Meanwhile, thinly slice half a red pepper, a handful of button mushrooms, and a stick of celery. Cube some leftover grilled chicken. Drain the pasta, add the vegetables and chicken, and pour over some reduced-fat creamy salad dressing. Top with chopped scallions and serve.

9. Tomato and Tuna Pasta

Boil some spaghetti, linguine, or angel-hair pasta. In a small pan, sauté some chopped parsley, garlic, and dried red-pepper flakes (optional) in a little oil until soft. Add a can of chopped tomatoes (undrained) and a small can of flaked tuna. Season with pepper and heat through. Serve the tuna and tomato sauce over pasta.

10. Mexican in Minutes

Brown a handful of 90 percent lean ground beef and a finely diced onion in a pan. Add a small can of white navy beans and taco seasoning if desired. Heat through. Serve with tomato salsa, shredded lettuce, avocado, and grated cheese in taco shells, tortilla wraps, or pita bread.

Desserts: A Low-GI Finish

It's fairly easy to give a meal a low-GI twist through dessert. This is because so many of the basic components of dessert, like fruit and dairy products, have low GI values.

Desserts can make a valuable contribution to our fruit

and dairy intake, foods underconsumed by many people. What's more, desserts are usually carbohydrate-rich, which means they add to our feelings of satiety, helping to signify the completion of eating.

Something Sweet

Sugar or sucrose, a common ingredient in traditional desserts, has a GI value of 68. Most sugary foods have low to moderate GI values. Cakes and cookies made with or without sugar have similar GI values. Recipes incorporating fruit for sweetness rather than sugar may have more fiber and lower GI values. Remember, fruits such as apples, pears, peaches, nectarines, cherries, and berries tend to have the lowest GI values.

Low-GI Desserts

Citrus Winter fruits that are an excellent source of vitamin C. Soak segments of a variety of citrus fruits in orange juice with a dash of brandy, scatter with raisins, and serve as winter fruit salad.

Cherries A classic summer fruit. Serve cherries around a dollop of low-fat plain yogurt drizzled with honey. Add a sprinkle of ground flaxseeds to increase your day's omega-3 intake.

Stone fruits Apricots, peaches, and nectarines in the grocery store or at farmers' markets signal the beginning of warmer weather. Fresh sliced peaches or nectarines are delicious with ice cream or yogurt. Sprinkle fresh peach halves with cinnamon or nutmeg and try them lightly grilled.

Pears and apples These are at their peak during autumn and winter but are available all year. To prepare, simply wash and slice—or grill or bake—however served, they provide the perfect finish to a meal.

Grapes One of the most popular fruits with children because they are so sweet and easy to eat (especially the seedless varieties). Put a bowl on the table after a meal, include them in a fruit salad, or freeze them for a fun snack.

Custard, pudding, ice cream, and yogurt Look for low-fat varieties for a cool and creamy accompaniment to your fruit.

Eight Quick and Easy Low-GI Desserts

1. Combine a pint of washed, hulled, and halved strawberries with a tablespoon of sugar in a small saucepan. Stir over medium heat for about 5 minutes until the strawberries soften and a syrup forms. Serve warm or chilled over low-fat vanilla ice cream.

2. Remove the core from large green apples and stuff with a combination of raisins, chopped dried apricots,

cinnamon, and a teaspoon of brown sugar. Serve with low-fat plain yogurt or vanilla pudding.

3. Drain a can of peaches. Spoon into bowls. Pour over some low-fat pudding, then stir in crumbled coconut macaroons.

4. Make a fruit crisp by topping cooked fruit with a mixture of toasted oats, wheat flakes, a little melted butter or margarine, and honey.

5. Slice a firm banana in half lengthways and top with 2 scoops of light vanilla ice cream. Spoon fresh fruit pureed in a food processor over the top and sprinkle with toasted almonds.

6. Top unsweetened canned fruit halves with a combination of shredded coconut, brown sugar, and cinnamon. Drizzle with a little of the juice from the can, then bake for 10 minutes till browned.

7. Brush 4–5 layers of phyllo pastry with low-fat milk (rather than butter or margarine). Place stewed or canned apple, raisins, currants, and mixed spice down the center and wrap as for a strudel. Brush the top with milk and bake in a hot oven for 15 minutes.

8. Lay a selection of sliced fresh fruits (e.g., mango, pineapple, strawberries, kiwi fruit, and cantaloupe) on a platter and serve with a cup of plain yogurt combined with a tablespoon of honey.

Snacks: Maintaining between Meals

The fine art of grazing! Hands up all those who thought that sensible eating meant keeping to three meals a day? Of course it may be, if the alternative is to skip breakfast, snack all day, and then feast before sleeping at night—certainly not the ideal pattern! New evidence, however, suggests that people who graze properly, eating small amounts of nutritious food throughout the day at frequent intervals, may actually be doing themselves a favor. Recent research indicates that frequent small meals stimulate the metabolic rate (the rate at which the body burns calories when it is at rest).

A study that compared people eating a diet of three meals a day with those who had three meals and three snacks showed that snacking stimulated the body to use up more energy for metabolism than to concentrating the same amount of food into three meals. It's as if the more often you give your body fuel, the more it will burn.

The problem with grazing is that often we turn to high-fat foods like cakes, chocolate, snack bars, chips, or pastries, which just add empty calories. Another criticism is that for those who tend to overeat, increasing the number of times they face food is tempting disaster. Choosing snack foods that are carbohydrate-rich and have low GI values, however, will reduce your chance of overeating. Using our snack suggestions, you can enrich the variety of foods in your diet and feel satisfied before you have overconsumed. Measure out your portions and eat slowly.

Sustaining Snacks

For a snack to keep you satisfied, make a smoothie with low-fat yogurt, milk, and a soft fruit like strawberries, cantaloupe, or banana. You could also try:

- cinnamon-raisin toast
- a juicy orange
- a bunch of grapes
- sourdough English muffin with jam
- an 8-ounce container of low-fat yogurt
- a can of unsweetened applesauce or diced peaches
- a glass of milk
- dried apricots
- a handful of raisins
- a big green apple
- a scoop of light ice cream in a cone

But if you're looking for something salty or strong tasting, try:

- baked tortilla chips and salsa
- hummus (process a can of chickpeas with 2 cloves of

garlic, 2 tablespoons of tahini, and 2 tablespoons of lemon juice) with pumpernickel bread

- raw vegetables (baby carrots, green beans, pepper strips, radishes, celery, cucumber) with a low-fat dip such as hummus

- a small can of baked beans

- marinated vegetables such as artichoke hearts, roasted peppers, or eggplant (blot off the oil on a paper towel) with toasted pita bread

7

Cooking the Low-GI Way

In this chapter we'll present you with the whole low-GI plate—a plate that incorporates low-GI carbohydrate with healthy fats, lean and nutritious sources of protein and nutrient-rich fruits and vegetables. Bear in mind the components of a healthy diet. A nutritious diet is based on a wide variety of foods, but *not* on a wide variety of fast foods and foods with empty calories! Eat these foods every day:

- Fresh vegetables, cooked and raw
- Fresh fruit
- Whole-grain bread and cereals
- Non-fat or low-fat milk and part-skim cheese
- Fish, lean meat, chicken, legumes, and soy

In addition, you should eat the following foods regularly (but not necessarily daily) and in moderation. These foods are rich in antioxidants, vitamins and minerals, and some of them, such as vinegar, have a specific effect on lowering the glycemic response to carbohydrate. Others, such as nuts, olive oil, and avocado, are rich in heart-healthy fats:

- Nuts and seeds
- Olive, canola, peanut oils
- Avocado, olives
- Dried fruit
- Vinegar (vinaigrette for salads)
- Red wine
- Fresh herbs and spices
- Shellfish and other seafood
- Soy products

We encourage you to include fish once or twice a week and legumes at least twice weekly. We include cooked vegetables or salad in all meals and recommend fruit for dessert.

The Six Dietary Guidelines of the New Glucose Revolution

1. Eat 3 or more servings of low-GI fruit and 4 or more servings of vegetables every day. It's also preferable to consume whole fruits rather than fruit juices.

2. Eat whole-grain breads and cereals with a low-GI value.

3. Eat more legumes (beans, peas and lentils) and use nuts in small amounts more frequently.

4. Eat more fish and seafood.

5. Eat lean meats and low fat dairy food.

6. Use high-omega-3 and monounsaturated oils such as olive, peanut, and canola oils.

----

1. Eat 3 or More Servings of Fruit and 4 or More Servings of Vegetables Every Day

Fruit and vegetables are a major part of low-GI eating. The greater the variety you eat, the better. Forget dinner plates full of plain boiled vegetables, salads of lettuce and tomato and the daily apple or orange: The variety of fruit and vegetables that we're talking about extends far beyond this!

Specifically, aim to eat four or more servings of vegetables and three servings of fruit every day. Include green vegetables, particularly green leafy vegetables. Choose among broccoli, spinach, green beans, cauliflower, Brussels sprouts, leeks, cabbage, peppers, kale, and bok choy. You can eat vegetables steamed or seasoned with fresh or dried herbs, or with a dressing made from olive oil, lemon juice, balsamic vinegar, and garlic.

What Is a Serving?

BREAD/CEREAL GROUP

1 slice bread

1 tortilla

½ cup cooked rice, pasta or cooked cereal

1 oz ready-to-eat cereal

2 medium cookies

3–4 small crackers

1 4-inch pancake

VEGETABLE GROUP

½ cup chopped raw or cooked vegetables

1 cup raw leafy vegetables

¾ cup (6 oz) vegetable juice

½ cup cooked potatoes

10 French fries

FRUIT GROUP

1 medium-size piece fruit

½ cup chopped, cooked or canned fruit

1 melon wedge

¼ cup dried fruit

DAIRY GROUP

1 cup (8 oz) milk or yogurt

1 ½ oz natural cheese

2 oz processed cheese

1½ cups ice cream (regular or reduced fat)

1 cup frozen yogurt

PROTEIN GROUP

2½–3 oz cooked red meat, poultry or fish

½ cup cooked beans

1 egg (equal to 1 oz meat)

2 tbsp. peanut butter (equal to 1 oz meat)

⅓ cup nuts (equal to 1 oz meat)

FATS, OILS, SWEETS GROUP

Use sparingly.

Adapted from the Food Guide Pyramid, U.S. Department of Agriculture
Human Nutrition Information Service.

Eat a salad daily. If you or your children don't enjoy salads very much, try serving it first to catch their appetites when they're most voracious. Try a tossed salad of mixed salad greens, tomatoes, cucumber, red onion, chickpeas and sliced mushrooms. You can even add fruit or nuts if you want. Mix up a large salad at the start of the weekend so you have it on hand for easy meals.

We Americans tend to overlook the natural sweetness of fruit as a perfect finale to our meals (all three of them!) or a quick pick-me-up snack. Fruits are widely available, inexpensive and easy to eat—just like other snack foods—without the added fat and sugar.

Fruit and vegetables have consistently been linked with protection from certain types of cancer. They also contain heart-healthy nutrients including unsaturated oils, fiber, vitamin B_6, folate, and vitamin E, which reduce our risk of heart disease. Eating more vegetables, especially salad and tomatoes, decreases the risk of prostate cancer.

Easy Ways to Eat More Vegetables

Getting more vegetables into your diet is easier than you think. Here's how to make every meal and snack extra-nutritious:

- Add extra vegetables (frozen are easy) to stir-fried meat, chicken, shrimp, fish, or tofu.

- Chop up leftover vegetables, heat, and use as omelet filling.

- Try stuffed vegetables—an extraordinary meal.

- Include salad ingredients in a pocket sandwich or tortilla wrap.

- Throw some veggies onto the grill with meat. Try zucchini, corn, peppers, mushrooms, eggplant, or thick slices of parboiled sweet potato or onion. (Use vegetable spray on a cold grill or a little olive oil to prevent sticking.)

- Drink low-sodium vegetable juices.

- Try a vegetarian main dish at least once a week. (This is what the American Heart Association recommends.)

- Add grated carrot and zucchini to quick breads and muffins.

- Choose take-out meals that include vegetables. Here are a few choices:

    - regular hamburger with salad
    - vegetarian chili
    - vegetable stir-fry
    - salad sandwiches or rolls

- pasta with a tomato-based sauce

- vegetable pizza

- stuffed potato with beans, salsa and cheese

- a side order of salad

- meat and vegetable fajitas

- For quick munching, keep celery, peppers, baby carrots, cucumbers, jicama, broccoli, or cauliflower florets and cherry or grape tomatoes on hand. Dip them in low-fat dip or salsa.

- Try vegetarian lasagna.

- Every week, try a vegetable that you haven't eaten before.

Easy Ways to Eat More Fruit

Most people find fruit sweet enough to recommend itself. But if you're having a little trouble getting your daily requirement, try these tips.

- Always include fruit (fresh, canned in fruit juice or dried) in or with low-GI breakfast cereals.

- Top yogurt with fresh fruit.

- Make fresh fruit smoothies or milkshakes.

- Add fruit to fresh salads (examples: apples, citrus, grapes, strawberries, pears).

- Use fruit salsas in omelets, with fish or pork, as a salad dressing or a chip dip.

- Stew fresh fruit for compotes or for pancake and waffle toppings.

- For a quick lunch, try an apple or pear with some cheese and whole-grain crackers.

- Make your own jam with your favorite in-season fruit.

- Bake, broil, grill, or microwave meaty fruits such as apples or pears for a warm dessert.

- Carry a piece of fresh fruit or a few dried apricots to work or when you travel for a quick and readily available snack (one that just happens to be nutritious and low-GI!).

Enjoy a Kaleidoscope of Fruits and Vegetables

The world of fruits and vegetables is colorful, indeed! Here are some examples of the wide variety of produce you can enjoy every day.

Green: Salad greens, asparagus, broccoli, celery, cucumber, green beans, kale, peas, peppers, scallions, spinach, apples, figs, honeydew melon, pears

Red: Kidney beans, peppers, pinto beans, radishes, tomatoes, apples, cherries, pears, plums, raspberries, strawberries

White: Cauliflower, cannellini beans, onions

Orange: Carrots, peppers, sweet potato, squash (acorn, butternut), apricots, cantaloupe, nectarines, oranges, peaches, tangerines

Yellow: Corn, spaghetti squash, bananas, grapefruit, pears

Brown: Garbanzo beans, mushrooms, pears

Purple: Eggplant, blackberries, blueberries, figs, plums

2. Eat Whole-Grain Breads and Cereals with Low GI Values

Cereal grains including rice, wheat, oats, barley, rye, and products made from them (including bread, pasta, breakfast cereal, and flours) are the most concentrated sources of carbohydrate in our diet, with carbohydrate amounts ranging from 50 to 80 percent of their weight. (Compare this to the carbohydrate content of fruit—around 10 to 15 percent—and root vegetables such as potato—around 15 to 20 percent.) Because of the significant amount of carbohydrate in cereal grains, they have a major impact on the glycemic index of our diet.

Some people might argue that the demise of the human diet began with the industrial revolution and the refining of cereal grains. Traditionally, preparing grains was simple, limited to grinding the grains between stones. So, for the most part, grains kept their original form, which meant they were slowly digested and absorbed. Our ancestors ate most of their carbohydrate like this, including fruits, vegetables, beans, and whole cereal grains—all sources of carbohydrate with low GI values.

The advent of high-speed steel roller mills in the 19th century made the production of fine white flours and their derivatives—such as soft breads, cakes, doughnuts and corn flakes—possible. Our modern Western diet tends to be based on these quickly digested carbohydrates, which results in much greater rises in blood sugar and insulin levels than most of our bodies have evolved to cope with. As a result, many of us now suffer from diseases such as diabetes, heart disease, and obesity in epidemic proportions.

So significant is the health impact of the glycemic index that the WHO/FAO now recommends that we should choose foods with low GI values. For these reasons, we think that low-GI breads and cereals are a crucial part of healthy eating.

Choose breads and cereals with a low GI values such as:

- low-GI breakfast cereals (based on wheat bran, psyllium, and oats);

- grainy breads made with barley, rye, linseed, triticale (a wheat and rye hybrid), sunflower seed, oats, soy, and cracked wheat;

- pasta products in place of potatoes; and

- low-GI rices such as long grain white rice and brown rice.

Not only do whole grains have a lower GI value than refined cereal grains but also they are nutritionally superior, containing higher levels of fiber, vitamins, minerals, and phytochemicals. Studies show that higher consumption of whole grains is associated with reduced incidence of cancer and heart disease. A large survey of post-menopausal women showed a clear relationship between their intake of whole grains and risk of death from some forms of heart disease: In fact, the risk of dying from heart disease was reduced by about one-third in those women eating one or more servings of whole-grain product each day.

3. Eat More Legumes (Beans, Peas, and Lentils) and Use Nuts (in Small Amounts) More Frequently

Legumes, including lentils, chickpeas, cannellini beans, soybeans, and kidney beans, are an important part of a low-GI diet; we suggest that you eat them at least twice a week. You can eat more legumes by including them in soups, salads, and sauces.

Legumes are nutrient dense, providing protein, iron, zinc, calcium, folate, and soluble fiber. They're also an excellent source of phytoestrogens such as lignans and isoflavones. Studies suggest that eating large amounts of foods rich in phytoestrogens can reduce the risk of several diseases: The activity of lignans and isoflavones, for example, may control some menopausal symptoms. What's more, lignans and isoflavones possess antiviral, antifungal, antibacterial, and anticancer properties. Flavones also have antihypertensive, anti-inflammatory, and antioxidant activities. Beans are high in folate, which lowers the level of homocysteine in the blood and reduces the risk of heart disease.

Legumes are:

- inexpensive
- low in calories
- free of saturated fat and cholesterol
- filling

Soybeans are particularly rich in ALA (the plant precursor of omega-3s), and also contain genistein—an anti-cancer phytochemical. Tofu (soy bean curd) is an easy way of using soy. It has a mild flavor itself but absorbs the flavors of other foods, making it delicious when it's been marinated in soy sauce, ginger and garlic and tossed into a stir-fry.

Legumes supply carbohydrate and protein but very little fat. They're high in fiber—both soluble and insoluble—and are a great source of vitamins. Although they will keep indefinitely, it's best to use dried legumes within one year of purchase. Young beans cook faster than old ones and will also be more vividly colored.

Making the Most of Nuts

In a Mediterranean diet, people eat nuts and seeds (including almonds, walnuts, pumpkin and sunflower seeds, tahini, and roasted chickpeas) once or twice a week. Research suggests that eating a small handful of nuts (1 ounce) several times a week can help lower cholesterol and reduce heart attack risk. Nuts are healthy because they contain:

- very little saturated fat (the fats are predominantly mono- or polyunsaturated)
- dietary fiber
- vitamin E, an antioxidant believed to help prevent heart disease

Walnuts and pecans also contain some omega-3 fats, while linseeds are very rich in omega-3s, lignans and plant estrogens. When freshly ground, linseeds have a subtle nutty flavor and make a great addition to breads, muffins, biscuits, and cereals.

Easy Ways to Eat More Nuts

■ Use nuts and seeds in food preparation: For example, use toasted cashews or sesame seeds in a chicken stir-fry, sprinkle walnuts or pine nuts over a salad, top fruity desserts, or granola with almonds.

■ Spread bread with peanut, almond, or cashew butter rather than butter or margarine.

■ Sprinkle a mixture of ground nuts and linseeds over cereal or salads, or add to baked goods such as muffins.

■ Enjoy nuts as a snack. Although high in fat, nuts make a healthy substitute for less nutritious high fat snacks such as potato chips, chocolate and cookies.

4. Eat More Fish and Seafood

In studies, weekly fish consumption is linked to a reduced risk of coronary heart disease. In fact, just one serving of fish a week may reduce the risk of a fatal heart attack by

40 percent. The likely protective components of fish are the very long chain omega-3 fatty acids: eicosapentanoic acid (EPA) and docosahexanoic acid (DHA). Our bodies only make small amounts of these fatty acids and so we rely on dietary sources, especially fish and seafood, for them. (See chapter 4 for more on the benefits of omega-3 fats.) The American Heart Association recommends that American adults eat fish at least twice a week.

Just remember not to cook your fish in solid (saturated) fat. That means that eating fried fish from a fast-food restaurant doesn't count, nor does eating pre-cooked breaded frozen-fish products that have been cooked in saturated oils.

Attention has recently focused on high levels of mercury in some fish and shellfish, including swordfish, shark, lobster, and white albacore tuna. We subscribe to the Food and Drug Administration's recommendation to avoid frequent consumption of these fish and shellfish if you are pregnant, planning to become pregnant, nursing, or feeding a young child.

Which Fish is Best?

Oily fish, which tend to have darker colored flesh and a stronger fishy flavor, are the richest source of omega-3 fats. (Don't be put off by the term "fatty" or "oily" fish: four ounces of the fattiest fish has about the same amount of fat as four ounces of very lean beef.)

Canned salmon, sardines, mackerel, and, to a lesser extent, tuna, are all very rich sources of omega-3s; look for canned fish packed in water or soybean, canola, or olive oil.

Fresh fish with higher levels of omega-3s are: Atlantic salmon and smoked salmon, Atlantic, Pacific and Spanish mackerel, sea mullet, Southern bluefin tuna, and swordfish. Eastern and Pacific oysters and squid (calamari) are also rich sources.

"But I Don't Like Seafood!"

If you don't like fish or seafood you'll get some omega-3 fatty acids when you eat lean red meat. If you don't want to eat meat, you can also get a precursor of these fatty acids from plants. This precursor is also an omega-3 fat known as alpha-linolenic acid (ALA). Our bodies can convert this plant-based omega-3 fat to EPA and DHA, but it takes about 10 grams of ALA to yield 1 gram of DHA and EPA. You can get ALA from linseed, canola, walnut, and soybean oils. There are also small amounts in walnuts, linseeds, pecans, soybeans, baked beans, wheat germ, lean meats, and green leafy vegetables.

You can also include more omega-3s in your diet by taking fish oil supplements, but it's unlikely that you would get the full benefit of increased omega-3 intake without changing your lifestyle in other ways as well, including getting more exercise, eating a high-fiber, low-fat balanced diet, and quitting smoking. (A supplement, no matter how helpful, can't substitute for a healthy diet and good exercise habits.) Choose a product with the largest amount of EPA and DHA. But be careful—in a 1,000-milligram capsule the amount of EPA and DHA can vary considerably. Look for a product that includes vitamin E, which will help prevent the fish oils from oxidizing.

Is Cod Liver Oil a Source of Omega-3 Fatty Acids?

Although cod liver oil contains some omega-3 fats, the amounts are quite small. But it does contain a lot of vitamins A and D, two fat-soluble vitamins that our bodies store. If you were to take enough cod liver oil to meet your omega-3 requirement, you'd also exceed the recommended intake of vitamins A and D.

5. Eat Lean Meats and Low-Fat Dairy Foods

Eating lean meats and low-fat dairy foods is a great way to lower the saturated fat content of your diet. Scientists have known for years that a diet high in saturated fat raises cholesterol levels and increases heart disease risk. More recently, research has also implicated these fats in both insulin resistance and obesity: We burn saturated fat more poorly than other fats, so it tends to be stored as fat more readily. In contrast, our bodies are more likely to use omega-3 PUFAs and MUFAs for energy rather than storage.

Saturated fats should comprise less than 10 percent of our total calorie intake: For an average adult eating around 1800 to 2100 calories, this means eating about 20 grams of saturated fat a day. Unfortunately, the message to "avoid saturated fat" has, for many people, translated into "avoid red meat and dairy products," removing primary sources of iron and calcium from their diets. While it is true that these two food groups could contribute saturated fat to our diets, avoiding these foods entirely will not result in a healthier way of eating.

We suggest eating lean meat two or three times a week, and accompanying it with salad and vegetables. Trim all visible fat from meat, especially pork, and remove the skin (and the fat just below it) from chicken. Game meat such as rabbit and venison are not only lean but are also good sources of omega-3 fatty acids, as are organ meats such as liver and kidney. Replacing full fat dairy foods with reduced-fat, low-fat or fat-free varieties will also help you reduce your saturated fat intake.

Much of the saturated fat we consume these days comes from pre-prepared packaged and take-out foods; in fact, many fast-food restaurants cook with highly-saturated fat.

Until these restaurants make an effort to reduce the saturated fat content of their products, it's best to eat as little fried fast food as possible.

The Place for Eggs and Other Cholesterol-Rich Foods

We used to think that eating high-cholesterol foods such as eggs, shrimp, and other crustaceans would raise our blood cholesterol levels. We now know that our livers compensate for the increased cholesterol intake by reducing cholesterol production (although a small percentage of people have an inherited condition called *familial hypercholesterolemia*, which impairs this self-regulation). This means that you could eat an egg a day, for example, without harming your heart. To enhance your intake of omega-3 fats we suggest that you eat omega-3 enriched eggs (if you can find them), which have about six times more ALA and DHA than regular eggs. These enriched eggs are produced by feeding hens a diet that is naturally rich in omega-3s (including canola and linseeds).

6. Use High Omega-3 and Monounsaturated Oils Such As Olive, Peanut and Canola Oils

The following oils are rich in monounsaturated fatty acids, which should supply the majority of fat in our diets.

Olive oil has been a part of the Mediterranean and Middle
Eastern diet for thousands of years, and is recognized
as a healthy alternative to other fats and oils because
it's high in monounsaturated fats and low in saturates.
Its minimal PUFA content is also an advantage because
it allows our bodies to make greater use of the omega-3
fats we obtain from other dietary sources, without any
competition from excessive polyunsaturated omega-6
fats. Olive oil has other virtues, too: It's rich in antioxidants and an anti-inflammatory substance called
squalene, slows blood clot formation and lowers
cholesterol.

Peanut oil is a multi-purpose, mild-tasting oil that oxidizes
slowly and can withstand high cooking temperatures.
About 50 percent of the fat in peanut oil is monounsaturated and another 30 percent is polyunsaturated. This
heart-healthy fat is frequently used in Asian cooking.

Canola oil, besides being high in monounsaturated fat,
contains significant amounts of alpha-linolenic acid
(ALA), the plant form of polyunsaturated omega-3 fat.
(Canola oil contains approximately 2 grams of ALA per
tablespoon.) You can buy margarines made from canola
and olive oils in supermarkets; some brand names
include: Take Control, Smart Beat, Benecol and Lee
Iacocca's Olivio Premium Spread.

Linseed oil is the richest plant source of ALA (one tablespoon provides approximately 9 grams) and it contains
very little omega-6 fat. But linseed oil is highly prone to
oxidation—meaning the fats it contains turn rancid
easily. For this reason, we suggest using linseeds as a
source of ALA rather than linseed oil.

Flaxseed, though not commonly used, is an excellent
source of omega-3s. When it's fresh, it tastes sweet and
nutty, but it does deteriorate quickly, making it taste
unpleasant. Flaxseeds are also loaded with omega-3s.
One tablespoon of flaxseed oil or 2 tablespoons of
ground flaxseeds daily provide you with an excellent
dose of omega-3s. In either form, they're a healthful
addition to cereals, salads, breads, muffins, and cookies.

Cold pressed oils are among those that have undergone
minimal processing. Recent research suggests that
these oils may be better for our hearts because they are
richer in antioxidant compounds called polyphenols.
"Cold pressed" means that the oil is extracted from the
seed, nut or fruit by mechanical pressing only, without
heat or solvents. Cold pressed oils have a stronger
flavor and color than their regular counterparts, and
they're also much richer in vitamin E (a natural
preservative present in oils) and other antioxidants. For
example, extra-virgin olive oil—the best quality oil

made from the first cold pressing of the olives—
contains 30 to 40 different antioxidants. It is dark-
colored and strong in flavor.

Light and extra light oils are light in color and flavor. The
terms "light" and "extra light" don't mean, however,
that the oil is lower in fat than any other oil.

Vinegar

Recent studies have shown that consuming vinegar or lemon
juice with a meal can significantly lower blood sugar. As little as one tablespoon of vinegar in a vinaigrette dressing,
eaten with an average meal, lowered blood sugar by as much
as 30 percent. The effect appears to be related to the food's
acidity, which may slow stomach emptying and carbohydrate
digestion. Certain studies showed the greatest effect with
red wine vinegar and lemon juice, but we've used a range of
vinegars in the recipes in this book. Some favorite types of
vinegar include:

Balsamic vinegar: Rich and dark, made from sweet wine
aged in wooden barrels. It has a sweet, sharp flavor.

Wine vinegar: Made from red or white grapes and popular
for salad dressings. It's often flavored with herbs such as
tarragon.

Rice wine vinegar: A mild-flavored vinegar distilled from
fermented rice.

The A to Z of Foods

In this section we highlight a host of foods that can feature in a low-GI diet. These foods have optimum flavor and nutritional value.

Apples Apples are a popular fruit choice among Americans and, like all fruits, make an excellent low-GI snack. In a large study of people with type 1 diabetes, those who ate the most apples had the lowest levels of glycated hemoglobin (one of the best measures of diabetes control). Aim to eat at least two servings of fruit every day.

Bacon Bacon is a flavorful ingredient in many dishes. You can make a little bacon go a long way by trimming off all fat and chopping it finely. Lean ham is often a more economical and leaner way to go. In casseroles and soups, a ham or bacon bone imparts a fine flavor without much fat.

Cheese At around 30 percent fat (most of this being saturated), cheese can contribute quite a lot of fat to a recipe. Although there are a number of reduced-fat cheeses available, some of these may lose a lot in flavor for a small reduction in fat. It is worth comparing fat per ounce between brands to find the tastiest one with the lowest fat content. Alternatively, a sprinkle of a grated, very tasty cheese, such as Parmesan, may do the job.

Part-skim ricotta and 2-percent cottage cheeses are 25–50 percent lower in fat. Try them in a sandwich. They yield a fraction of the fat. It's worth trying some fresh ricotta from a deli—you may find the texture and flavor more acceptable than that of the ricotta available in tubs in the supermarket. Try ricotta in lasagna instead of a creamy white sauce. Flavored cottage cheeses are ideal low-fat toppings for crackers.

Cream and sour cream Keep to very small amounts as these are high in saturated fat. An 8-ounce container of cream can be poured into ice-cube trays and frozen, providing small amounts of cream when you need it. Adding one ice cube (about ⅔ ounce) of cream to a dish adds 7 grams of fat. You could also try light cream or reduced-fat sour cream; even low-fat, evaporated milk is a wonderful alternative for creamy pasta dishes.

Dried beans, peas and lentils These all have low GI values and are very nutritious. Incorporate them in a recipe, perhaps as a partial substitution for meat, and try a vegetarian dish (such as chickpea curry, hummus, red lentil soup, Mexican burritos, or a bean salad) at least once a week. Canned beans, chickpeas, and lentils are now widely available. They are convenient to use and a great time-saver.

Eggs Although the yolk is high in cholesterol, the fat in eggs is predominantly monounsaturated and there is no harm in consuming as much as an egg a day within the context of a low-fat diet. To enhance your intake of omega-3 fats we suggest using omega-3-enriched eggs.

Fish Seafood is generally a healthy choice, but salmon, anchovies, mackeral, trout, herrings, and sardines are richest in beneficial omega-3 fatty acids. Include fish at least once a week.

Grilling Grilling and barbecuing are excellent low-fat cooking methods (take care not to burn the meat!). Lean cuts of meat, chicken, and fish can be quickly cooked this way. Marinating first or basting during cooking will add flavor, moisture, and tenderness.

Herbs Fresh herbs are easily grown at home in pots or gardens and are available in most supermarkets these days, and there really is no substitute for the flavor they impart.

Ice cream A source of carbohydrate, calcium, riboflavin, retinol, and protein. Higher-fat varieties have the lowest GI values—but don't use that as an excuse. It's better to choose lower-fat varieties.

Jam A tablespoon of jam on toast contains far fewer calories than lightly spreading butter or margarine on toast.

Keep jars of minced garlic, hot peppers, or ginger in the refrigerator to spice up your cooking in an instant.

Lemon juice Try a fresh squeeze with ground black pepper on vegetables rather than butter. Lemon juice provides acidity that slows gastric emptying and lowers the GI value of a food.

Meat Lean meat is the best source of iron (the nutrient used in carrying oxygen in our blood), so we suggest including it at least two to three times a week. It is important that all visible fat is trimmed from meat before cooking and that the portions be kept moderate.

Nuts Research suggests that those who regularly eat nuts have a lower risk of heart attack. Nuts are high in poly- and monounsaturated fats, vitamin E, and fiber. Try some sprinkled over your breakfast cereal, salad, or dessert and enjoy a small snack of unsalted nuts occasionally. Also, try adding soy "nuts" (dry roasted soy beans) and/ or Chick Nuts (see recipe on page 296) to a nut mix.

Olive oil Rich in monounsaturates and antioxidants, extra virgin olive oil is the perfect base for vinaigrette dressing, marinades, and Mediterranean-style cooking.

Pasta A food to be eaten as often as desired—just remember to moderate portions. Fresh or dried, the preparation is easy. Simply boil in water until just tender or al dente, drain, and toss with pesto, a tomato sauce, or a sprinkle of Parmesan, pepper, and olive oil. Pasta is a carbohydrate rich in B vitamins.

Questions? Ask your dietitian for more recipe ideas. (See page 30 for guidance on finding one.)

Red wine A traditional part of the Mediterranean diet, red wine has been found to be cardioprotective, when consumed in moderation. This means no more than 5–10 ounces in a day, preferably with meals. Wine is a great flavoring in cooking, too.

Stock Make your own vegetable, beef, chicken, or fish stock. Prepare it in advance, refrigerate it, then skim off any accumulated fat from the top. Prepared stock is available in cartons, cubes, and powders in the super-market. Look for brands that have reduced salt.

Tomatoes Tomatoes and tomato sauces can be used with great versatility. They have a low GI value and are rich in health-giving lycopenes, a form of vitamin A that also serves as an antioxidant.

Unsaturated fats are good for you, but eat them in moder-ation. Avoid the saturated fats found in fried fast foods and bakery products. Enjoy the monounsaturated fats in avocados and olive and canola oils.

Vinegar A vinaigrette dressing (1 tablespoon of vinegar and 2 teaspoons of oil) with your salad can lower the blood-glucose response to the whole meal by up to 30 percent.

The best types of vinegars for this purpose are red- or white-wine vinegar, or use lemon juice.

Whole grains This includes barley, bulgur (cracked wheat), corn, oats, rice and wheat. Most whole grains have a lower GI value than refined cereals and they are also nutritionally superior, containing higher levels of fiber, vitamins, minerals, and phytoestrogens. Eating one or more servings a day is associated with improvements in insulin sensitivity and with a lower risk of cancer and heart disease.

Yogurt Yogurt is a valuable food in many ways. It is a good source of calcium, gut-friendly bacteria, protein, and riboflavin. Unlike milk, it is suitable for those who are lactose intolerant. Low-fat plain yogurt is a suitable substitute for sour cream. If using yogurt in a hot sauce or casserole, add it at the last minute and do not let it boil, or it will curdle. It is best if you can bring the yogurt to room temperature before adding to the hot dish. To do this, mix a small amount of yogurt with a little sauce from the dish, then stir this mixture back into the bulk of the sauce.

Zero fat is unhealthy, so learn how to get just the right amount you need. Our bodies need essential fatty acids that can't be synthesized and must be supplied in the diet. Fat adds flavor—use monounsaturated fats such as olive oil, canola oil, and flaxseed oil in your cooking.

Your Low-GI Foods

To make low-GI choices easy choices, you need to stock the right foods. Here are some ideas for what to keep in your pantry, fridge, and freezer.

▶ *What to keep in your pantry*

Rolled oats Besides their use in oatmeal, oats can be added to desserts, cakes, breads, and cookies

Rice Basmati or Uncle Ben's® Converted® long grain

Dried pasta Short or long types such as spaghetti or fettucine and spirals or macaroni

Dried noodles

Couscous Ready in minutes; serve it with casseroles, stews, or stir-fries

Dried legumes Split red lentils, for example, which take only 20 minutes to cook; other examples are brown lentils, split peas, or garbanzo beans

Canned legumes Kidney beans, mixed beans, baked beans, pinto beans, lima beans, and chickpeas

Canned vegetables Canned string beans, tomatoes, asparagus, carrots, and mushrooms are always handy to boost the vegetable content of a meal

Canned fish Tuna, crabmeat, or sardines in spring water; salmon

Tomato paste Use in soups, sauces, and casseroles plus bottled tomato pasta sauces

Bottled vegetables Sun-dried tomatoes, grilled eggplant or peppers, marinated artichoke hearts, and mushrooms are handy to keep as flavorful additions to pastas and breads

Prepared stock Beef, chicken, or vegetable stocks come in liquid, cube, and powder forms, regular or low-sodium versions

Dried fruits Dried apricots, fruit medley, raisins, prunes, cherries, and berries

Unsweetened canned fruit Peaches, pears, applesauce

Canned evaporated skim milk Makes an excellent creamy pasta sauce

Oils Canola for general use, some extra virgin olive oil for salad dressings and sesame or peanut oils for Asian-style stirfries

Black pepper

Mustard Seeded or whole-grain mustard is useful for a sandwich spread, in salad dressings and sauces

Asian sauces Hoisin, oyster, soy, and fish sauces

Vinegar White-wine vinegar, red-wine vinegar, and balsamic vinegar are excellent for salads

Curry pastes A tablespoon or so makes a delicious curry base

Honey Can be used in place of table sugar; keeps baked goods moist

Herbs and spices Oregano, basil, thyme, parsley, rosemary, marjoram, ginger, garlic, hot peppers are most commonly used either fresh or dried. Ground cumin, turmeric, cinnamon, nutmeg, etc. should be bought in small quantities as they lose pungency with age and incorrect storage

Capers, olives and anchovies Can be bought in jars and kept in the fridge once opened. They are tasty (though salty) additions to pasta dishes, salads, sauces, and pizzas

▶ *What to keep in your fridge*

Milk Skim or 1%

Yogurt Fat free or low fat, plain and with added fruit

Eggs Certified organic or omega-3-enriched

Cheese Grated light mozzarella is very handy for adding to a toasted sandwich or sprinkling over a baked dish.

A block of fresh Parmesan is indispensable for grating over pasta and will keep for months if refrigerated. Reduced-fat cottage and ricotta cheeses have a short life so are best bought as needed

Fresh pasta or noodles A great standby for a quick meal

▶ *What to keep in your freezer*

Low-fat ice cream Always ideal for a quick dessert, served with fresh fruit

Spinach Great for adding to pastas

Canned beans Can be added to curries and stir-fries

Peas and corn Handy to add to a quick meal

Berries Make any dessert special

_____

Your Low-GI Food Fact Finder

Use this to quickly identify low-GI foods and discover their other nutritional benefits.

Breads

Although none of these breads have been specifically tested for their GI values, it is likely that the values are lower than in ordinary bread. They also offer the nutritional benefits of any whole-grain food.

Alvarado Farms 100% Sprouted Wheat

Arnold Stoneground 100% Whole Wheat

Martins Dutch Country 100% Stoneground Whole
Wheat Sandwich Roll

Pepperidge Farm Sprouted Wheat™

Pritikin Whole Grain Whole Wheat Rye™

Shiloh Farms Cracked Wheat, 100% Whole Grain
Wheat

Taystee 100% Stoneground Whole Wheat

Toufayan 100% Whole Wheat Pita

Vermont Bread Company 100% Whole Wheat, Alfalfa
Sprouts, Sprouted Wheat, etc.

Pita bread (GI value of 57) Unleavened flat bread was
found to have a slightly lower GI value than regular
bread in a Canadian study. Sold in supermarkets in
packets of flat rounds.

Pumpernickel bread (GI value of 41) Also known as rye
kernel bread because the dough it is made from contains
80 to 90 percent whole rye kernels. It has a strong
flavor and is usually sold thinly sliced. Because it is not
made with fine flour, its GI value is much lower than
that of ordinary bread. Available in supermarkets and
delicatessens.

Breakfast Foods

Breakfast cereals The high degree of cooking and processing of commercial breakfast cereals tends to make
the starch in them more rapidly digestible, giving a
higher GI value. Less-processed cereals (muesli, rolled
oats) tend to have lower GI values. All-Bran™ and
varieties (GI value of 30–51), Frosted Flakes™ (GI
value of 55), Kellogg's Complete™ (GI value of 48),
muesli (GI value of 39–55), oat bran (GI value of 55),
rice bran (GI value of 19) are all rated low GI.

Oatmeal Published GI values range from a low 42 up to 75
for one-minute oats. The additional cutting of rolled
oats to produce quick-cooking oats probably increases
the rate of digestion, causing a higher GI value.

Dairy Foods

Custard (GI value of 35) Made with milk, so provides
calcium, protein, and B vitamins plus a little sugar,
vanilla flavoring, and a starch thickener.

Ice cream (GI value of 36–80) Go for the lower-fat varieties.
Most dairy products have very low GI values. When we
eat dairy foods, a protein curd forms in the stomach and
slows down its emptying. This has the effect of slowing
down absorption and lowering the GI value.

Milk (GI value of 31) Lactose, the sugar occurring naturally in milk, is a disaccharide that must be digested into its component sugars before absorption. The two sugars that result, glucose and galactose, compete with each other for absorption. This slows down absorption and lowers the GI value. The presence of protein and fat in milk also lowers the GI value.

Yogurt (GI value of 14–36) A concentrated milk product, soured by the use of specific bacteria. All varieties have a low GI value, including those containing sugar. Artificially sweetened brands have a lower GI value and contain fewer calories.

Fruit

Apples (GI value of 38) Easy to incorporate into the diet as a low-GI food—an average apple will add 3 grams of fiber to your diet. They are also high in pectin, which lowers their GI value.

Apple juice (GI value of 40) The main sugar occurring in apples is fructose (6.5 percent), which itself has a low GI value. The high concentration of sugars is known to slow the rate of stomach emptying, hence slowing the absorption and lowering GI value.

Apricots (GI value of 64, canned; 30, dried) Apricots are an excellent source of beta-carotene and dried apricots in particular are high in potassium. Like apples, they are high in fructose (5 percent), which lowers their GI value.

Cherries (GI value of 22) The GI value for cherries is based on European cherries. Other cherries may have a higher GI value.

Grapefruit (GI value of 25) The low GI value of grapefruit may be due to its high acid content, which slows absorption from the stomach.

Grapes (GI value of 46) An equal mix of fructose and glucose and a high acid content are characteristics of fruits with a low GI value. Grapes are a good example.

Kiwi fruit (GI value of 58) Kiwi fruits contain equal proportions of glucose and fructose and high acidity, all of which contribute to a reasonably low GI value. They are also a wonderful source of vitamin C, with one kiwi fruit meeting the total recommended daily intake.

Oranges (GI value of 42) Well known as a good source of vitamin C, most of the sugar content of oranges is sucrose. This, along with their high acid content, probably accounts for their low GI value.

Peaches (GI value of 42, fresh; 52, canned in light syrup) Most of the sugar in peaches is sucrose (4.7 percent). Other aspects, such as their acid and fiber content, may account for their low GI value.

Pears (GI value of 38, fresh; 43, canned) Another fruit with a high fructose (7 percent) content, accounting for the low GI value.

Pineapple juice (GI value of 46) Mainly sucrose (8 percent).

Plums (GI value of 39) The GI value for plums comes from a European study. In general, plums may contain a fairly equal mixture of glucose, fructose, and sucrose. The higher the concentration of sugars, the slower the food is emptied from the stomach and hence the slower the absorption. This may account for the low GI value.

Raisins (GI value of 64) Raisins are less acidic than grapes and this may account for their higher GI values since increased acidity is associated with lower GI values.

Grains

Barley (GI value of 25) "Pearled" barley, which has had the outer brown layers removed, is most commonly used. It is high in soluble fiber, which probably contributes to its low GI value. Available in supermarkets.

Basmati rice (GI value of 58) Has a low GI value attributable to its high amylose-starch content. Available in supermarkets.

Buckwheat (GI value of 54) Also known as groats or kasha, buckwheat is available from health-food stores and some supermarkets. It can be cooked as a breakfast cereal, or steamed and served with vegetables in place of rice. It can also be ground and used as flour for making pancakes and pasta. Buckwheat in this form is likely to have a higher GI value than when whole.

Bulgur (GI value of 48) Made by roughly grinding previously cooked and dried wheat. Most commonly recognized as a main ingredient in tabbouleh. The intact physical form of the wheat contributes to its low GI value.

Uncle Ben's® Converted® Rice (GI value of 44) Converted or parboiled rice is second only to brown rice in its nutritional quality. In addition, its high amylose-starch content gives it its low GI value. Use parboiled rice in any of the same ways you would other types of rice.

Oat bran (GI value of 55) Unprocessed oat bran is available in the cereal section of supermarkets, or loosely packed in plastic bags in health-food stores. Its carbohydrate content is lower than that of oats and it is higher in fiber, particularly soluble fiber, which is probably responsible for its low GI value. A soft, bland product, it is useful as a partial substitution for flour in baked goods to lower the GI value.

Oats See Oatmeal under Breakfast cereals.

Parboiled rice (GI value of 38–87) Parboiling involves steeping rice in hot water and steaming it prior to drying and milling. Nutrients from the bran layer are retained in the grain and the cooked product has less tendency to be sticky. Some studies have found par-boiled rice to have a lower GI value than non-parboiled rices. The overriding determinant of the GI value of rice is the type of starch present in the grain.

Quick-cooking wheat (GI value of 54) Whole-wheat grains that have been physically treated to allow short cooking times, quick-cooking wheat is most often used as a substitute for rice. The whole-grain structure also acts as a barrier and so reduces its digestibility and hence lowers the GI value.

Rice bran (GI of 19) Rich in fiber (25 percent by weight) and oil (20 percent by weight), rice bran has an extremely low GI value. It is available in the cereal section of supermarkets and health-food stores.

Legumes

Legumes (GI value of 10–70) These include dried peas, beans, and lentils; most have a GI value of 50 or less. Canned varieties have a slightly higher GI value than their home-cooked counterparts due to the higher temperature during processing.

Soy beans (GI value of 14–20) These have one of the lowest GI values, possibly due to their higher protein and fat content. Their viscous fiber, as in other legumes, reduces physical availability of starch to digestive enzymes.

Nuts

Nuts Contain relatively little carbohydrate, so they do not have a GI value. Cashews are an exception and have a GI value of only 22. Most nuts average about 50 percent fat, but this is predominantly healthy fat of the mono- and polyunsaturated varieties. Research suggests that a small handful of unsalted nuts (1 ounce) on most days of the week is beneficial in lowering cholesterol and reducing risk of heart attack.

Peanuts (GI value of 14) are not nuts at all, but legumes. They contain about 25 percent carbohydrate but have minimal effect on blood-glucose levels.

Pasta

Pasta (GI value of 32–78) Pasta is made from hard wheat semolina with a high protein content, which makes for a strong dough. Protein–starch interactions and minimal disruption to the starch granules during processing contribute to the low GI value. There is some evidence that thicker pasta has a lower GI value than thin types.

Spaghetti (GI value of 38) While both fresh and dried pastas have low GI values, this is not the case for canned spaghetti. Canned spaghetti is generally made from flour rather than high-protein semolina and is very well cooked—two factors that are likely to give it a high GI value.

Vegetables

Most vegetables are low in carbohydrate, which makes their GI value *irrelevant*. Even those for which a GI value has been measured have little effect on blood-glucose levels in the quantities one usually eats.

Peas (GI value of 48) Peas are high in fiber and also higher in protein than most other vegetables. Protein–starch interactions may contribute to their lower GI value. They also average 4 percent sucrose, giving them a sweet flavor.

Sweet corn (GI value of 54) Raw, fresh, frozen, or canned varieties would be suitable to use. Corn on the cob has a lower GI value than tortilla chips or cornflakes. The intact whole kernel makes enzymic attack more difficult.

Sweet potato (GI value of 44) Belonging to a different plant family than regular white potatoes, sweet potatoes are mainly available either white or yellow-orange in color. Their sweetness comes from a high sucrose content. Sweet potato is high in fiber. It has a lower GI value than regular potato varieties.

8

Recipes

All the recipes in this book have been analyzed using a computerized nutrient-analysis program*, and the GI value, calorie, carbohydrate, fat, and fiber content per serving are shown. The following information will help put this nutritional profile into context for you. Where a range of servings is given for the recipe, the nutritional information relates to the higher number.

GI We have given each recipe a GI rating, which is our best estimate of the range in which the GI value falls. A calculated GI value is not realistic for all recipes because the carbohydrate may be used in the recipe in a different form from that in which the original GI value of the food was tested.

*Foodworks™, Xyris Software (Australia) Pty Ltd.

Energy This is a measure of how many calories a serving provides. A moderately active woman aged 18 to 54 years requires about 1,900 calories a day; a man, about 2,400 calories. Those who burn lots of energy through exercise need a higher calorie intake than those who live more sedentary lives.

Carbohydrate It is not necessary to calculate how many grams of carbohydrate you eat on a daily basis; however, if you're an athlete or you have diabetes, you may find this information useful. To consume around 50 percent of energy from carbohydrate, on average, women need about 200 grams a day, while men need about 300 grams. Athletes can consume anywhere from 300 to 700 grams of carbohydrate a day, providing 50–60 percent of their energy needs. To have an idea of the impact the carbohydrate in the recipe may have on your blood-sugar level and insulin response, multiply the carbohydrate content per serving of the recipe by its GI value to give you the glycemic load. See pages 54–57 and 430–432 for a discussion of the glycemic load and the tables in Part 4 for glycemic load values.

Fat We have aimed to keep our recipes low in fat, in particular low in saturated fat. For this reason we have used mono- and polyunsaturated margarines and oils. Omega-3 fatty acids from fish and seafood have many health benefits, so we have included a number of recipes containing these foods and used omega-3-enriched eggs.

The amount of fat that is appropriate in your diet depends on your calorie intake and the overall composition of your diet. A low-fat diet for most people could contain somewhere between 30 and 60 grams of fat per day. If you are not trying to lose weight, there is no harm in consuming larger amounts of fat, so long as it is predominantly unsaturated.

Fiber Most of the recipes are high in fiber, both soluble and insoluble. Dietary guidelines recommend a daily fiber intake of at least 25 grams. People with diabetes should aim for 25–30 grams of fiber, as the American Diabetes Association recommends. A slice of whole-wheat bread provides 2 grams of fiber, an average apple 4 grams. The average American consumes only about 11 grams of fiber a day.

Breakfasts

Honey Banana Smoothie

■

Sweet Potato and Corn Hotcakes
with Pan-fried Tomato and Basil

■

Muesli with Mixed Fresh Fruit

■

Raisin-studded Oatmeal

■

Buttermilk Pancakes
with Glazed Fruit

HONEY BANANA SMOOTHIE

The "smoothie"—a quick but sustaining breakfast. Many variations are possible using different combinations of fruits, milks, and yogurts.

LOW GI
Per serving:

cal 190

carb .... 35 g

fat .... 0.5 g

fiber .... 2 g

1 large, ripe banana

1 tablespoon All-Bran™ breakfast cereal

1 cup low-fat milk, chilled

½ cup evaporated low-fat milk, well chilled

2 teaspoons honey

few drops vanilla extract

1. Peel banana and coarsely chop.

2. Combine with remaining ingredients in a blender and blend for 30 seconds or until smooth and thick.

3. Serve immediately.

Serves 2

For this recipe, the evaporated milk must be chilled to froth up well.

SWEET POTATO AND CORN HOTCAKES WITH PANFRIED TOMATO AND BASIL

These hotcakes make a very delicious breakfast or brunch item.

LOW GI
Per serving:

cal 90
carb .... 15 g
fat .... 1 g
fiber .... 2 g

½ cup self-rising flour

½ cup rolled oats

1 egg, lightly beaten

½ cup low-fat milk

1 8-ounce can corn kernels, drained

1 small (5 oz) sweet potato, peeled and grated

freshly ground black pepper

3–4 ripe tomatoes, cut into ½-inch-thick slices

handful of fresh basil leaves

1. Combine the flour and rolled oats in a medium-sized bowl. Using a whisk, stir in the beaten egg and milk, mixing until combined. Stir in the corn kernels and grated sweet potato with the pepper.

2. Brush a nonstick frying pan or griddle with oil or spray with cooking spray over medium heat. Add large spoonfuls of the mixture to the pan. Cook 2 minutes or until bubbles begin to form. Turn and cook 1–2 minutes on the other side. Repeat with remaining mixture. Set aside cooked hotcakes in a warm place.

3. Once you are finished cooking the hotcakes, regrease the frying pan and place over medium heat. Add the sliced tomatoes, cooking for a couple of minutes until browned on one side, then turn, sprinkle with basil and cook until softened. Serve the fried tomatoes and basil over the hotcakes.

Makes 10 hotcakes

MUESLI WITH MIXED FRESH FRUIT

Creamy rolled oats, plump raisins, and crunchy almonds combined with plain yogurt and milk.

LOW GI
Per serving:

cal 365
carb .... 50 g
fat .... 11 g
fiber .... 6 g

1 cup rolled oats

⅔ cup low-fat milk

1 tablespoon raisins

½ cup (4 oz) low-fat plain yogurt

¼ cup whole almonds, chopped

1 apple, grated

lemon juice (optional)

mixed fresh fruit, such as strawberries, pear, plum, blueberries

1. Combine the oats, milk, and raisins in a bowl. Cover and refrigerate overnight.

2. Add the yogurt, almonds, and apple; mix well.

3. To serve, adjust the flavor with lemon juice. Serve with fresh fruit.

Serves 2

RAISIN-STUDDED OATMEAL

A quick and easy breakfast with a lot of stick-to-your-ribs character.

LOW GI
Per serving:

cal 210
carb .... 38 g
fat .... 3 g
fiber .... 3 g

⅔ cup rolled oats

1 cup low-fat milk, approximately

1 small ripe banana, mashed

1 heaping tablespoon raisins

1. Place the oats in a saucepan or large microwaveable bowl. Add sufficient water to cover, plus about ⅔ cup of the milk.

2. Bring to a boil and boil for 2 minutes or microwave on high for 1 to 2 minutes.

3. Add the banana and cook 1 to 2 minutes more.

4. Add the remaining milk to make a smooth consistency and stir in raisins.

Serves 2

BUTTERMILK PANCAKES WITH GLAZED FRUIT

Golden light pancakes served with warm, soft summer fruits.

LOW GI
Per serving:

cal 420
carb .... 60 g
fat .... 12 g
fiber .... 6 g

1 cup 1-minute oats or unprocessed oat bran

2 cups buttermilk

½ cup dried-fruit medley, chopped

½ cup white flour, sifted

2 teaspoons sugar

1 teaspoon baking soda

1 egg, lightly beaten

2 teaspoons mono or polyunsaturated margarine, melted

low fat milk (optional)

GLAZED FRUIT

1 tablespoon mono or polyunsaturated margarine

1 tablespoon brown sugar

6 medium peaches or apricots or nectarines

1. Combine the oats and buttermilk in a bowl and let stand 10 minutes.

2. Stir in the dried fruit, flour, sugar, baking soda, egg, and margarine; mix thoroughly. Let stand for about 1 hour.

3. After standing, add a little low-fat milk if the mixture is too thick.

4. Heat a nonstick frying pan or griddle and spray with cooking spray or grease lightly with margarine. Pour in about 3 tablespoons of batter, cook over moderate-high heat until bubbly on top and lightly browned underneath. Turn pancake to brown on other side. Repeat with remaining batter.

5. Set aside to keep warm.

6. To make the glazed fruit, melt the margarine and sugar together over medium heat in frying pan. Stir until sugar is dissolved. Add the sliced fruit and cook over medium heat 2–3 minutes until softened. Serve warm over the pancakes.

Serves 4

Dried-fruit medley is a mixture of dried fruit and is available from supermarkets and health-food stores.

Light Meals

Pasta with Roasted Butternut
Squash and Pepper in a
White Wine Sauce

■

Marinated Mushroom and
Cracked Wheat Salad

■

Lentil and Barley Soup

■

Minestrone

■

Split Pea Soup

■

Tabbouleh

■

Vegetable Lasagna

■

Creamy Mushrooms and Pasta

■

Pasta and Red Bean Salad

■

Pasta with Tangy Tomatoes

■

Spicy Noodles

PASTA WITH ROASTED BUTTERNUT SQUASH AND PEPPER IN A WHITE WINE SAUCE

Here is a tasty and easy way to eat fiber and some anti-oxidants.

LOW GI
Per serving:

cal 410

carb .... 63 g

fat .... 8 g

fiber .... 5 g

1.5 lbs butternut squash

1 large red pepper, halved lengthways, seeds removed

2 sprigs fresh rosemary

1 clove garlic

1 tablespoon olive oil

8 oz bowtie pasta

WHITE WINE SAUCE

1 teaspoon olive oil

1 teaspoon margarine

1 large red onion, halved and thinly sliced

1 clove garlic, crushed

2 teaspoons seeded mustard

1 sprig fresh rosemary, chopped

½ cup white wine

approximately 1 cup low-fat evaporated milk

fresh basil leaves

1. Preheat the broiler part of the oven to medium-high.

2. Cut the squash into 3 wedges. Peel and then slice each wedge into ¼-inch-thick slices, to create small triangular-shaped pieces of squash. Toss the sliced squash and pepper in the olive oil with the rosemary and garlic to coat. Lay the squash in a single layer, and the pepper skin-side-up, on a sheet of parchment paper on a tray. Broil 4 inches from the heat for 10 minutes.

3. Cook the pasta according to package directions.

4. Remove the pepper from the oven and place in a paper bag, fold down the top, and set aside. Turn over the squash pieces and return to the oven for another 5–10 minutes or until they are browned and tender.

5. Heat the olive oil and margarine in a large frying pan and sauté the onion and garlic over moderate heat for 2 minutes. Add the mustard, rosemary, and white wine and simmer for 2 minutes to reduce slightly.

6. While the wine is reducing, remove the pepper from the bag and peel off the skin (which should lift easily). Slice into strips.

7. Add the evaporated milk to the frying pan and a handful of fresh basil leaves, stirring over low heat as they wilt. Add the drained hot pasta, stirring to coat with the sauce. Then add the pepper strips and squash and serve.

Serves 4

MARINATED MUSHROOM AND CRACKED WHEAT SALAD

A super-nutritious high-fiber salad.

LOW GI
Per serving:

cal 195
carb .... 22 g
fat .... 10 g
fiber .... 5 g

4 oz button mushrooms, sliced

2 green onions, finely chopped

1 cup cracked wheat (bulgur)

MARINADE

3 tablespoons lemon juice

3 tablespoons olive oil

1 teaspoon brown sugar

1 clove crushed garlic

2 tablespoons parsley, finely chopped

1 tablespoon mint, finely chopped

1. Combine ingredients for marinade in a bowl. Add mushrooms and green onions, stirring to coat. Cover and refrigerate for about 1 hour for the mushrooms to soften and the flavors to develop.

2. Meanwhile, place the bulgur in a bowl and cover with hot water and let it stand for about half an hour until the water is absorbed and the bulgur softens.

3. Drain the bulgur and squeeze out excess water by wrapping in a paper towel. Toss the bulgur with the marinated mushrooms and spoon into a serving dish.

Serves 4 to 6

LENTIL AND BARLEY SOUP

A zesty, satisfying winter soup that is a meal in itself.

LOW GI
Per serving:

cal 180
carb .... 25 g
fat .... 5 g
fiber .... 5 g

1 tablespoon oil

1 large onion, finely chopped

2 cloves garlic, crushed, or 2 teaspoons minced garlic

½ teaspoon turmeric

2 teaspoons curry powder

½ teaspoon ground cumin

1 teaspoon minced hot peppers

6 cups water

1½ cups prepared chicken stock

1 cup red lentils

½ cup pearl barley

1 15-ounce can tomatoes, undrained and crushed

salt

freshly ground black pepper

chopped fresh parsley or coriander, to serve

1. Heat the oil in a large saucepan. Add the onion, cover, and cook gently for about 10 minutes or until beginning to brown, stirring frequently.

2. Add the next 5 ingredients (garlic through hot peppers) and cook, stirring, for 1 minute.

3. Stir in the water, stock, lentils, barley, tomatoes, and salt and pepper to taste. Bring to a boil, cover, and simmer about 45 minutes or until the lentils and barley are tender.

4. Serve sprinkled with parsley or coriander.

Serves 4 to 6

MINESTRONE

Serve this hearty soup with crusty bread and a green salad for a delicious balanced meal.

LOW GI
Per serving:

cal 120
carb .... 18 g
fat .... 2 g
fiber .... 7 g

15-ounce can cannellini beans, rinsed and drained

oil

2 medium onions, chopped

2 cloves garlic, crushed

1 small ham bone

10 cups water

5 beef bouillon cubes

3 carrots, diced

2 sticks celery, sliced

2 small zucchini, chopped

4 tomatoes (approximately 1 lb), diced

⅓ cup (2 oz) small macaroni pasta

2 tablespoons fresh parsley, chopped

freshly ground black pepper

grated Parmesan cheese, to serve (optional)

1. Heat a little oil in a large heavy-based saucepan. Add the onions and garlic and cook for about 5 minutes or until soft. Add the ham bone, water, bouillon cubes, and drained beans. Bring to a boil.

2. Add the carrots, celery, zucchini, and tomatoes to the stock. Reduce heat and simmer, covered, for 1 hour.

3. Remove the lid, take out the ham bone, and add the macaroni and stir. Continue to simmer for 10 to 15 minutes or until the macaroni is tender.

4. Stir in the parsley and add pepper to taste. Serve with Parmesan cheese.

Serves 6

SPLIT PEA SOUP

Begin this full-flavored favorite a day ahead, allowing the split peas to soak overnight.

LOW GI
Per serving:

cal 260
carb .... 39 g
fat .... 3 g
fiber .... 9 g

2 cups split peas

1 ham bone

12 cups (3 quarts) water

1 teaspoon oil

1 medium onion, finely chopped

1 medium carrot, finely chopped

1 stick celery, finely chopped

1 bay leaf

½ teaspoon dried thyme leaves

juice of ½ lemon

freshly ground black pepper

1. Wash the split peas, place in a large saucepan with the ham bone and water. Bring to a boil. Allow to cool, refrigerate overnight.

2. Next day, skim any fat from the top and bring to a boil and simmer, covered, for 2 hours.

3. Remove the ham bone from the soup and trim any meat from it. Return the meat to the soup.

4. Heat the oil in a frying pan, add the onion, carrot, and celery, and cook for about 10 minutes or until lightly browned. Add the onion mixture to the soup with the bay leaf and thyme. Simmer, covered, for 20 minutes. Remove the bay leaf.

5. Puree the soup in a food processor or blender, adding extra water if necessary to make a soup consistency.

6. Add the lemon juice and season to taste with pepper. Reheat if needed before serving.

Serves 6

TABBOULEH

Tabbouleh is best if you make it ahead, allowing time for the flavors to develop. It keeps a couple of days in the refrigerator.

LOW GI
Per serving:
cal 160
carb .... 15 g
fat .... 10 g
fiber .... 5 g

½ cup cracked wheat (bulgur)

1 cup fresh flat-leafed parsley or continental parsley, finely chopped

1 small onion or 3–4 green onions, finely chopped

1 medium tomato, finely chopped

DRESSING

2 tablespoons fresh lemon juice

2 tablespoons olive oil

pinch salt

½ teaspoon freshly ground black pepper

1. Cover the bulgur with hot water and soak for 20–30 minutes to soften. Drain well and roll in a clean, lint-free kitchen towel to squeeze out excess water.

2. Combine the bulgur, parsley, onion, and tomato in a bowl.

3. For the dressing, combine all the ingredients in a screw-top jar; shake well.

4. Add the dressing to the bulgur mixture and toss lightly to combine.

Serves 4

Variations include the addition of a chopped cucumber, a crushed clove of garlic, or 2 tablespoons of chopped fresh mint. You can use half lemon juice and half vinegar if preferred.

VEGETABLE LASAGNA

Soft layers of spinach, cheese, and lasagna noodles with a luscious vegetable sauce.

LOW GI
Per serving:

cal 340

carb .... 44 g

fat .... 10 g

fiber .... 9 g

1 bunch spinach, washed and stalks removed

8 oz instant lasagna sheets

2 tablespoons grated Parmesan cheese or low-fat cheddar cheese

VEGETABLE SAUCE

2 teaspoons oil

1 medium onion, chopped

2 cloves garlic, crushed, or 2 teaspoons minced garlic

8 oz mushrooms, sliced

1 small green pepper, chopped

1 6-ounce can tomato paste

1 1-lb can beans, any variety, rinsed and drained

1 15-ounce can tomatoes, undrained and mashed

1 teaspoon mixed herbs

CHEESE SAUCE

1½ tablespoons poly or mono-unsaturated margarine

1 tablespoon white flour

1½ cups low-fat milk

½ cup grated low-fat cheese

pinch ground nutmeg

freshly ground black pepper

1. Blanch or lightly steam the spinach until just wilted; drain well.

2. For the vegetable sauce, heat the oil in a nonstick frying pan. Add the onions and garlic and cook for about 5 minutes or until soft. Add the mushrooms and pepper and cook a further 3 minutes, stirring occasionally. Add the tomato paste, beans, tomatoes, and herbs. Bring to a boil and simmer, partly covered, for 15 to 20 minutes.

3. Meanwhile, for the cheese sauce, melt the margarine in a saucepan or a microwave bowl. Stir in the flour and cook 1 minute, stirring (for 30 seconds on high, in microwave). Remove from the heat. Gradually add the milk, stirring until smooth. Stir over medium heat until the sauce boils and thickens, or in microwave on high until boiling, stirring occasionally. Remove from heat, stir in the cheese, nutmeg, and pepper.

4. To assemble, pour half the vegetable sauce over the base of a lasagna pan or ovenproof dish (about 6½ by 10½ inches). Cover with a layer of lasagna sheets, then half the spinach. Spread a thin layer of cheese sauce over the spinach. Top with the remaining vegetable sauce and remaining spinach. Place over a layer of lasagna sheets and finish with the remaining cheese sauce. Sprinkle with Parmesan or cheddar cheese.

5. Cover with aluminum foil and bake in a moderate oven (350°F) for 40 minutes. Remove foil and bake for a further 30 minutes or until the top is beginning to brown.

Serves 6

Dipping the lasagna sheets briefly in hot water before use helps to soften them prior to cooking.

CREAMY MUSHROOMS AND PASTA

Put this dish together quickly with staples from the pantry.

LOW GI
Per serving:
cal 440
carb .... 68 g
fat .... 7 g
fiber .... 8 g

2 cups macaroni or other small pasta

2 tablespoons fresh parsley, finely chopped

2 tablespoons finely grated Parmesan cheese

SAUCE
2 teaspoons olive oil

1 medium onion, thinly sliced

1 clove garlic, crushed, or 1 teaspoon minced garlic

1 lb mushrooms

1 teaspoon paprika

2 teaspoons Dijon mustard

2 tablespoons tomato paste

1 12-ounce can evaporated
  skim milk

¼ cup grated low-fat
  cheddar cheese (1 oz)

½ cup chopped green
  onions

freshly ground black pepper

1. Add the pasta to a large saucepan of boiling water and boil, uncovered, until just tender. Drain and keep warm.

2. While the pasta is cooking, begin the sauce. Heat the oil in a nonstick frying pan. Add the onions, garlic, and mushrooms, and cook for about 5 minutes or until softened.

3. Combine the paprika, mustard, tomato paste, and milk in a small bowl. Stir into the mushroom mixture with the cheese and cook, stirring frequently, over low heat for 5 minutes.

4. Add the onions with pepper to taste.

5. Pour the sauce over the pasta and toss gently to combine. Serve sprinkled with the parsley and Parmesan cheese.

Serves 4

Mushrooms are a good source of niacin and can be a source of vitamin B_{12} if they are grown on a mixture containing animal compost.

PASTA AND RED BEAN SALAD

A summer salad full of flavor. Easy to prepare with canned beans.

LOW GI
Per serving:
cal 130
carb .... 15 g
fat .... 5 g
fiber .... 4 g

1 cup cooked pasta (e.g., shells, elbows, twists)

1 cup cooked or canned red kidney beans, well drained

3 green onions, finely chopped

1 tablespoon fresh parsley, finely chopped

DRESSING

1 tablespoon olive oil

1 tablespoon wine vinegar

1 teaspoon Dijon mustard

1 clove garlic, crushed

freshly ground black pepper

1. Combine the pasta, beans, onions, and parsley in a serving bowl.

2. For the dressing, combine the oil, vinegar, mustard, garlic, and pepper in a screw-top jar; shake well to combine.

3. Pour the dressing over the pasta mixture and toss well.

Serves 4

PASTA WITH TANGY TOMATOES

A simple, light pasta dish that can be on the plate in about 15 minutes.

LOW GI
Per serving:

cal 415
carb .... 65 g
fat .... 10 g
fiber .... 7 g

5 oz uncooked spaghetti or other pasta

3 medium tomatoes

1 tablespoon olive oil

1 tablespoon capers, drained

1 clove garlic, crushed, or 1 tablespoon minced garlic

juice of 1 lemon

1 tablespoon hot sauce

black pepper

fresh basil leaves, shredded

1. Cook the spaghetti according to package directions.

2. Meanwhile, dice the tomatoes. Combine in a bowl with the olive oil, capers, garlic, lemon juice, hot sauce, olives, pepper, and basil.

3. Drain the spaghetti and return to its saucepan. Add the tomato combination to it and stir in. Serve hot or warm.

Serves 2

SPICY NOODLES

Good-tasting and good for you too.

LOW GI
Per serving:
cal 280
carb .... 45 g
fat .... 6 g
fiber .... 4 g

8 oz dried thin egg noodles

2 teaspoons oil

2 cloves garlic, crushed, or 2 teaspoons minced garlic

1 teaspoon minced ginger

1 teaspoon minced hot peppers

6 green onions, sliced

1 tablespoon smooth peanut butter

2 tablespoons soy sauce

1 cup prepared chicken stock

1. Add the noodles to a large saucepan of boiling water and boil, uncovered, for about 5 minutes or until just tender.

2. While the noodles are cooking, heat the oil in a nonstick frying pan, add the garlic, ginger, chili, and onions and stir-fry for 1 minute. Remove from the heat.

3. Stir in the peanut butter and soy sauce and gradually add the stock, stirring until smooth. Stir over heat until simmering, and simmer for 2 minutes.

4. Drain the noodles and add to the spicy sauce, stirring to coat. Serve immediately.

Serves 4 as an accompaniment

Add strips of stir-fried chicken or meat with a packet of Asian-style mixed vegetables.

Main Meals

Moroccan Chicken over Couscous

■

Steamed Mussels over Ratatouille
and Basmati Rice

■

Spicy Beef Stew

■

Spinach, Feta, and Bean Frittatas

■

Whitefish Fillets over Sweet Potato
Chips with Oven-roasted
Basil Tomatoes

■

Thai Tuna and Sweet Potato Tart

■

Pork and Noodle Stir-fry with
Cashews

Glazed Chicken with Sweet Potato
Mash and Stir-fried Greens

■

Warm Lamb and Chickpea Salad

■

Spicy Pilaf with Chickpeas

■

Moroccan Kebabs

■

Winter Hotpot

■

Carrot and Thyme Quiche

■

Parsley Cheese Pie

■

Beef and Lentil Burgers

MOROCCAN CHICKEN OVER COUSCOUS

Make extra; this recipe is great for day-after leftovers.

MODERATE GI
Per serving:

cal 360
carb .... 43 g
fat .... 9 g
fiber .... 4 g

2 teaspoons ground cumin

2 teaspoons ground coriander

1 teaspoon ground fennel

1 15-ounce can chickpeas, drained and patted dry

2 cloves garlic, finely chopped

2 hot red peppers, finely chopped

1 tablespoon olive oil

1 lb chicken-breast cutlets, sinews removed

½ bunch flat-leafed parsley, coarsely chopped

1 lemon, pits removed, rinsed and thinly sliced

½ cup dry white wine

1 cup couscous, uncooked

½ cup raisins

juice of 1 lemon

salt

freshly ground black pepper

1. Combine the cumin, coriander, and fennel in a mixing bowl, and toss the chickpeas in the spices.

2. Heat the olive oil in a large wok or frying pan. Add the garlic and hot peppers and cook, stirring, for 1 minute.

3. Toss the chickpeas into the pan and cook until the aroma of the spices comes through—approximately 2 minutes. Place chickpeas in a large bowl and set aside.

4. Add 1 tablespoon olive oil to the pan and cook the chicken cutlets for approximately 4 minutes or until just cooked through. Add to the chickpeas, and stir in the chopped parsley and lemon slices.

5. To make a sauce, deglaze the pan with the wine, simmering for 2 minutes.

6. Pour over the chicken mixture and keep warm.

7. Place the couscous in a large mixing bowl and pour 1 cup of boiling water over the top. As the couscous plumps up, gently mix in the raisins, lemon juice, and salt and pepper.

Serves 6

STEAMED MUSSELS OVER RATATOUILLE AND BASMATI RICE

MODERATE GI
Per serving:
cal 390

carb .... 56 g

fat .... 7 g

fiber .... 6 g

1 large eggplant, diced small

1 large red pepper, halved, seeded and diced (½-inch pieces)

4 zucchini, sliced into 1-inch rings

1 large brown onion, roughly chopped

3 cloves garlic, roughly chopped

1 tablespoon mustard seed oil

1 15-ounce can chopped tomatoes, undrained

2 cups water

4 bay leaves

2 sprigs fresh thyme

salt

freshly ground black pepper

8 leaves fresh basil

1 cup Basmati rice

1 lb mussels (approximately 20)

1 cup dry white wine

1 cup water

2 bay leaves

10 black peppercorns

1. Place the eggplant in a colander, sprinkle with salt, and leave for 30 minutes. Wash under cold water, drain, and pat dry with a paper towel.

2. Heat the oil in a large saucepan and add the eggplant, pepper, zucchini, onion, and garlic. Toss in the hot oil for 2 minutes, then add the tomatoes, water, and herbs. Season with salt and pepper. Reduce the heat and simmer for 45 minutes, stirring occasionally. Remove the bay leaves and thyme sprigs. Chop the basil leaves and stir through the ratatouille.

3. Bring 2 quarts of salted water to a boil and cook the rice for 11 minutes. Immediately drain and keep warm.

4. Prepare the mussels by discarding any broken shells and soaking in cold water. Pull the "beard" from the side of the shell with a sharp tug toward the pointed end of the mussel.

5. Bring the wine and water, bay leaves, and peppercorns to a boil, reduce the heat, and add the mussels. Cover the saucepan with the lid, and simmer for approximately 2 minutes, removing each mussel as it fully opens. Discard any unopened shells.

6. To serve, arrange half a cup of rice in the middle of the plate, top with spoonfuls of ratatouille and arrange the cooked mussel shells over the top.

Serves 4

The ratatouille flavor improves with time, so make it the day before and reheat gently.

SPICY BEEF STEW

Here's a warm comfort food, rich in taste and nutrients.

LOW GI
Per serving:

cal 320
carb .... 40 g
fat .... 7 g
fiber .... 8 g

1 lb rump steak, diced

⅓ cup white flour

salt

freshly ground black pepper

1 tablespoon olive oil

2 medium brown onions, finely diced

3 cloves garlic, coarsely chopped

1 red hot pepper, coarsely chopped

3 large (1½ lbs) sweet potatoes, peeled and coarsely diced

1½ quarts beef stock

2 tablespoons tomato paste

1 tablespoon grainy mustard

2 stalks celery, sliced

2 large red peppers, halved, seeded, and coarsely diced

1 cup corn kernels

1 28-ounce can peeled chopped tomatoes, undrained

1 15-ounce can pinto beans, drained

1 cup spiral noodles, cooked

½ cup kalamata olives

½ bunch parsley, coarsely chopped

1. Toss the steak in flour seasoned with salt and black pepper in a large mixing bowl.

2. Heat the oil in a large 6-quart casserole dish or metal pan and gently cook the onions, garlic, and hot pepper for 1 minute. Add the steak and brown on all sides.

3. Add the sweet potato, beef stock, tomato paste, grainy mustard, celery, pepper, corn kernels, and tomatoes. Season with salt and pepper. Simmer gently, with lid on, for 1½ hours, stirring occasionally.

4. Remove the lid and add the pinto beans, noodles, and olives. Simmer for 5 minutes, stir in the parsley, and serve immediately.

Serves 8

SPINACH, FETA, AND BEAN FRITTATAS

Much more than a muffin, despite its muffiny look.

LOW GI
Per serving:
cal 227
carb .... 13 g
fat .... 13 g
fiber .... 5 g

1 10-ounce package chopped frozen spinach, thawed

1 teaspoon nutmeg

5 oz reduced-fat feta, crumbled

1 15-ounce can red kidney beans, drained

½ bunch green onions, finely chopped

2 cloves garlic, finely chopped

¼ cup canola oil

5 omega-3-enriched eggs, lightly beaten

salt

pepper

¾ cup self-rising flour

1. Preheat the oven to 350°F.

2. Lightly oil 8 × ¾ cup capacity large muffin tins.

3. In a large mixing bowl, combine the spinach with nutmeg, feta, beans, green onion, and garlic.

4. Stir in the canola oil, eggs, salt, pepper, and flour.

5. Fill the 8 muffin tins and bake immediately for 35–40 minutes, till golden brown and puffy. Serve hot or cold.

Makes 8

WHITEFISH FILLETS OVER SWEET POTATO CHIPS WITH OVEN-ROASTED BASIL TOMATOES

Everyone will love the delicate combination of flavors in this dish.

LOW GI
Per serving:

cal 310

carb .... 26 g

fat ....11 g

fiber .... 4 g

6 large ripe plum tomatoes, halved lengthways

1 teaspoon olive oil

2 cloves garlic, finely chopped

6 basil leaves, finely sliced

salt

freshly ground pepper

6 small whitefish* fillets (about 1½ lbs)

⅓ cup white flour, seasoned with salt and freshly ground black pepper

2 omega-3-enriched eggs, lightly whisked

3 large (1¾ lbs) sweet potatoes, peeled and thinly sliced

2 tablespoons olive oil

3 cups (2 oz) baby spinach leaves

1 tablespoon toasted sesame seeds

6 lemon wedges

*Whitefish includes flounder, halibut, and turbot.

1. Preheat the oven to 350°F.

2. Place the tomatoes, cut side up, on a lightly oiled baking tray. Top the tomatoes with a little olive oil, half the garlic, and the basil leaves and seasonings. Place in the oven and bake for 30 minutes.

3. Dip the whitefish fillets in the seasoned flour and eggs. Cover and set aside in the refrigerator.

4. Peel the sweet potato and slice thinly.

5. Heat 1½ tablespoons olive oil in a heavy-based frying pan and spread the sweet potato slices over it, seasoning the layers with salt and pepper and the remaining garlic. Cook until the underside turns golden brown and slightly crisp, then turn once and cook the other side. Keep warm.

6. Heat ½ tablespoon olive oil in a heavy-based frying pan and cook the whitefish fillets for approximately 4 minutes, turning once only, until golden brown and flaky.

7. Serve with a bed of baby spinach, and then the sweet potato chips topped with the whitefish. Sprinkle with toasted sesame seeds and serve with lemon wedges and oven-roasted basil tomatoes.

Serves 6

THAI TUNA AND SWEET POTATO TART

This entree is packed with flavorful, nutrient-dense ingredients that are easy to have on hand.

LOW GI
Per serving:

cal 327
carb .... 33 g
fat .... 12 g
fiber .... 4 g

1 teaspoon canola oil

2 medium sweet potatoes (1 lb)

5 omega-3–enriched eggs

1 14-ounce can lite coconut milk

grated zest of 1 lemon

3 tablespoons fresh coriander, finely chopped

½ bunch green onions, roughly sliced

2 cloves garlic, finely sliced

½ cup self-rising flour

salt

freshly ground black pepper

½ cup cooked Basmati rice

2 6-ounce cans water-packed tuna chunks, drained

1 1-lb can corn niblets, drained

1. Preheat the oven to 350°F.

2. Oil a 12-inch round tart pan (fluted, metal or ceramic) with 1 teaspoon canola oil or, alternatively, oil a 12 × ¾ cup capacity large muffin tin.

3. Peel and steam whole sweet potato until just tender, approximately 20 minutes. Drain and cut the sweet potato into chunks.

4. Whisk the eggs, coconut milk, lemon zest, coriander, green onions, garlic, self-rising flour, and seasonings together in a large bowl until well combined.

5. Arrange chunks of cooked sweet potato, tuna, rice, and corn niblets over the base of the ovenproof dish, or in the muffin tins. Pour over the egg and coconut mixture.

6. Place the tart (or muffin) tin into the preheated oven, and bake for 1 hour (45 minutes for muffins) until puffed and golden brown.

7. Serve cut into wedges or as individual tarts, either hot or cold, with a leafy green salad.

**Makes 1 large tart for
8 or 12 individual tarts**

PORK AND NOODLE STIR-FRY WITH CASHEWS

A classic, flavorful dish that is easy to prepare.

LOW GI
Per serving:

cal 580
carb .... 56 g
fat .... 19 g
fiber .... 8 g

1 tablespoon oil

1 lb pork strips

10 oz Chinese plain noodles

1 medium red pepper, sliced into thin strips

8 oz broccoli, chopped into small florets

1 clove garlic, crushed

2 teaspoons finely grated fresh ginger

5 oz snow peas, ends cut off and sliced diagonally into thirds

8 oz button mushrooms, thinly sliced

1 baby bok choy, washed, trimmed, and cut lengthways into 8

6 green onions, chopped diagonally

1 tablespoon salt-reduced soy sauce

1 tablespoon hoisin sauce

1 tablespoon honey

½ cup roasted cashew nuts

1. Heat a large frying pan or wok over high heat. Add half the oil and when the oil is hot, add one-third of the pork strips and stir-fry for 1–2 minutes until just cooked. Repeat with the remaining 2 batches of pork, transferring to a plate covered loosely with foil to keep warm.

2. Prepare the noodles according to package directions and drain.

3. Add the remaining oil to the pan over high heat. Add the pepper, broccoli, garlic, and ginger and stir-fry for about 1 minute. Add the remaining vegetables and stir-fry 1–2 minutes until the vegetables are tender-crisp, sprinkling in a little water if necessary.

4. Combine the sauces and honey together in a bowl.

5. Return the pork to the pan with the noodles and sauces. Toss until well combined and heated through. Put into bowls to serve, and sprinkle with the cashew nuts.

Serves 4

GLAZED CHICKEN WITH SWEET POTATO MASH AND STIR-FRIED GREENS

Here's a yummy stir-fry ready in no time.

LOW GI
Per serving:

cal 530

carb .... 49 g

fat .... 15 g

fiber .... 9 g

SWEET POTATO MASH

1 medium sweet potato (1 lb), peeled and cut into chunks

⅓ cup low-fat milk

1 tablespoon sweet chili sauce

GLAZED CHICKEN

2 12-oz chicken breasts, sliced into strips across the grain

1 teaspoon oil

1 cup chicken stock

2 teaspoons salt-reduced soy sauce

1 tablespoon duck sauce

1 tablespoon cornstarch

2 teaspoons grated fresh ginger

few sprigs of fresh coriander leaves

STIR-FRIED GREENS

1 teaspoon oil

large handful of snow peas

bunch of Chinese greens such as baby bok choy

2 medium zucchini

1. Boil or microwave the sweet potato until tender. When cooked, drain and mash with milk and sweet chili sauce. Keep warm.

2. Heat a wok or large frying pan with the oil and stir-fry the chicken until browned. Remove from pan and set aside to keep warm.

3. Heat a further teaspoon of oil in the wok or frying pan. When hot, add the green vegetables (chopped stalks and sliced zucchini first). Stir-fry until lightly cooked. Combine remaining ingredients in a separate bowl and add to the pan with the cooked chicken and stir until thickened slightly.

4. Serve the chicken and greens over the sweet potato mash.

Serves 2

WARM LAMB AND CHICKPEA SALAD

A delicious new way to prepare lamb.

LOW GI
Per serving:

cal 430
carb .... 23 g
fat .... 25 g
fiber .... 9 g

1 lb lamb cutlets

1 tablespoon olive oil

1 onion, finely chopped

3 garlic cloves, crushed

½ teaspoon ground cumin

½ teaspoon ground coriander

½ teaspoon ground ginger

½ teaspoon paprika

2 15-ounce cans chickpeas, drained and rinsed

salt and black pepper to taste

1 tomato, diced

1 cup fresh coriander, finely chopped

1 cup fresh flat-leafed parsley, finely chopped

1 cup fresh mint, finely chopped

3 tablespoons extra virgin olive oil

juice of 1 lemon

baby spinach leaves, washed, to serve

1. Cook the lamb cutlets in a lightly oiled frying pan, over medium heat, about 3 minutes each side. Transfer to a plate and cover with foil to keep warm. Set aside.

2. Heat the tablespoon of olive oil in the frying pan and cook the onion for 5 minutes or until soft. Add the garlic and spices and cook for 5 minutes over low heat, stirring occasionally. Add the chickpeas and heat through, stirring until warm and well coated with the spice mixture. Remove from the heat and add the salt and pepper, tomato, chopped herbs, extra oil, and lemon juice.

3. Cut the lamb cutlets into thick slices, diagonally. Toss in the chickpea/herb mixture.

4. Arrange the baby spinach leaves on plates and top with the chickpeas and lamb. Serve immediately.

Serves 4

The fat in this recipe is predominantly from the olive-oil dressing and is highly monounsaturated.

SPICY PILAF WITH CHICKPEAS

A meatless rice dish that serves three to four people for a light meal or 6 as a side dish.

LOW GI
Per serving:

cal 230
carb .... 32 g
fat .... 8 g
fiber .... 4 g

1 teaspoon poly- or monounsaturated margarine

2 teaspoons olive oil

1 medium onion, peeled and finely diced

6 oz button mushrooms, quartered or halved

1 clove garlic, crushed

⅔ cup Basmati rice

1 teaspoon garam masala*

⅓ 15-ounce can chickpeas, drained

1 bay leaf

1½ cups chicken stock

1 tablespoon slivered almonds, toasted**

1. Heat margarine and oil in a medium-sized frying pan over medium heat. Add the onion, cover, and cook 3 minutes, stirring occasionally. Add mushrooms and garlic and cook, uncovered, a further 5 minutes, stirring occasionally.

2. Add the rice and spice, stirring to combine until aromatic. Add the chickpeas and bay leaf and pour over stock. Bring to a boil. Reduce heat to very low. Cover with a tight-fitting lid and simmer (without lifting the lid) for at least 12 minutes or until rice is tender and all liquid has been absorbed.

3. Sprinkle with toasted almonds and serve with a salad.

Serves 3 to 4

*Garam masala (pronounced gah-RAHM mah-SAH-lah) is a blend of Indian spices (peppercorns, cardamom, cinnamon, cloves, coriander, nutmeg, turmeric, and/or fennel seeds), found in Indian specialty shops, markets, or international sections of large super-markets.

**Slivered almonds can be toasted easily by placing in a dry pan over medium heat. Once the pan gets hot, toss the almonds around to toast them. This will take no more than a minute. Don't leave unattended because the almonds toast rapidly.

MOROCCAN KEBABS

Here are some North African flavors right from your own kitchen in 20 minutes.

LOW GI
Per serving:

cal 470
carb .... 65 g
fat .... 9 g
fiber ....11 g

4 large pieces of pita bread	3 medium tomatoes, diced
12 oz lean ground beef	1 tablespoon mint, roughly chopped
½ cup cracked wheat (bulgur)	2 teaspoons olive oil
2 teaspoons Moroccan seasoning*	2 teaspoons red-wine vinegar
1 medium white onion, very finely chopped	lettuce
1 egg, lightly beaten	hummus (optional)**

1. Wrap the pita bread in foil and heat in the oven for 15 minutes.

2. Meanwhile, combine beef, bulgur, seasoning, onion, and egg in a bowl. Shape mixture into 8 patties.

3. Heat a nonstick frying pan with cooking spray and cook patties about 4 to 5 minutes each side.

4. Combine tomato and mint with olive oil and vinegar in a bowl and serve with the patties and lettuce on the pita bread. Spread with hummus.

Serves 4

*Moroccan seasoning is available in jars in the spice section of the supermarket. Alternatively, flavor the patties with 1 clove of crushed garlic and ½ teaspoon each of ground coriander, cumin, paprika, black pepper, and dried rosemary.

**Hummus can be purchased in the refrigerated section of the supermarket or in delicatessens. Alternatively, see recipe on p. 159.

WINTER HOTPOT

A hearty vegetarian meal that can be prepared in around 30 minutes.

LOW GI
Per serving:

cal 260
carb .... 47 g
fat .... 1.5 g
fiber .... 12 g

1 15-ounce can kidney beans, rinsed and drained

5 cups water

1 bay leaf

1 teaspoon oil

1 onion, finely chopped

2 cloves garlic, crushed, or 2 teaspoons minced garlic

2 sticks celery, sliced

2 squash or 2 small zucchini, sliced

8 oz button mushrooms

1 28-ounce can tomatoes, undrained and chopped

1 teaspoon minced hot pepper

2 tablespoons tomato paste

1½ cups prepared vegetable stock

1¼ cups small macaroni pasta

freshly ground black pepper

chopped fresh parsley, to serve

1. Heat the oil in a nonstick frying pan, add the onion and garlic and cook for about 5 minutes or until soft.

2. Add the celery, squash, or zucchini and mushrooms and cook, stirring, for 5 minutes. Stir in the beans, tomatoes, hot pepper, tomato paste, and stock, and bring to a boil.

3. Add the pasta, reduce heat, and simmer for about 20 minutes or until the pasta is tender. Add pepper to taste and serve sprinkled with parsley.

Serves 4 to 6

This is a complete meal in itself but you could serve it with a dinner roll or bread.

CARROT AND THYME QUICHE

Warm or cold this quiche is as flavorful as it is colorful.

LOW GI
Per serving:

cal 209
carb .... 11 g
fat .... 15 g
fiber .... 6 g

2 lbs carrots, peeled and
  grated

1 large onion, peeled and
  grated

2 cloves garlic, grated or
  finely chopped

2½ oz low-fat cheddar
  cheese, grated

⅓ cup canola oil

3 eggs, lightly beaten

1 teaspoon ground nutmeg

salt and freshly ground
  black pepper

1 tablespoon fresh thyme
  leaves, or 1 teaspoon
  dried

½ cup self-rising flour

1. Preheat the oven to 350°F.

2. Lightly oil a 12-inch round shallow quiche or pie dish.

3. Grate the carrots, onion, garlic, and cheese (using the
   grating disc of your food processor makes this step quick
   and easy).

4. In a large mixing bowl beat together the oil, eggs, nut-meg, salt and pepper, and thyme leaves. Stir in the flour until combined, then add the carrots, onion, garlic, and cheese.

5. Spoon into the prepared dish and bake for 45 minutes, until golden brown and cooked through.

Serves 6 to 8

PARSLEY CHEESE PIE

A cheese and egg dish incorporating rice. Cheese and eggs make a refreshing alternative to meat in this dish. Serve with a tossed salad.

LOW GI
Per serving:

cal 207

carb .... 27 g

fat .... 4 g

fiber .... 3 g

½ cup Basmati rice

1 cup chopped fresh parsley

1 cup grated low-fat cheddar cheese

1 medium onion, finely chopped

½ cup creamed corn

½ cup corn kernels

1 large zucchini, grated

3–4 mushrooms, finely chopped

3 eggs

2 cups low-fat milk

¼ teaspoon ground nutmeg

1 teaspoon ground cumin

1 egg white, lightly beaten

1. Add the rice to a saucepan of boiling water and boil, uncovered, for about 12 minutes or until just tender; drain.

2. Combine the rice, parsley, half the cheese, onion, creamed corn, corn kernels, zucchini, and mushrooms in a bowl and spoon into a greased 9inch pie dish.

3. Whisk the eggs, milk, nutmeg, and cumin in a bowl. Fold in the lightly beaten egg white and pour evenly over the rice mixture. Sprinkle the remaining cheese on top.

4. Bake in a moderate oven (350°F) for about 1 hour or until set in the center.

Serves 6

BEEF AND LENTIL BURGERS

Serve these succulent patties hot, with vegetables or salad and mustard or chutney.

LOW GI
Per patty:

cal 56
carb .... 4 g
fat .... 2 g
fiber .... 1 g

½ cup dried brown or red lentils

1 lb lean ground beef

1 small onion, finely chopped

½ small green pepper, finely chopped

1 clove garlic, crushed, or 1 teaspoon minced garlic

2 teaspoons dried mixed herbs

⅓ cup tomato sauce

1 egg, lightly beaten

freshly ground black pepper

about ½ cup unprocessed oat bran

1. Cook the lentils in a saucepan of boiling water for about 20 minutes or until soft; drain well.

2. Combine the lentils with the beef, onion, green pepper, garlic, herbs, sauce, egg, and ground black pepper in a bowl; mix well.

3. Add enough oat bran to form a burger consistency. Shape the mixture into 24 patties and place on a lightly greased baking tray.

4. Bake in a hot oven (400°F) for about 40 minutes, or until cooked through, turning halfway through cooking time. Alternatively, cook the patties in a nonstick frying pan over medium-high heat until browned and cooked through.

Makes 24 small patties

Reheat the leftovers and serve in pita bread with chutney, tomato, cucumber, grated carrot, and lettuce.

Desserts

Fruit Bread and Butter Pudding

■

Oat Bran and Honey Loaf Chocolate Pudding

■

Ginger Nectarine Ice Cream

■

Mixed Berry and Cinnamon Compote

■

Apple Crumble

■

Apricot, Honey, and Coconut Slice

■

Fresh Fruit Cheesecake

■

Creamy Rice with Sliced Pears

■

Winter Fruit Salad

■

Yogurt Berry Jelly

FRUIT BREAD AND BUTTER PUDDING

Served with a mixed-berry compote, this is an ideal early-autumn dessert.

LOW GI
Per serving:
cal 175
carb .... 25 g
fat .... 4 g
fiber .... 1 g

2½ cups 1% milk

3 omega-3-enriched eggs

2 tablespoons sugar

1 teaspoon vanilla extract

4 slices spicy fruit bread (cinnamon-raisin)

1 tablespoon margarine

½ cup raisins, soaked in 2 tablespoons brandy

1 teaspoon ground cinnamon

1. Preheat the oven to 325°F.

2. Lightly grease a 6-cup (1½-quart) ovenproof dish.

3. Boil 4–6 cups of water.

4. Whisk the milk, eggs, sugar, and vanilla extract in a large mixing bowl.

5. Remove the crusts from the fruit bread and spread generously with the margarine, cutting each slice in half diagonally. Stack the triangles of bread upright across the prepared dish. Scatter the cut slices with the presoaked raisins, and pour over the custard mixture. Gently push the slices down to soak up the custard. Sprinkle with cinnamon.

6. Place a deep baking dish in the oven and position the bread and butter pudding dish in the center. Pour the boiling water slowly into the baking dish to come at least three-quarters of the way up the sides of the ovenproof dish.

7. Bake for approximately 1 hour or until the custard is set, puffy, and a light golden brown.

8. Serve with the warm Mixed Berry and Cinnamon Compote (see page 276).

Serves 6 to 8

OAT BRAN AND HONEY LOAF CHOCOLATE PUDDING

Why not make this a standard item on your brunch menu?

LOW GI
Per serving:

cal 340

carb .... 55 g

fat .... 7 g

fiber .... 2 g

1 tablespoon raisins

1 tablespoon rum (optional)

4 slices sourdough bread

2 tablespoons Nutella®
hazelnut spread

2 eggs, lightly beaten

½ teaspoon ground
cinnamon

½ cup sugar

1 cup 1% milk

1 tablespoon pudding mix

1. If you want to plump the raisins with rum, place them in a small bowl with the alcohol and heat in the microwave for 20 seconds or until the fruit is swollen.

2. Spread the Nutella® thickly over 2 slices of the bread. Dot with the raisins and sandwich together with the remaining 2 slices of bread. Cut each sandwich into 4 triangular quarters and stand upright in a 1-quart baking dish, squashing together to fit.

3. Combine the beaten eggs with the remaining ingredients by whisking together in a deep bowl. Pour the egg mixture over the sandwiches in the baking dish and let stand for 10 minutes while the bread absorbs the custard.

4. Stand the baking dish into another ovenproof dish and add hot water to the larger dish to come halfway up the sides (hot-water-bath style). Bake for 40 minutes at 400°F until the custard around the bread is set and golden in color.

Serves 4

GINGER NECTARINE ICE CREAM

Keep this on hand in your freezer for an impromptu, yet classy, dessert.

LOW GI
Per serving:

cal 148
carb .... 27 g
fat .... 3 g
fiber .... 2 g

2 medium nectarines, peeled and pitted

1 quart low-fat vanilla ice cream

2 teaspoons honey

½ cup (4 oz) plain low-fat yogurt

4 oz diced dried-fruit medley

4 gingersnaps, crushed

almond or ginger thins for garnish

1. Dice the nectarine.

2. Remove ice cream from freezer and let stand at room temperature for about 10 minutes or until softened slightly. Scoop out into a large bowl.

3. Stir the honey into the yogurt. Add to the softened ice cream with the dried fruit, ginger snaps and nectarine, mixing together quickly. Pour the ice cream into a metal loaf tin, cover with plastic wrap, and return to freezer for at least 4 hours until set.

4. To serve, remove the ice cream from the freezer and stand the tin in a sink of hot water for 20–30 seconds to soften the outside of the ice cream. Tip the ice cream out onto a board and cut thick slices through it with a knife dipped into hot water between cuts. Lay on plates and garnish with almond or ginger thins.

Serves 8

MIXED BERRY AND CINNAMON COMPOTE

Fifteen minutes is all it takes for this scrumptious dessert.

LOW GI
Per serving:
cal 145
carb .... 36 g
fat .... negligible
fiber .... 2 g

¾ cup freshly squeezed
orange juice

1 cup sugar

2 cinnamon sticks

zest of 1 orange, finely
sliced

4 cups mixed berries
(raspberries, blackberries,
blueberries, strawberries)

1. Place the orange juice, sugar, cinnamon sticks, and orange zest in a large stainless-steel saucepan, and slowly bring to a boil.

2. Add the mixed berries and simmer gently for 2 minutes, just until the berries warm through and swell.

3. Serve with Fruit Bread and Butter Pudding (see page 270).

Serves 6 to 8

Before you squeeze the oranges for juice, zest the skin using a zester or vegetable peeler.

APPLE CRUMBLE

A quick and easy version that makes a delicious low-GI dessert.

LOW GI
Per serving:

cal 365
carb .... 60 g
fat .... 12 g
fiber .... 7 g

3 large Granny Smith apples, peeled, cored, and sliced

½ teaspoon mixed spice

CRUMBLE

1 cup rolled oats

½ cup unprocessed oat bran

½ cup brown sugar

1 teaspoon cinnamon

3 tablespoons poly or monounsaturated margarine

1. Combine the apples and spice. Place in a 10-inch pie dish.

2. In a food processor, combine the crumble ingredients.

3. Mix to form a crumble and sprinkle over the apples. Bake in a 350°F oven for 30 minutes.

Serves 4 (generously)

Unprocessed oat bran is available in supermarkets and health-food stores.

APRICOT, HONEY, AND COCONUT SLICE

Apricots, honey, and yogurt on a coconut-cookie base.

LOW GI
Per serving:

cal 255

carb .... 32 g

fat .... 12 g

fiber .... 2 g

BASE

¼ cup dried, shredded coconut, toasted*

16 Fifty 50 Hearty Oatmeal cookies†, finely crushed

4 tablespoons poly or monounsaturated margarine, melted

TOPPING

1 cup dried apricots

½ cup boiling water

2 8-ounce containers low-fat apricot yogurt

¼ cup honey

2 eggs

1. Line a 6½-by-10½-inch rectangular baking pan with foil.

2. For the base, combine the ingredients in a bowl and mix well. Press the mixture evenly over the base of the prepared pan.

3. Bake in a moderate oven (350°F) for about 10 minutes or until browned. Remove from oven and allow to cool.

4. For the topping, cover the apricots with the boiling water, let stand 30 minutes or until soft. Process in a blender or food processor until smooth. Add the yogurt, honey, and eggs and blend until smooth.

5. Spread the topping mixture over the prepared base. Bake in a moderate oven (350°F) for about 30 to 35 minutes or until set.

6. Cool, then refrigerate several hours before serving.

Serves 8

*To toast coconut, cook in a nonstick frying pan over low heat, stirring for 2 minutes or until just golden. Remove from the pan to cool.

†Available at supermarkets nationally.

FRESH FRUIT CHEESECAKE

A delicious lower-fat cheesecake that leaves you feeling good after you eat it—not weighed down with fat.

LOW GI
Per serving:

cal 335

carb .... 35 g

fat .... 14 g

fiber .... 1 g

BASE

32 Fifty 50 Hearty Oatmeal cookies†, crushed

6½ tablespoons poly or monounsaturated margarine, melted

FILLING

2 teaspoons gelatin

2 tablespoons boiling water

1 8-ounce container low-fat fruit yogurt

1 8-ounce container low-fat pineapple cottage cheese

¼ cup honey

½ teaspoon vanilla extract

1 cup chopped fresh fruit (e.g., apple, orange, cantaloupe, strawberries, pear, grapes)

1. For the base, combine the cookie crumbs and margarine in a bowl. Press evenly into a 9-inch pie dish. Bake in a moderate oven (350°F) for 10 minutes. Cool.

2. For the filling, sprinkle the gelatin over the boiling water in a cup, stand cup in a small pan of simmering water and stir until dissolved; cool slightly.

3. Process the cooled gelatin with the yogurt, cottage cheese, honey, and vanilla extract in a blender or food processor until smooth.

4. Arrange the chopped fruit over the prepared crust and pour over the yogurt mixture. Refrigerate for about 1 hour or until set.

Serves 8

Don't use papaya, pineapple, or kiwi fruit, as these tend to prevent gelatin from setting.

†Available at supermarkets nationally.

CREAMY RICE
WITH SLICED PEARS

A rice pudding with a healthy twist.

LOW GI
Per serving:

cal 295

carb .... 65 g

fat .... negligible

fiber .... 3 g

2 cups water

1 cup Uncle Ben's®
Converted® or Basmati
rice

¾ cup canned evaporated
skim milk

¼ cup firmly packed brown
sugar

1 teaspoon vanilla extract

1 16-ounce can pear slices,
drained

1. Bring the water to a boil in a saucepan, add the rice and
boil for 15 minutes; drain.

2. Return the rice to the saucepan with the milk. Stir over
low heat until all the milk is absorbed. Stir in the sugar
and vanilla extract; cool.

3. Using an ice cream scoop, serve scoops of rice with the
pear slices fanned out next to it.

Serves 4

WINTER FRUIT SALAD

Oranges, apples, and bananas tend to be available year-round, and this combination is ideal when other fruits are out of season.

LOW GI
Per serving:

cal 150
carb .... 33 g
fat .... 1 g
fiber .... 5 g

1 orange, peeled and separated into segments

1 medium red apple, cut into bite-size cubes

2 teaspoons sugar

1 teaspoon fresh lemon juice

1 small banana

1 tablespoon shredded coconut

1. Cut orange segments in half. Place apple and orange chunks in a bowl. Sprinkle with the sugar and lemon juice and mix thoroughly. Cover and refrigerate at least 1 hour.

2. Just before serving, stir in the sliced banana. Sprinkle with coconut to serve.

Serves 2

YOGURT BERRY JELLY

An easy dessert. You could make it with sugar-free gelatin if you wanted to reduce the calories.

LOW GI
Per serving:

cal 85
carb .... 16 g
fat .... negligible
fiber .... 1 g

1 3-ounce package berry-flavored gelatin powder

1 cup strawberries or frozen raspberries

1 cup boiling water

1½ cups low-fat berry yogurt

1. Stir boiling water into gelatin in a bowl, stir until completely dissolved; cool, but do not allow to set.

2. Roughly chop the strawberries (frozen raspberries will tend to break up on stirring).

3. Fold the yogurt and berries into the gelatin; mix well. Pour into serving dishes, cover, and refrigerate until set.

Serves 4

Snacks

Walnut, Banana,
and Sesame Seed Loaf

■

Cinnamon Muesli Cookies

■

Oat and Apple Muffins

■

Mini Cheese and
Herb Oat Scones

■

Granola Bars

■

Chick Nuts

■

Oat Munchies

■

WALNUT, BANANA, AND SESAME SEED LOAF

A versatile quick bread that can be toasted for breakfast or eaten as a snack.

MODERATE GI
Per serving:

cal 255
carb .... 30 g
fat .... 12 g
fiber .... 5 g

3 tablespoons honey

1 tablespoon canola oil

3 omega-3–enriched eggs

3 large bananas, roughly mashed

1 teaspoon ground cinnamon

1 cup whole-wheat self-rising flour

1 cup white self-rising flour

1 cup whole walnuts

1 tablespoon sesame seeds

1. Preheat the oven to 350°F.

2. Lightly oil a 5-by-9-by-2¾-inch metal loaf tin, and line with a strip of parchment paper.

3. Combine the honey, oil, and eggs in a large mixing bowl and whisk together well.

4. Whisk the bananas into the mixture with the cinnamon, and add the flours, 1 cup at a time, whisking quickly.

5. Stir in the walnuts and quickly spoon the mixture into the prepared loaf tin. Sprinkle with sesame seeds.

6. Place on the middle shelf in the preheated oven and bake for 45 minutes.

7. Test with a skewer inserted into the center of the loaf. If it comes out clean, and the loaf is golden brown, it is ready.

8. Turn out onto a wire rack to cool and slice.

Makes 1 loaf

Serves 10

CINNAMON MUESLI COOKIES

Good-tasting and good-for-you cookie treats.

MODERATE GI
Per cookie:

cal 130
carb .... 21 g
fat .... 4 g
fiber .... 2 g

2 tablespoons canola oil

3 tablespoons maple syrup

⅓ cup orange juice

1 cup unsweetened
   rolled-oat muesli

1 cup self-rising flour

1 tablespoon cinnamon

powdered sugar

1. Preheat the oven to 350°F.

2. Line a cookie tray with parchment paper.

3. Measure the oil and maple syrup into a large mixing bowl. Add the orange juice and mix.

4. Add the muesli, flour, and cinnamon and mix to a soft dough.

5. Place spoonfuls of the mixture onto the prepared tray, leaving about 1 inch between each cookie.

6. Bake immediately for 15–20 minutes, until just golden brown. Cool on a wire rack and sprinkle with a little powdered sugar.

Makes approximately 12 cookies

OAT AND APPLE MUFFINS

These are a delicious low-fat muffin, with moist chunks of apple.

LOW GI
Per serving:

cal 100
carb .... 22 g
fat .... 1 g
fiber .... 2 g

½ cup All-Bran™ cereal

⅔ cup 1% milk

½ cup self-rising flour

2 teaspoons baking powder

1 teaspoon mixed spice

½ cup unprocessed oat bran

½ cup raisins

1 Granny Smith apple, peeled and diced

1 egg, lightly beaten

¼ cup honey

½ teaspoon vanilla extract

1. Combine the All-Bran™ and milk in a bowl and let stand for 10 minutes.

2. Sift the flour, baking powder, and mixed spice into a large bowl. Stir in the oat bran, raisins, and apple.

3. Combine the egg, honey, and vanilla in a bowl. Add the egg mixture and All-Bran™ mixture to the dry ingredi-

ents and stir with a wooden spoon until just combined. Do not overmix.

4. Spoon the mixture into a greased 12-hole muffin tray. Bake in a moderate oven (350°F) for about 15 minutes or until lightly browned and cooked through. Serve warm or cold.

Makes 12 muffins

If you find these too dry when cold, warm in the microwave on high for 10 seconds before serving. Also, warm the honey first to make measuring easy.

MINI CHEESE AND HERB OAT SCONES

These tasty scones make a delicious light lunch with salad, or a tasty snack on their own. They are ready to eat as they are!

MODERATE GI
Per serving:

cal 125
carb .... 17 g
fat .... 5 g
fiber .... 3 g

1 cup self-rising flour, sifted

1½ teaspoons baking powder

1 cup unprocessed oat bran

2 tablespoons poly or monounsaturated margarine

½ cup 1% milk

2 tablespoons water

½ cup (2 oz) grated low-fat cheddar cheese

2 teaspoons chopped fresh parsley

2 teaspoons chopped fresh basil or 1 teaspoon dried basil leaves

1 teaspoon dried rosemary leaves

1. Sift the flour and baking powder into a large bowl, stir in the oat bran. Cut in the margarine.

2. Make a well in the center and add the milk and half the water. Mix lightly with a knife, adding extra water if necessary, to make a soft dough. Turn the dough onto a lightly floured board and knead gently.

3. Roll out the dough to a rectangle about ½ inch thick. Scatter half the cheese and all the herbs over the entire surface.

4. Beginning from a long side, roll up like a jelly roll to make a thick sausage. Cut into 1-inch slices to make little rounds.

5. Place the rounds side by side on a greased baking tray and sprinkle with the remaining cheese. Bake in a hot oven (400°F) for about 20 minutes or until golden brown. Serve hot or cold.

Makes 10 scones

GRANOLA BARS

These bars have a heavy, wholesome texture and make a very sustaining snack.

LOW GI
Per serving:

cal 140
carb .... 15 g
fat .... 8 g
fiber .... 3 g

½ cup whole-wheat flour

½ cup self-rising flour

1 teaspoon baking powder

½ teaspoon mixed spice

½ teaspoon ground cinnamon

1½ cups rolled oats

1 cup dried-fruit medley or dried fruit of choice, chopped

¼ cup sunflower seed kernels

½ cup apple juice

¼ cup oil

1 egg, lightly beaten

2 egg whites, lightly beaten

1. Line an 8-by-12-inch baking pan with parchment paper.

2. Sift the flours, baking powder, and spices into a large bowl. Stir in the oats, fruit, and seeds and stir to combine.

3. Add the apple juice, oil, and whole egg; mix well. Gently mix in the egg whites until combined.

4. Press the mixture evenly into the prepared pan and press firmly with the back of a spoon. Mark the surface into 12 bars using a sharp knife.

5. Bake in a hot oven (400°F) for about 15 to 20 minutes or until lightly browned. Cool and cut into bars.

Makes 12 bars

CHICK NUTS

Toasted chickpeas make a terrifically healthy low-GI nibble. Spice them up with the flavorings suggested or your own combinations. All you need is some chickpeas.

LOW GI
Per ½ cup:

cal 320
carb .... 45 g
fat .... 6 g
fiber .... 15 g

1 1-lb package dry chickpeas

Flavor Variations

CHICK DEVILS

Sprinkle a mixture of cayenne pepper and salt over the hot chick nuts.

RED CHICKS

Sprinkle a mixture of paprika and garlic salt over the hot chick nuts.

1. Soak the chickpeas in water overnight. Next day, drain and pat dry with paper towels.

2. Spread the chickpeas in a single layer over a baking tray. Bake in a moderate oven (350°F) for about 45 minutes or until completely crisp. (They will shrink to their original size.)

3. Toss with a flavoring (see previous page) while hot, or cool and serve plain.

Makes 6 cups

After seasoning these, allow them to air dry for a few days to ensure all residual moisture has evaporated.

OAT MUNCHIES

Crunchy cookies that make handy low-GI snacks.

LOW GI
Per serving:
cal 140
carb ....17 g
fat .... 6 g
fiber .... 3 g

6½ tablespoons poly or monounsaturated margarine

¼ cup honey

1 egg

½ teaspoon vanilla extract

2½ cups rolled oats

2 tablespoons sunflower seed kernels

¼ cup self-rising flour, sifted

1. Melt the margarine and honey in a small saucepan.

2. Whisk the egg and vanilla extract together in a large bowl.

3. Add the margarine mixture, oats, sunflower seed kernels, and flour to the egg mixture; stir until combined.

4. Place small spoonfuls of the mixture onto a lightly greased baking tray, spacing evenly.

5. Bake in a moderately hot oven (375°F) for about 10 minutes or until golden brown. Let stand on tray until firm, then loosen and place on a wire rack to cool.

Makes 16 cookies

Part

3

The Glycemic Index and You

All the latest information on how the glycemic index can help you with weight control, diabetes, heart health, and the metabolic syndrome (Syndrome X)—and its relevance for children and athletes

9

The Glycemic Index and Weight Control

Obesity is now recognized as a serious and growing health concern for a large section of the American population. Between 1991 and 2000, obesity in the United States rose 60 percent. Two in three American adults are overweight and one in three is obese. Even children are affected—over 15 percent of American children are overweight. We need to tackle the problem on many fronts, including exercise and diet. The glycemic index can play an important role in weight management by helping to control appetite and insulin levels.

If you are overweight, or consider yourself overweight, chances are that you have looked at countless books, brochures, and magazines offering a solution to losing weight. New diets or miracle weight-loss solutions seem to appear weekly. They are clearly good for selling magazines, but for the majority of people who are overweight the "diets" don't work—if they did, there wouldn't be so many!

At best—while you stick to it—a diet will reduce your calorie intake. At its worst, a diet will change your body composition for the fatter. This is because many diets employ the technique of drastically reducing your carbohydrate intake to bring about quick weight loss. The weight you lose, however, is mostly water (that was trapped or held with stored carbohydrate) and muscle (as it is broken down to produce the glucose you need to fuel your brain). Once you return to your former way of eating, your body contains a little less muscle mass. With each repetition of a diet you lose more muscle. Over years, the resultant change in body composition to less muscle and proportionately more fat makes weight control increasingly difficult. Your body requires less and less energy to keep the engine idling. This is nature's way of helping animals adapt to the environment in which they live.

> **The real aim in losing weight is losing body
> fat. Perhaps it would be better described as
> "releasing" body fat. After all, to lose
> something suggests that we hope to find it
> again some day!**

This chapter is not prescribing yet another diet for you to try; instead we will give you some important facts about food and how your body uses it. Not all foods are equal. When it comes to losing weight, it is not necessarily a matter of reducing how much you eat. Research has shown that the type of food you give your body determines what it is going to burn and what it is going to store as body fat. It has also revealed that certain foods are more satisfying to the appetite than others.

This is where the glycemic index plays a leading role. Low-GI foods have two essential advantages for people trying to lose weight:

1. They fill you up and keep you satisfied for longer.
2. They help you burn more body fat and less muscle.

Eating to lose weight with low-GI foods is easier because you don't have to go hungry and what you end up with is true fat release.

Why Is Being Overweight a Problem?

If you are overweight you are at increased risk of a range of health problems. Among these are heart disease, diabetes, high blood pressure, gout, gallstones, sleep apnea (when breathing stops for a significant period of time; snoring is a good sign of this), and arthritis. Along with this list of complications, there is an equal number of emotional and psychological problems associated with being overweight.

The proportion of overweight people in our society is increasing; in fact, Americans are living in an obesity epidemic despite the expanding weight-loss industry and an ever-increasing range of "diet" or "lite" foods. It is clear that the answer to preventing obesity or becoming overweight is not a simple one. Nor is losing weight easy to do. *The New Glucose Revolution* can make it easier, however. We can tell you which foods satisfy hunger for longer and are the least likely to encourage weight gain. When you use the glycemic index as the basis for your food choices, there is no need to:

- overly restrict your food intake

- obsessively count calories

- starve yourself

Learning which foods your body works best on is what using the glycemic index is all about.

It is also worthwhile to take control of aspects of your lifestyle that have an impact on your weight. You may not create a new body from your efforts, but you will feel better about the body you've got. Eating well and exercising is the aim of the game.

Why Do People Become Overweight?

Is it genetic?

Is it hormonal?

Is it our environment?

Is it a psychological problem?

Or is it due to an abnormal metabolism?

For most of us, even without much conscious effort, our bodies maintain a constant weight, even if that's higher than we'd prefer. This is despite huge variations in how much we eat. It's as if there's a weight to which our body naturally gravitates. For a proportion of people who are overweight, this balancing of energy intake and output is operating at a higher threshold. So, regardless of all apparent efforts to control it—every fad diet, every exercise program, even operations and medications—body weight is regained over the years.

Our weight is a result of how much we take in and how much we burn. So, if we take in too much and don't burn enough, we are likely to put on weight.

The question is: How much, of what, is too much?

The answer is not a simple one: Not all foods are equal and no two bodies are the same.

People are overweight for many different reasons. Some people believe they only have to look at food, others put on weight from just walking past the bakery, others blame themselves because they just can't refuse highly palatable food. Research has made it clear that a combination of social, genetic, dietary, metabolic, psychological, and emotional factors combine to influence our weight.

Before we talk more about food, let's look at the role *genetics* plays in weight control. There are many overweight people who tell us resignedly:

- "Well, my mother's/father's the same"
- "I've always been overweight"
- "It must be in my genes"

Weight Gain in Pregnancy

Did you gain a lot of weight during pregnancy and have never lost it all? A new study suggests that weight gain during pregnancy is influenced greatly by the GI values of the diet. Women who followed a low-GI diet from early on in pregnancy gained only 20 pounds, compared to 44 pounds gained by those eating an otherwise equivalent high-GI diet. What's more, the baby's birth weight and body-fat content were also higher if the mother's diet was high-GI. This study requires confirmation, but it's not all that surprising. It's been known for a long time that a baby's birth weight is related to the mother's blood-glucose levels. Women with diabetes (or at risk of developing it) have heavier babies than those without diabetes. Now it seems that *all* the maternal tissues may respond to the high levels of glucose and insulin that occur after eating high-GI foods. That includes the fat stores laid down to sustain lactation. While we await more studies, low-GI diets during pregnancy can do no harm.

Research shows us that these comments have much truth behind them. A child born to overweight parents is much more likely to be overweight than one whose parents were not overweight. It may sound like an excuse, but there is a lot of evidence to back up the idea that our body weight and shape is at least partially determined by our genes.

Much of our knowledge in this area comes from studies in twins. Identical twins tend to be similar in body weight even if they are raised apart. Twins adopted out as infants show the body-fat profile of their biological parents rather than that of their adoptive parents. When twins were given 1,000 extra calories a day for 100 days, some gained 9 pounds and some gained 26 pounds, but amazingly, one twin invariably gained similar amounts to that of his/her twin. These findings suggest that our genes are a stronger determinant of weight than our environment (which includes the food we eat). It seems that information stored in our genes governs our tendency to burn off or store excess calories.

Our genetic make-up also underlies our *metabolism* (basically how many calories we burn per minute). Bodies, like cars, differ in this regard. A V-8 consumes more fuel to run than a small four-cylinder car. A bigger body, generally, requires more calories than a smaller one. When a car is stationary, the engine idles—using just enough fuel to keep the motor running. When we are asleep, our engine keeps running (for example, our brain is still at work) and we use a minimum number of calories. This is our *resting metabolic rate*—the amount of calories we burn without any exercise (when we are at rest). Most of it is necessary fuel for our large brains. When we start exercising, or even just moving around, the number of calories, or the amount of fuel we use, increases. The largest amount (around 70 percent) of the calories used in a twenty-four-hour period, however, are those used to maintain our resting metabolic rate.

Since our resting metabolic rate is how most of the calories we eat are used, it is a significant determinant of our body weight. The lower your resting metabolic rate, the greater your risk of gaining weight and vice versa. We all know someone who appears to eat like a horse but is positively thin! Almost in awe we comment on their fast metabolism, and we may not be far off the mark! Men's bodies, for example, contain more muscle mass and are expensive to run; body fat, on the other hand, is just a storehouse. Maintaining muscle mass by exercising is therefore important for weight control. New research also suggests that our genes dictate the fuel mix we burn from minute to minute. A mix that contains *more energy derived from fat and less from carbohydrate* (even if the total energy burned per minute is the same) may aid weight control.

All this doesn't mean that if your parents were overweight

you should resign yourself to being overweight too. But it may help you understand why you have to watch what you eat while other people seemingly don't have to.

Measuring the Fuel We Need

Remember, calories are a measure of the energy in food and the energy we require to keep us alive. Our bodies need a certain number of calories every day to keep our hearts beating and our brains working, just as a car needs so many gallons of gasoline to run for a day. Food and drink are our source of calories. If we eat and drink too much we may store the additional calories as extra body fat and protein. If we consume fewer calories than we need, our bodies will break down their stores of fat and protein to make up for the shortfall.

So, if you were born with a tendency to be overweight, why does it matter what you eat? The answer is that foods (or more correctly, nutrients) are not equal in their effect on body metabolism. In particular, the foods you eat dictate the fuel mix that you burn for several hours after eating. If you are burning more fat and less carbohydrate, even if the energy content of the food is the same, then chances are you'll be less hungry and less likely to gain body fat over the course of the day. Consequently, your choice of foods is critical for weight control.

Among all four major sources of calories in food (protein, fat, carbohydrate, and alcohol), fat has the highest energy content per gram, twice that of carbohydrate and protein. A high-fat food is therefore said to be "energy dense," meaning there are a lot of calories in a relatively small amount of food. A typical croissant made with wafer-thin layers of buttery pastry contains about 500 calories (which equates to about 20–25 percent of total energy needs for most people for the day!). To eat the same amount of energy in the form of apples, you have to eat about six large apples. So, getting more energy—calories—than your body needs is relatively easy when eating an energy-dense food.

What You Need to Know about Energy Density

A food's "energy density" (calories per gram) is more important to weight control than its fat content.

Assessing a food's energy density has become more important than knowing its fat content. Some diets, such as traditional Mediterranean diets, contain quite a lot of fat (mainly from olive oil), but are still bulky because

survey conducted at the University of Michigan where obese men and women listed their favorite foods, men preferred mainly fatty meats and women listed cakes, cookies, and doughnuts. The unifying trait was a lot of energy per gram of food.

How Can the Glycemic Index Help?

One of the biggest challenges to losing weight can be feeling hungry all the time, but this gnawing feeling is not a necessary part of losing weight. Foods with low GI values are among the most filling of all foods and delay hunger pangs for longer.

In the past, it was believed that protein, fat, and carbohydrate foods, taken in equal quantities, satisfied our appetite equally. We now know from recent research that the satiating capacity—the degree to which foods make us feel full—of these three nutrients is not equal.

Fatty foods, in particular, have only a weak effect on satisfying appetite relative to the number of calories they provide. This has been demonstrated clearly in experimental situations where people are asked to eat until their appetite is satisfied. They overconsume calories if the foods they are offered are high in fat. When high-carbohydrate and low-fat foods are offered, they consume fewer calories when given the opportunity to eat until satisfied. So, *conventional* carbohydrate foods are the best for satisfying our appetite without over-satisfying our caloric requirement.

> *Satiety* is the feeling of fullness and satisfaction
> we experience after eating. Conventional
> carbohydrate foods provide the best satiety.

In studies we conducted, people were given a range of individual foods that contained equal numbers of calories, then their satiety responses were compared. We found that the most filling foods were those that contained fewer calories per gram, i.e., the least energy dense. This included potatoes, oatmeal, apples, oranges, and pasta. Eating more of these foods satisfies appetite without providing excess calories. Foods that provided a lot of calories per gram, like croissants, chocolate, and peanuts, were the least satisfying. These foods are more likely to leave us wanting more and to lead to what scientists call passive overconsumption—overeating without realizing it.

After energy density, the second best predictor of satiety was a food's GI value—the lower the GI value, the more the food satisfied people's hunger. Indeed, there are now more than seventeen studies that confirm low-GI foods are able to suppress hunger for longer than high-GI foods.

There are probably several mechanisms responsible for this.

- Low-GI foods remain longer in the small intestine, triggering receptors that tell the brain there's food still in the gut to be digested.

- High-GI foods may stimulate hunger because the rapid rise and then fall in blood-glucose levels appears to stimulate counter-regulatory responses to reverse the decline.

- Stress hormones like adrenaline and cortisol are released when glucose levels rebound after a high-GI food. Both hormones tend to stimulate appetite.

- Low-GI foods may be more satiating simply because they are often less energy dense than their high-GI counterparts. The naturally high fiber content of many low-GI foods increases their bulk without increasing their energy content.

What's more, even when the calorie intake is the same, people eating low-GI foods may lose more weight than those eating high-GI foods. In a South African study, the investigators divided overweight volunteers into two groups: one group ate a low-calorie, high-GI diet and the other, a low-calorie, low-GI diet. The amount of calories, fat, protein, carbohydrate, and fiber in the diet was the same for both groups. Only the GI values of the diets were different. The low-GI group included foods like lentils, pasta, oatmeal, and corn in their diet and excluded high-GI foods like potatoes and bread. After twelve weeks, the volunteers in the group eating low-GI foods had lost, on average, 20 pounds—4 pounds more than people in the group eating the diet of high-GI foods.

How did the low-GI diet work? The most significant finding was the different effects of the two diets on the level of insulin in the blood. Low-GI foods resulted in lower levels of insulin over the course of the day and night.

Insulin is a hormone that is not only involved in regulating blood glucose levels, but also plays a key part in determining the fuel mix that we burn from minute to minute. High levels of insulin mean the body is *forced* to burn carbohydrate rather than fat. Thus, over the day, even if the total energy burned is the same, the proportions of fat and carbohydrate are not.

Obese individuals appear to have high glycogen (carbohydrate) stores that undergo major fluctuations during the day. This suggests that glycogen is a critical source of fuel for obese people. If glycogen is burning, this makes it hard to burn the fat in food as well as the fat stored in the body. The next meal restores glycogen to its former high level (especially if the food has a high GI value) and the cycle repeats itself.

Are Potatoes Fattening?

In spite of their high GI value, potatoes are highly filling during the first 2 hours after consumption. One explanation for this is their low energy density—to eat 250 calories, you need to eat 7 medium-sized potatoes! It is possible, however, that in the period 3 to 4 hours after consumption, the high insulin response caused by potatoes may cause lower levels of glucose and free fatty acids in the blood. In turn, this may increase the levels of the stress hormones cortisol and noradrenaline, and thereby stimulate appetite—a finding that has been shown in previous studies. So if potatoes are your favorite food, don't cut them out—instead, eat them in moderation, cut your usual portion in half, and substitute sweet potatoes, which have a low GI value. Boiled potatoes are a much better choice for weight control than french fries or potato chips or similar high-calorie foods with a high energy density.

———

> In our experience of looking at the diets of people who want to lose weight, the change required is often to eat more.

There are other reasons why low-GI diets might aid weight loss. When people first begin a diet, their metabolic rate drops in response to the reduction in food intake. One study, however, found that the metabolic rate had dropped less after one week on a low-GI diet than a conventional high-carbohydrate diet. The same study suggested that the low-GI diet helped to preserve lean body mass better, which could explain the higher metabolic rate.

New findings also provide evidence that low-GI diets are able to reduce abdominal fat specifically. In a French study, overweight men were given, in succession, a high and low-GI weight-maintaining diet (in random order), equivalent in energy and macronutrient composition. After five weeks on each diet, their body-fat mass was measured using sophisticated X-ray methods. Those allocated to the low-GI diet had lost 1 pound of fat from the abdomen. There was no difference in subcutaneous fat (i.e., the fat under the skin). That evidence was backed up by a large observational study in Europe of people with type 1 diabetes. It found that those who had naturally self-selected a low-GI diet had not only better blood-glucose control values, but the men in the group had lower waist circumferences, a good index of abdominal fat.

In the table on the next page, foods of high and low energy density but equal calorie value are compared. On the left are small amounts of energy dense foods that provide the same number of calories as the larger amounts of low energy-dense foods on the right.

———

High Energy Dense	Low Energy Dense
2 Chips Ahoy chunky chocolate-chip cookies	2 graham crackers spread with light ricotta cheese and jam
A hot fudge sundae	A frozen fruit bar
An 8-ounce container of full-fat yogurt	An 8-ounce container of light yogurt and 1 banana
A snack pack of raisins	A small bunch (½ cup) of grapes and a medium-sized apple
6 Ritz® crackers and cheddar cheese	2 WASA® crackers topped with ham, tomato, and cucumber
Small, medium, or large fries	1 large baked potato with ½ cup steamed broccoli, grated cheese, a small orange juice, and an apple.

Four Tips for Losing Weight

Tip 1. Focus on what to eat, rather than what not to eat

Typically people approach weight management by looking at which foods they could eat less of. An alternative is to focus on meeting the recommended fruit and vegetable intake first, and then see how much space you have left to fit in the extras.

To eat a healthy diet, ensure you eat at least the minimum of these foods:

1. **Vegetables and legumes—at least 5 servings every day.**

    1 serving means:

    ½ cup cooked vegetables

    1 small potato

    ½ cup cooked dried beans, peas, or lentils

    1 cup salad vegetables

2. **Fruit—at least 2 servings every day.**

    1 serving means:

    1 medium piece (apple, banana, orange)

    2 small pieces (apricots, kiwi fruit, plums)

    ½ cup diced pieces or canned fruit

    ¼ cup dried fruit

    ¾ cup fruit juice

3. **Breads/cereals/rice/pasta and noodles—4 servings or more every day.**

   1 serving means:

   1 ounce ready-to-eat cereal

   ½ cup cooked pasta, noodles, or rice

   ½ cup cooked cereal

   1 slice bread

   ½ bread roll

Tip 2. Eat at Least One Low-GI Food at Each Meal

Reducing the GI value of your diet will reduce insulin levels and increase the potential for fat burning. You can achieve an effective reduction by replacing at least one high-GI carbohydrate choice at each meal with a low-GI type. It's the carbohydrate foods you eat the most of that have the greatest impact—so check your intake using the following table.

What Type of Carbohydrate Did You Eat Yesterday?

1. Recall the carbohydrate-rich foods you ate yesterday. Remember to think of snacks as well as the main meals!

2. Check the boxes below for the types of foods you ate.

HIGH-GI	LOW-GI

Fruit
- ☐ Papaya
- ☐ Pineapple
- ☐ Cantaloupe
- ☐ Watermelon

Fruit
- ☐ Apples
- ☐ Oranges
- ☐ Bananas
- ☐ Grapes
- ☐ Kiwi fruit
- ☐ Peaches, plums, apricots, cherries

Starchy foods
- ☐ Potato, including baked, mashed, steamed, boiled, and chips
- ☐ Rice
- ☐ Rice cakes
- ☐ French fries

Starchy foods
- ☐ Sweet corn
- ☐ Baked beans
- ☐ Sweet potato
- ☐ Chickpeas, kidney beans, lentils
- ☐ Pasta
- ☐ Noodles
- ☐ Basmati or Uncle Ben's® Converted® rice

Bread products
- ☐ White bread
- ☐ Whole-wheat bread
- ☐ Hamburger buns
- ☐ Rolls
- ☐ Scones
- ☐ Bagels
- ☐ French bread

Bread products
- ☐ Whole-grain bread
- ☐ Sourdough bread

HIGH-GI	LOW-GI
Cereals	**Cereals**
☐ Corn Flakes™	☐ Special K™
☐ Rice Krispies™	☐ Old-fashioned oatmeal
☐ Cocoa Puffs™	☐ Muesli
☐ Froot Loops™	☐ All-Bran™
☐ Puffed Wheat	☐ Frosted Flakes™
Cookies	**Cookies**
☐ Sugar wafer with creme filling	Social Tea™ biscuits
☐ Oreo®, reduced fat	Oatmeal
Snacks	**Snacks**
☐ Fruit bars	☐ Dried apricots
☐ Hard candy	☐ Dates
☐ Popcorn	☐ Prunes
☐ Pretzels	☐ Nuts
	☐ Yogurt

3. Now add up the number of checks in each column of foods. The foods in the left column have high GI values. If most of your checks are in this column, you are eating a high-GI diet. Consider altering some of your choices to include more of the foods from the column on the right.

Tip 3. Reduce Your Fat Intake, Especially Saturated Fat

Reducing the amount of fat we eat is an effective way to lower the energy density of our diet. Because fat contains more calories per gram than any other food, it can provide lots of energy for little fill-up value. It is, however, unnecessary and unwise to cut out fat completely. The priority is to reduce sources of saturated fat (butter, cream, cheese, cookies, cakes, fast foods, chips, sausages, most cold cuts, fatty meats), looking at your consumption of foods high in unsaturated, healthier fats (most oils, margarines, nuts, avocados) only if further calorie reduction is necessary.

Remember, too, that while a low-fat diet is important, the calories from other sources are important too. Rice and bread contain little fat, but when your body is burning the carbohydrate in these foods, it doesn't burn as much fat. So even if you do truly follow a low-fat diet, you won't lose weight if your caloric intake is still high.

Is Your Diet Too High in Fat?

Use this fat counter to tally up how much fat your diet contains.

Circle all the foods that you could eat in a day, look at the serving size listed, and multiply the grams of fat up or down to match your serving size. For example, with milk, if you estimate you might consume 2 cups of regular milk in a day, this supplies you with 20 grams of fat.

FOOD	FAT CONTENT (GRAMS)	HOW MUCH DID YOU EAT?
▶ Dairy foods		
Milk, 1 cup		
whole	8	
2%	5	
1%	3	
fat free (skim)	0	
Yogurt, 8-ounce container		
regular	7	
nonfat light or low fat	2–3	
Ice cream, vanilla, ½ cup	0	
regular	7	
reduced fat	2	
Cheese		
American, regular, 1 oz	9	
American, low fat	3	
Cottage cheese, 2%, 2 tablespoons	1	
Ricotta, 2 tablespoons		
whole milk	8	
part skim	3	
light	2	
Cream/sour cream, 1 tablespoon		
regular	2	
reduced fat	1	
fat free	0	

FOOD	FAT CONTENT (GRAMS)	HOW MUCH DID YOU EAT?
◗ **Fats and oils**		
Butter/margarine, 1 teaspoon	4	
Oil, any type, 1 tablespoon	14	
Cooking spray, ⅓-second spray	0	
Mayonnaise, 1 tablespoon		
regular	11	
light	5	
cholesterol free	5	
Salad dressing, 2 tablespoons		
regular	5–10	
reduced fat	2–5	
◗ **Meat**		
Beef, 5 ounces		
top sirloin	12	
ground, lean	18	
top round roast	9	
London broil	9	
Pork		
baked ham, 5 oz	8	
sausage, 2 oz	8	
tenderloin, 5 oz	9	
center cut, 5 oz	12	
bacon, 3 strips	9	
Veal		
cutlets, 5 oz	9	

FOOD	FAT CONTENT (GRAMS)	HOW MUCH DID YOU EAT?
Lamb		
leg, roast, 5 oz	12	
Chicken		
breast, skinless, 5 oz	6	
drumstick, with skin, 2 oz	6	
thigh, with skin, 2½ oz	10	
nuggets, breaded & fried,		
6 pieces	20	
➧ **Fish**		
Grilled fillet, 3 oz	1	
Salmon, 3 oz	11	
Fish sticks, breaded & fried,		
3 oz	10	
➧ **Snack foods**		
Chocolate bar, 1 oz	5	
Potato chips, 1 oz	10	
Tortilla chips, 1 oz	10	
Peanuts, 1 oz	14	
French fries, 10 pieces	4	
Pizza, cheese, 1 slice, 4 oz	11	
Pretzels, 1 oz	1	

Total **➡ How did you rate?**	
Less than 40 grams	Excellent. Thirty to 40 grams of fat per day is an average range recommended for those trying to lose weight.
41–60 grams	Good. A fat intake in this range is recommended for most adult men and women.
61–80 grams	Acceptable if you are very active, i.e., doing hard physical work or athletic training. It is too much if you are trying to lose weight.
More than 80 grams	You're possibly eating too much fat, unless of course you are Superman or Superwoman!

Tip 4. Eat Regularly

Regular consumption of low-GI foods increases satiety at meals and decreases subsequent energy intake to help prevent excess weight gain. Snacking can help prevent overeating at mealtimes and helps control appetite. Of course, the choice of foods is important.

Planning Low-GI Meals

Here are some basic tips for low-GI meals. Part 2 has more comprehensive information about changing to a low-GI diet, as well as some fabulous low-GI recipes.

Breakfast

- Start with a bowl of low-GI cereal served with skim or low-fat milk or yogurt.

- Try All-Bran® or rolled oats (raw or cooked).

- If you prefer granola, keep to a small bowl of low-fat granola—check that it doesn't contain added fats.

- Add a slice of toast made from a low-GI bread (or 2 slices for a bigger person) with a tablespoon of jam, sliced banana, honey, or light cream cheese with sliced apple. Keep butter or margarine to a minimum, or use none at all.

- If you like a hot breakfast, try a boiled or poached egg, or a Western egg-white omelet with your toast.

Lunch

- Try a sandwich or roll, with only a small amount of margarine. Choose a bread with lots of whole grains in it (not just sprinkled on top) if you can, for a low GI value. Add plenty of salad fillings.

■ For the filling, choose from a thin slice of ham, lean roast beef or grilled chicken or turkey, or a slice of low-fat cheese, salmon or tuna (water packed), or an egg. An extra container of salad or vegetable soup will help to fill you up.

■ Finish your lunch with a piece of fruit, or fruit salad with a low-fat yogurt, or a low-fat flavored or plain milk.

Dinner

■ The basis of dinner should be high-carbohydrate grains and root vegetables.

■ Eat many vegetables with meat, chicken, or fish as a side dish rather than the main ingredient.

■ Use lean meat like London broil, veal, fresh pork, lean lamb, chicken breast, fish fillets, turkey. Red meat is a valuable source of iron—just choose lean types. A piece of meat, chicken, or fish that fits in the palm of your hand (no fingers) meets the daily protein requirements of an adult.

■ If you prefer not to eat meat, a cup of cooked dried peas, beans, lentils, or chickpeas can provide protein and iron without any fat. At the same time they supply low-GI carbohydrate and fiber.

■ High-protein legumes like soy beans and peanuts are good meat alternatives.

■ Boost your fruit intake and get into the habit of finishing your meal with fruit—fresh, stewed, or baked.

Snacks

■ It is important to include a couple of dairy food servings each day for your calcium needs. If you haven't used yogurt or cheese in any meals, you may choose to make a low-fat milkshake or fruit smoothie. One or two scoops of low-fat ice cream or pudding can also contribute to daily calcium intake.

■ If you like grainy breads, a slice of toast makes a very good choice for a snack. Other snacks can include toasted English muffin halves, or half a bagel.

■ Fruit is always a low-calorie option for snacks. You should aim to consume at least two servings a day. It may be helpful to prepare fruit in advance to make it accessible and easy to eat.

■ Low-fat crackers (like reduced-fat Triscuits®) are a low-calorie snack if you want something dry and crunchy, although they may not be as sustaining as a grainy bread.

■ Keep vegetables (such as celery and carrot sticks, cherry or grape tomatoes, radishes and florets of blanched cauliflower or broccoli) ready-prepared to snack on too.

10

The Glycemic Index and Diabetes

Diabetes is on its way to becoming one of the most common health problems in the world. Currently, in many developing and newly industrialized nations there is an epidemic of diabetes, and the World Health Organization predicts that the rates of diabetes will double in the next fifteen to twenty years. Already in some developing countries half of the adult population has diabetes. Even in developed countries, the rate of diabetes is increasing at an alarming pace. More than 18 million Americans have diabetes—5 million of them are unaware that they have the disease. Sixteen million Americans are estimated to have pre-diabetes, and at current rates of growth, more than 10 percent of all Americans will have diabetes by 2010.

The glycemic index has far-reaching implications for

diabetes. Not only is it important in treating people with diabetes, but it may also help prevent people from developing diabetes in the first place and possibly even prevent some of the complications of diabetes.

What is Diabetes?

Diabetes is a chronic condition in which there is too much glucose in the blood. Keeping the glucose level normal in the blood requires the right amount of a hormone called insulin. Insulin gets the glucose out of the blood and into the body's muscles, where it is used to provide energy for the body. If there is not enough insulin, or if the insulin does not do its job properly, diabetes develops.

Children and young adults usually develop diabetes because they cannot make enough insulin. This is called *type 1 diabetes*. In this type of diabetes the pancreas does not produce enough insulin, and insulin injections are needed to replace the insulin deficit. Five to 10 percent of people with diabetes have type 1 diabetes.

Typically, *type 2 diabetes*, or non-insulin-dependent diabetes mellitus, develops after the age of forty. With our society's increasing trend to physical inactivity and obesity, however, this type of diabetes is being found in younger and younger people, and, in some ethnic groups, even in children less than ten years of age.

People get type 2 diabetes because their insulin does not work properly (the process whereby this happens is called insulin resistance). At first the body will struggle to make extra insulin, but later people with type 2 diabetes develop a shortage of insulin. The aim of treatment is to help people with type 2 diabetes make the best use of the insulin they have and to try to make it last as long as possible. Overeating, being overweight, and not exercising enough are important lifestyle factors that can lead to this type of diabetes, especially when there is someone else in the family with diabetes. Oral medications or insulin injections may be necessary to treat this type of diabetes. Ninety to 95 percent of people with diabetes have type 2 diabetes.

Are You at Risk?

You are at particular risk for type 2 diabetes if any of the following apply to you:

- over the age of 55
- with a family history of diabetes
- overweight
- have high blood pressure
- had diabetes during pregnancy (gestational diabetes)
- of one of the following ethnic backgrounds: African American, Latino, Native American, Pacific Islander, Asian American

If you fit into one of these categories, you can reduce your chances of getting diabetes by controlling your weight, exercising more, and eating more foods with low GI values. A reduction of the GI value of your diet reduces the demand on your pancreas to produce more insulin, perhaps prolonging its function and delaying the development of diabetes. Research from Harvard University has shown that eating low-GI foods that are high in fiber is associated with the lowest risk of developing type 2 diabetes (see pages 340 to 343 in this chapter for more information).

Why Do We Get Diabetes?

To find the answer we need to look back in time. Our ancestors lived and evolved in a very cold climate. Over the last 2 million years there have been many ice ages—the last ended only 10,000 years ago. During these ice ages there was very little edible plant food around and people had to hunt animals for survival. This gave them a lot of protein in their diet. In other words, during the ice ages our ancestors were carnivores (meat eaters). Their bodies adapted to this way of life to help them survive on this diet—and also to help them survive times when food was scarce.

As it turned out, this protein-based diet would also have favored those people with genes for insulin resistance. This is because the main way the body copes when there is not much carbohydrate (glucose) in the diet is to make sure that the important parts, such as the brain, get what little glucose is available. To do this the body redirects glucose away from muscles to the brain. The mechanism of doing this involves making the muscles insulin resistant. Thus the natural-selection process benefited those who were genetically insulin resistant.

Since the end of the last ice age there have been many changes to the type and amount of food that we eat. First, our ancestors began to grow food crops. Agriculture changed their eating pattern from one based on animal protein to one based on carbohydrate in the form of whole cereal grains, vegetables, and beans. A dietary change like this would also have changed the glucose levels in their blood. While they ate a high-protein diet, the glucose levels in their blood would not have risen significantly after a meal. When they started eating carbohydrate regularly, the blood-glucose level would have increased after meals. The amount by which the glucose levels in the blood increased after a meal would have depended on the GI value of the carbohydrate. Crops such as spelt wheat grain, which our ancestors grew, had a low GI value. These foods would have had minimal effects on glucose levels in the blood and the demand for insulin would have been similarly low.

The second major change came with industrialization and the advent of high-speed steel roller mills. Instead of whole-grain products, the new milling procedures produced highly refined carbohydrate, which we now know increases the GI value of a food, and transforms a low-GI food into one with a high GI value. When this highly refined food is eaten it causes a greater increase in blood-glucose levels. To keep the blood-glucose levels normal, the body has to make large amounts of insulin. The vast majority of the commercially packaged foods and drinks with which we now fill our shopping carts have a high GI value. All this strains the body's insulin-making capabilities.

Third, the dramatic increase over the past fifty years in the quantity of high-fat takeout and fast foods that we regularly eat has made matters even worse. To our already high-GI foods, we have added a lot of fat as well. As we explained in chapter 9, eating a lot of fat will increase body weight, which in turn makes it harder for the insulin to clear the glucose from the blood. In other words, the body becomes even more resistant to the effect of insulin. Continually eating carbohydrate foods with a high GI value places enormous pressure on the body's ability to keep producing large amounts of insulin to control the blood-glucose levels. Add to this worsening insulin resistance, and you have the perfect recipe for eventually exhausting the body's insulin supply and developing diabetes.

It takes eons of time for our bodies to adapt to such major changes in diet. Because our European ancestors had thousands of years to adapt to a diet with a lot of carbohydrate, they were in a better position to cope with the changes in the GI values of foods. That is why people of European descent have a lower prevalence of type 2 diabetes than people whose diets have recently changed to include lots of high-GI foods. There is, however, only so much that our bodies can take. As we continue to consume increasing quantities of foods with high GI values, plus excessive amounts of fatty foods, our bodies are coping less well. The result can be seen in the significant increase of people developing diabetes.

Studies from Harvard University, in which thousands of men and women were studied over many years, have shown that people who ate large amounts of refined, high-GI foods were two to three times more likely to develop type 2 diabetes or heart disease. The most dramatic increases in diabetes, however, have occurred in populations that have been exposed to these lifestyle changes over a much shorter period of time. In some groups of Native Americans and populations within the Pacific region, up to one adult in two has diabetes because of the rapid dietary and lifestyle changes they have undergone in the twentieth century.

Treating Diabetes

Watching what you eat is essential if you have diabetes. For some people with type 2 diabetes, this is all they have to do to keep their blood- glucose levels in the normal range (of

70–140 milligrams per deciliter [mg/dl]). Others also need to take diabetes medication or injections of insulin. People with type 1 diabetes must have insulin injections. But no matter what the treatment, everyone with diabetes must carefully consider what they eat in order to keep their blood-glucose levels under control. Keeping the blood glucose near the normal range helps prevent such complications of diabetes as heart attacks, strokes, blindness, kidney failure, and amputations.

For more than a hundred years, people with diabetes have been given advice on what to eat. Many diets were based more on unproven (although seemingly logical) theories than actual research. In 1915, for example, the *Boston Medical and Surgical Journal* wrote that the best dietary treatment for someone with diabetes was "limitation of all components of the diet." This translated into a very low-calorie diet interspersed with days of fasting. Unfortunately, malnutrition was often the result.

In the 1920s doctors began recommending high-fat diets for their diabetic patients. Ignorant of the dangers of a high-fat diet, they knew that fat, at least, didn't break down to become blood glucose. We now know that high-fat diets only hastened the development of heart disease, the most frequent cause of death among people with diabetes.

It was not until the 1970s that carbohydrate was considered to be a valuable part of the diabetic diet. Researchers found that not only did the nutritional status of patients improve with a higher carbohydrate intake, but their insulin sensitivity improved as well.

The only part of food that directly affects blood-glucose levels is carbohydrate. When we eat carbohydrate foods, they are broken down into glucose and cause the blood-glucose levels to rise. The body responds by releasing insulin into the blood. The insulin clears the glucose from the blood, moving it into the muscles where it is used for energy, so the blood-glucose level returns to normal.

Some people think that because carbohydrate raises the blood-glucose level, it should not be eaten at all by people who have diabetes. This is not correct. Carbohydrate is a normal part of the diet and helps maintain insulin sensitivity and physical endurance. Mental performance is also superior when meals contain carbohydrate rather than just protein and fat.

The secret to the diabetic diet is not only the *quantity* but also the *type* of carbohydrate.

Traditionally sugar was excluded from diabetic diets because it was thought to be the worst type of carbohydrate. The simple structure of sugar supposedly made it more rapidly digested and absorbed than other types of carbohydrate, such as starch. This assumption was not correct. Even in the late 1970s, test meal studies showed that there was a great deal of overlap between the blood-glucose responses to sugary and starchy foods. Fifty grams of carbohydrate eaten as potato caused a rise in blood glucose similar to that of 50 grams of sugar. Ice cream resulted in a lower blood-glucose response than potato! Findings like these sparked research into the glycemic index in an effort to learn more about how the body actually responds to different carbohydrate foods.

▶ Case Study

I'm 54 and the CEO of a very large public-sector organization with all that that entails, including missed meals, incorrect eating (often a single meal at night), long work hours, stress, etc.

After not feeling well for some time, I consulted my family doctor, who ordered blood tests. They showed a relatively mild onset of type 2 diabetes and a couple of other disorders that, in the scheme of things, were not what you would consider serious but all of which could be attributed to my crazy lifestyle.

My doctor referred me to a dietitian who, thankfully with my knowledge now, was well versed in the glycemic index.

Well, to cut the inevitable story short, three months later I have lost almost 26 pounds, am within 5 pounds of my goal weight, and feel significantly improved healthwise, in all respects including self-esteem. My wonderful wife has also lost about 15 pounds, and she too doesn't need to lose much more.

Although I have yet to go back for blood tests, neither I nor Penny, my dietitian, have any doubt that there will be a major improvement in the results, since I feel so much better.

At my first appointment with Penny, I indicated to her that I was not there just to lose some weight and reduce my type

2 symptoms. That was certainly the primary objective, but my main goal was to change for the long term my eating and lifestyle habits.

Thanks primarily to your book I now believe I have achieved that. Both the philosophy and the practice of the glycemic index are relatively simple and easy to understand and very much common sense. I have read and continue to refer to your books and I'm a fairly regular drop-in to your website.

So that's my story thus far. Keep up the great work.

Regards,
Paul

———

The emphasis through the 1970s, and for much of the 1980s, was on the quantity of carbohydrate in the diet. "Exchanges" were used to prescribe a set amount of carbohydrate to be eaten at every meal. (A carbohydrate exchange is an amount of carbohydrate-rich food that contains 15 grams of carbohydrate.)

An underlying assumption of the carbohydrate-portions theory was that equivalent amounts of carbohydrate, regardless of the type, cause an equal change in the blood-glucose level. This reasoning had no scientific backing and has since clearly been shown to be incorrect. Fortunately, high-quality scientific research supports today's dietary recommendations for people with diabetes. While the GI research has not negated the significance of the quantity of carbohydrate in the diet, it has shown us the importance of considering the *type* of carbohydrate food as well.

The glycemic index has shown us that the way to increase the quantity of carbohydrate in the diabetic diet, without increasing the glucose levels in the blood, is to choose carbohydrate foods with low GI values.

▶ Case Study

At 50 years of age, Helen had tried to lose weight many times. Her neighbors had started walking on a regular basis, but she felt tired all the time and had no energy to do anything more than what she absolutely had to. Being 209 pounds and only 5 feet 5 inches tall ruined her morale. Her mother had diabetes and she knew being overweight put her at greater risk, but every time she lost weight she ended up regaining it. Finally, it was no surprise to her when she was diagnosed with diabetes. In fact, it was some relief—here at last was a reason for her tiredness.

At her doctor's suggestion, Helen saw a dietitian for help with her diet. At first glance, what Helen was eating appeared reasonable. Breakfast was a slice of whole-wheat toast or a whole-wheat cracker with margarine and black tea. Lunch was a light meal such as celery, lettuce, a slice of cheese, a slice of ham, an egg, and a couple of crackers spread with margarine. For dinner she was having soup and a piece of steak with vegetables. She limited herself to a small potato. The meal was finished by a piece of fruit.

A closer look at her food record showed that Helen's diet was in fact poorly balanced. It was dominated by protein and saturated fat and contained insufficient carbohydrate. It didn't contain enough food to provide a good range of nutrients. What's more, Helen herself was struggling with it and often felt hungry since she had cut candy and cookies out of her diet.

To improve things, we first looked at the frequency of eating. Helen kept to three meals a day because she had been brought up to believe that was better for her. She agreed to try a small snack of fruit or a slice of bread between meals. Even though she wasn't on medication for diabetes, the effect of spreading her food intake more evenly across the day, between small meals and snacks, could help to stabilize her blood-glucose level and help her lose weight.

We then revised the amount of carbohydrate she ate, and listed a range of low-GI carbohydrate foods that were to be her first priority at each meal. The satiating value of the carbohydrate left her with less space for the proteins that used to dominate her diet.

Breakfast began with a freshly squeezed orange juice and a bowl of oatmeal with raisins and low-fat milk. Helen added a slice of 100% whole-grain toast if she was still hungry.

Lunch was usually a sandwich on whole-grain bread with a slice of lean meat and salad and a piece of fruit or a muffin to finish. Sometimes she had a vegetable soup, or pasta with a vegetable sauce and salad.

The proportion of foods on her **dinner** plate was rearranged, shrinking in the meat department and filling out on the vegetable side. She began to think of carbohydrate food as the basis of the meal and varied between pasta, rice and potato. Twice a week she made a vegetarian dish with legumes, such as a minestrone soup or a vegetable lasagne. An evening snack was usually yogurt or fruit.

After a month on her new eating plan Helen felt better—in fact she felt well enough to tackle some exercise. Taking a serious look at her day, she decided to commit the half-hour after dinner to a walk, five nights a week.

Over the next six months Helen's weight dropped from 209 pounds to 176 pounds. Her blood-glucose levels were mainly within the normal range. She no longer struggled with hunger and felt good about the food she was eating.

Lowering the GI values of your diet as Helen did is not as hard as it seems, because nearly every carbohydrate food that we typically consume has an equivalent food with a low GI value. Our research has shown that blood-glucose levels in people with diabetes are greatly improved if foods with a low GI value are substituted for high-GI foods.

We studied a group of people with type 2 diabetes and taught them how to alter their diet by replacing the high-GI foods they were normally eating for carbohydrate foods with a low GI value. After three months, there was a significant drop in their average blood-glucose levels. They did not find the diet at all difficult and in fact commented on how easy it had been to make the change and how much more variety had been introduced to their diet.

Substituting Low-GI Foods for High-GI Foods

High-GI Food	Low-GI Alternative
Bread, whole wheat or white	Whole-grain breads such as 100% stone-ground and sourdough breads
Processed breakfast cereal	Unrefined cereal such as old-fashioned oatmeal, or check the GI tables in Part 4 for processed cereals with a low GI value, e.g., All Bran™ or Special K™
Cakes, cookies, crackers, doughnuts, pastries	Fruit, fresh, canned, and dried; milk; yogurt
Potato, rice	Sweet potato, pasta, legumes, noodles, Basmati and Uncle Ben's converted rice

Similar results have been reported by other researchers in both type 1 and type 2 diabetes. For example, large studies in Australia, Europe, and Canada of people with type 1 diabetes have shown that the lower the GI values of the diet, the better the diabetes control. In fact the improvement in diabetes control seen after changing to a low-GI diet is often better than that achieved with some of the newer and expensive diabetes medications and insulins.

Making this type of change in your everyday diet does not mean that your diet has to be restrictive or unpalatable. There are lots of recipes in Part 2 of this book that can help you reduce the overall GI value of your diet. The following case study is an example of the results you could achieve.

▶ Case Study

Bill, a 62-year-old man, was taking every care with his diabetes. He had changed his diet by reducing his total food intake, had lost weight, and was exercising regularly. He was doing finger-prick blood-glucose level tests at home. Despite his best efforts, he could not achieve a blood-glucose level in the desired range of less than 140 mg/dl after breakfast. At first glance he was eating what most dietitians would consider to be a good breakfast for someone with diabetes: about a cup of cornflakes with 8 ounces of milk, plus two slices of whole-wheat toast with a bit of margarine. His blood glucose after breakfast, however, was consistently around 200 mg/dl. He was advised to make one simple change—to lower the GI value of the carbohydrate by changing the cornflakes to a bowl of rolled oats. This had an immediate impact, and his glucose levels after breakfast fell to 125 mg/dl.

If you are having trouble controlling your blood-glucose level after a meal, look up the GI value for the carbohydrates it contains in Part 4. See if you can find substitutes with a lower GI value from the list. Eating a meal with a lower GI value can lower the blood-glucose rise after the meal.

Although we haven't mentioned them yet, don't think that fatty foods are not important. They are, especially in people who are overweight. But fatty foods do not increase the glucose levels. Only carbohydrate foods do. Being overweight and eating fatty foods, however, prevents the body's insulin from doing its job and indirectly causes the blood-glucose levels to rise. So, eating chips or fries (mixtures of high-GI carbohydrate and fat) causes double trouble. Not only does the high GI value of potato increase the blood-glucose levels, but the extra fat will also eventually stop the body's insulin from working properly and make it less effective in clearing the glucose from the blood. Persistently high blood-glucose levels may be evident the day after a very high-fat evening meal.

The Glycemic Index and Snacks

The glycemic index is especially important when carbohydrate is eaten by itself and not as part of a mixed meal. Carbohydrate tends to have a stronger effect on our blood-glucose level when it is eaten alone. This is the case with between-meal snacks, which most people with diabetes should eat. When choosing a between-meal snack, pick one with a low GI value. For example, an apple with a GI value of 36 is better than a slice of white toast with a GI value of around 70, and will result in less of a jump in the blood-glucose level.

Some snack foods with a very low GI value (such as peanuts with a GI value of 14) have a very high fat content and are not recommended for people with a weight problem. As an occasional snack they're fine (especially as their fat is monounsaturated), but not every day, since it is hard to stop at just one small handful.

Try the following low-fat and low-GI snack foods instead:

- fruit smoothie
- a low-fat milkshake
- an apple
- low-fat fruit yogurt
- 5 to 6 dried apricot halves
- a small banana
- 1 to 2 oatmeal cookies
- an orange
- a scoop of low-fat ice cream in a cone
- a glass of low-fat milk

Many people with diabetes have to resort to oral medication to control blood-glucose levels. An increased intake of low-GI carbohydrate foods can sometimes make these drugs unnecessary. Sometimes, however, despite your best efforts with diet, medication will still be needed to obtain good blood-glucose control. This is eventually the case for most people with type 2 diabetes as they grow older and their insulin-secreting capacity declines further.

Using the Glycemic Index When You Exercise

It is sometimes necessary with diabetes to eat extra carbohydrate when you exercise depending on the type of diabetes you have and the type and amount of medication you take. Often, you won't want to increase your food intake—because the exercise is intended to burn off some earlier overconsumption! (For people with type 1 diabetes, remember this will only work if you have enough insulin in your body and your blood sugars aren't too high to start with.)

You may need extra carbohydrate before you exercise, or, if the exercise is prolonged over an hour or more, you may need extra carbohydrate while you exercise, too. Whether or not you need to eat extra, and how much to take, depends on your blood sugar level before, during, and after the exercise, and how your body responds to the exercise—all of which you learn from experience. Discuss your situation and how best to manage it with a dietitian, diabetes educator, or doctor.

If you need to eat immediately before exercise to bring your blood sugar up during exercise, it makes sense to eat some high-GI carbohydrate, such as a slice of regular bread, a couple of cookies, or a ripe banana.

If you plan to eat your last meal or snack one to two hours before your exercise, it makes sense to eat a low-GI meal to sustain you through the exercise, such as a sandwich made with low-GI bread, lowfat protein such as turkey breast or boiled ham, a container of yogurt, or an apple.

If you need to eat something quickly after or during exercise to restore your blood sugar level, use high-GI food—crispbread or rice cakes, a bowl of corn flakes or Rice Krispies, or a slice of watermelon, for example.

NOTE: Always remember to measure your blood sugar when you exercise to assess your body's response and judge your carbohydrate needs.

Hypos—the Exception to the Low-GI Rule

In people with diabetes who are treated with insulin or oral medication the blood glucose may sometimes fall below 70 mg/dl, which is the lower end of the normal range. When this happens you might feel hungry, shaky, and sweaty, and be unable to think clearly. This is called hypoglycemia.

Hypoglycemia, or low blood sugar, is a potentially dangerous situation and must be treated immediately by eating some carbohydrate food. In this case, you should pick a carbohydrate with a high GI value because you need to increase your blood glucose quickly. Jelly beans (GI value of 80) are a good choice. If you are not due for your next meal or snack, you should also have some low-GI carbohydrate, like an apple, to keep your blood glucose from falling again until you next eat.

▶ Case Study

Low blood sugars in the night were a particularly worrisome problem for Jane. Her evening insulin doses had been adjusted in an effort to stop her blood glucose from going too low at night, but she believed experimenting with her supper carbohydrate could also help.

After trying all sorts of different foods and many 3 a.m. blood tests, she struck the answer that the glycemic index predicted would work—milk! Jane found that a large glass of milk before going to bed, rather than her usual plain crackers, was easy to have and maintained her blood glucose at a good level through the night.

Diabetes Complications

If blood-glucose levels are not properly controlled, diabetes can cause damage to the blood vessels in the heart, legs, brain, eyes, and kidneys. For this reason, heart attacks, leg amputations, strokes, blindness, and kidney failure are more common in people with diabetes. It can also damage the nerves in the feet, causing pain and irritation in the feet and numbness and loss of sensation.

In addition to high glucose levels, many researchers believe that high levels of insulin also contribute to the damage of the blood vessels of the heart, legs, and brain. High insulin levels are thought to be one of the factors that might stimulate the muscle in the wall of the blood vessel to thicken. Thickening of the muscle wall causes the blood vessels to narrow and can slow the flow of blood to the point that a clot can form and stop the blood flow altogether. This is what happens to cause a heart attack or stroke.

We know that foods with a high GI value cause the body to produce larger amounts of insulin, resulting in higher levels of insulin in the blood. Therefore, for people with type 2 diabetes, it makes sense that eating foods with low GI values will have the effect of helping to control blood-glucose levels, and will do this with lower levels of insulin. This may have the added benefit of reducing the large vessel damage which accounts for so many of the problems of diabetes.

A Word of Advice

There are many factors that can affect your blood-glucose levels. If you have diabetes and you are struggling to control your blood-glucose level, it is important to seek medical help. How much exercise you do, your weight, stress levels, total dietary intake, and need for medication may have to be assessed.

The Optimum Diet for People with Diabetes

Plenty of whole-grain cereals, breads, vegetables, and fruits

A low-fat, low-GI diet emphasizes lots of whole-grain breads; cereals like oats, barley, couscous, cracked wheat; legumes like kidney beans and lentils; and all types of fruits and vegetables.

Only small amounts of fat, especially saturated fat

Limit cookies, cakes, butter, potato chips, take-out fried foods, full-fat dairy products, fatty meats, and sausages, which are all high in saturated fat. Poly- and monounsaturated oils like olive, canola, and peanut are healthier types of fats.

A moderate amount of sugar and sugar-containing foods

It's okay to include your favorite sweetener or sweet food—small quantities of sugar, honey, maple syrup, jam—to make meals more palatable and pleasurable.

Only a moderate quantity of alcohol

Only two drinks for men and one drink for women per day, with at least two alcohol-free days a week.

Only a moderate amount of salt and salted foods

Try lemon juice, freshly ground black pepper, garlic, chili, herbs, and other flavors rather than relying on salt.

Diabetes and the Glycemic Index: Frequently Asked Questions

Q. Why is the glycemic index so important in diabetes management?

A. As mentioned, if blood sugar levels are not properly controlled, diabetes can cause damage to the blood vessels in the eyes, kidneys, and nerves. For this reason, heart attacks, strokes, kidney failure, and blindness are more common in people with diabetes. High blood sugar levels can also damage the nerves in the feet, which can cause pain, irritation, and loss of sensation in the feet.

High insulin levels can also damage the blood vessels of the heart, legs, and brain. In fact, some researchers think that high insulin levels might cause the muscle in the walls of blood vessels to thicken. This thickening would cause the blood vessels to narrow and slow the flow of blood. A clot could form and stop the blood flow altogether, causing a heart attack or stroke.

Q. How does the glycemic index help control insulin and blood sugar levels?

A. In general, studies show an excellent correlation between the glycemic index of a food and its insulin response. With low-GI foods, there's a reduced secretion of the hormone insulin over the course of the day. With high-GI foods, the body produces larger amounts of insulin, resulting in higher levels of insulin in the blood.

It makes sense for people with type 2 diabetes to eat foods with low GI values to help control blood sugar levels, and do so with lower levels of insulin. (A low-GI diet improves the body's sensitivity to insulin, so the insulin you do have works better.) This may have the added benefit of reducing the large vessel damage that accounts for many of the problems that diabetes can cause.

We also know that a low-GI diet in conjunction with a low fat intake can help keep your blood vessels healthy by keeping your levels of blood fats down. Studies have shown that people have lower levels of blood fats (such as cholesterol and triglycerides) when they eat lower-GI foods.

Q. Does sugar cause diabetes?

A. No. There is absolute consensus that sugar in food does not cause diabetes. Type 1 diabetes (insulin-dependent diabetes) is an autoimmune condition triggered by unknown environmental factors such as viruses. Type 2 diabetes (non-insulin-dependent diabetes) is strongly inherited, but lifestyle factors, such as lack of exercise and being overweight, increase the risk of developing it. Because the dietary treatment of diabetes in the past involved strict avoidance of sugar, many people wrongly believed that sugar was in some way implicated as a cause of the disease. While sugar is off the hook, high-GI foods are not. Studies from Harvard University indicate that high-GI diets increase the risk of developing both diabetes and heart disease.

Q. Why are people with diabetes now allowed some sugar in their diet?

A. For a long time, strict avoidance of sugar was the mainstay of diabetes diets. Health-care professionals were taught that simple sugars were solely responsible for high blood-glucose levels. But research has proven that people with diabetes can eat the same amount of sugar as the average person without compromising diabetes control. It is important, however, to remember that "empty calories"—whatever the source: sugar, starch, fat, or alcohol—won't keep the engine running smoothly. "Moderation in all things" is a good motto. The upper limit should be no more than 10 percent of your total daily calories. This translates into about 3 tablespoons of sugar a day for women and about 4½ tablespoons for men. Keep in mind that this refers not only to the sugar *you* add to coffee or cereal but also to the sugar already added *into* the foods you eat.

Try to spread your sugar budget over a variety of nutrient-rich foods that sugar makes more palatable. Remember, sugar is concealed in many foods—a can of soft drink contains about 40 grams of sugar.

Most foods containing sugar do not raise blood sugar levels any more than most starchy foods. Golden Grahams (GI value of 71) contain 39 percent sugar while Rice Chex (GI value of 89) contain very little sugar. Many foods with large amounts of sugar have GI values close to 60—lower than white bread.

Sugar can be a source of enjoyment and help you limit your intake of high-fat foods, but the blood sugar response to a food is hard to predict. Use the tables in this book and your own blood sugar monitoring as a guide.

Q. Can GI values obtained from tests on healthy people be applied to people with diabetes?

A. Yes, several studies show a good correlation between values obtained in healthy people and people with diabetes (type 1 and type 2). By its very nature, GI testing takes into account differences in glucose tolerance between people. Although people with diabetes have defects in glucose metabolism, there is usually nothing wrong with their gastrointestinal digestion. High-GI foods are still digested quickly and low-GI foods are still digested slowly. Some people with diabetes have gastroparesis, a disorder in which the emptying of the stomach slows down. The ranking of foods according to their GI values is still applicable.

Q. If a food has a high glycemic index, should someone with diabetes avoid it?

A. Some foods like bread and potatoes have high GI values (70–80). But, potatoes and bread can play a major role in a high-carbohydrate and low-fat diet. You only have to exchange about half the carbohydrate (from high to low GI values) to achieve lower blood sugar levels. So, there's plenty of room for bread and potatoes. Some breads have lower GI values than others. Choose these if your goal is to lower the GI numbers as much as possible. You can't predict the GI value of a food from its composition. To test the GI number, you need real people and real foods. Standardized methods are always followed so that results from one group of people can be directly compared with those from another.

Q. Some vegetables, such as pumpkin, appear to have a high GI value. Does this mean that a person with diabetes shouldn't eat them?

A. Most definitely not, because, unlike potatoes and cereal products, these vegetables are very low in carbohydrate. So, despite their high GI value, their glycemic load (GI × carbohydrate per serving divided by 100) is low. Carrots, broccoli, tomatoes, onions, salad vegetables, etc., which contain only a small amount of carbohydrate but loads of micronutrients, should be seen as "free" foods for everyone. Eat them to your heart's content.

Q. Some breads and potatoes have high GI values (70–80). Does this mean a person with diabetes should avoid all breads and potatoes?

A. Potatoes and bread can play a major role in a high carbohydrate and low fat diet, even if a secondary goal is to reduce the overall GI value. Only about half the carbohydrate has to be exchanged from high glycemic index to low glycemic index to achieve measurable improvements in diabetes control. So, there is still room for bread and potatoes. Of course, some types of bread and potatoes have lower GI values than others and these should be preferred if the goal is to lower the glycemic index as much as possible.

In the overall management of diabetes, the most important message is that the diet should be low in fat and high in carbohydrate. This will help people not only to lose weight, but to keep it off and improve their overall blood glucose and lipid control.

Q. Why should people with diabetes watch out for fatty foods?

A. With diabetes, being overweight and eating fatty foods prevents insulin from doing its job. When insulin can't work properly (or there isn't enough of it) blood sugar levels rise. Most type 2 diabetes is associated with an excess of abdominal fat (a "pot belly").

Breaded or battered foods, French fries, fried rice, pastries, or other such fatty foods are often the cause of elevated blood sugar. The high glycemic index of potato, rice, or flour tends to increase blood sugar levels, and the extra fat interferes with the action of insulin and makes it less effective in clearing sugar from the blood.

Some foods high in fat have a low glycemic index and may seem all right to eat because of this. The glycemic index is low because fat tends to slow the rate of stomach emptying (and therefore the rate at which foods are digested in the small intestine). Some high fat foods, therefore, tend to have lower GI values than their low fat equivalents (potato chips, 54 compared with a dry baked potato, 85). This doesn't make them better foods.

Q. Could a high-protein diet be harmful to a person with diabetes?

A. Yes. People with diabetes should avoid high-protein diets because eating large amounts of protein can tax the kidneys and bring on renal failure more quickly. (Renal failure is one possible complication of diabetes.) It's much healthier for people with diabetes to control their blood sugar by eating a low-GI diet.

Q. Would a person with diabetes need to reduce their insulin dose if they changed to low-GI foods?

A. Most studies have not shown a need for a significantly reduced insulin dose when consuming a low-GI diet. This is probably because the insulin dose is dictated not just by carbohydrates in the diet but by protein and fat as well. A few studies in subjects using insulin pumps have suggested that they could reduce their insulin dosage and maintain the same blood-glucose levels. Further studies are needed to say this confidently.

11

The Glycemic Index and Hypoglycemia

Hypoglycemia has become a popular diagnosis for all sorts of problems that cannot be attributed to a more specific diagnosis. There has been considerable publicity about hypoglycemia, which is often blamed for many nonspecific health problems, ranging from tiredness to depression. Unfortunately, hypoglycemia is often wrongly blamed, which can delay a proper diagnosis and correct treatment.

Nevertheless, genuine hypoglycemia does occur in a few people, and the glycemic index has a role to play in treating some forms of this condition. The most common form of hypoglycemia occurs after a meal is eaten. This is called *reactive hypoglycemia*.

Normally, when a meal containing carbohydrate is eaten, the blood-glucose level rises. This causes the pancreas to make insulin, which pushes the glucose out of the blood and into the muscles where it provides energy for you to carry out your regular tasks and activities. The movement of glucose out of the blood and into the muscles is finely controlled by just the right amount of insulin to drop the glucose back to normal. In some people, the blood-glucose level rises too quickly after eating and causes an excessive amount of insulin to be released. This draws too much glucose out of the blood and causes the blood-glucose level to fall below normal. The result is hypoglycemia.

Hypoglycemia causes a variety of unpleasant symptoms. Many of these are stress-like symptoms such as sweating, tremor, anxiety, palpitations, and weakness. Other symptoms affect mental function and lead to restlessness, irritability, poor concentration, lethargy, and drowsiness.

──────────

Hypoglycemia is a condition in which the glucose level in the blood falls below normal levels. It derives from the Greek words "hypo" meaning under and "glycemia" meaning blood glucose—hence blood-glucose level below normal.

──────────

The diagnosis of true reactive hypoglycemia cannot be made on the basis of vague symptoms. It depends on detecting a low blood-glucose level when the symptoms are actually being experienced. A blood test is required to do this.

Because it may be difficult—or almost impossible—for someone to be in the right place at the right time to have a blood sample taken while experiencing the symptoms, a glucose-tolerance test is sometimes used to try to make the diagnosis. This involves drinking pure glucose, which causes the blood-glucose levels to rise. If too much insulin is produced in response, a person with reactive hypoglycemia will experience an excessive fall in their blood-glucose level. Sounds simple enough, but there are pitfalls.

Testing must be done under strictly controlled conditions—e.g., a low blood glucose is best demonstrated by measuring properly collected capillary (not venous) blood samples. Home blood-glucose meters are not sufficient for the diagnosis of hypoglycemia in people without diabetes.

Treating Hypoglycemia

The aim of treating reactive hypoglycemia is to prevent sudden large increases in blood-glucose levels. If the blood-glucose level can be prevented from rising quickly, then excessive, unnecessary amounts of insulin will not be produced and the blood-glucose levels will not plunge to abnormally low levels.

Smooth, steady blood-glucose levels can be readily achieved by changing from high to low-GI foods in the diet. This is particularly important when eating carbohydrate foods by themselves. Low-GI foods like whole-grain bread, low-fat yogurt, and low-GI fruits are best for snacks.

If you can stop the big swings in blood-glucose levels, then you will not get the symptoms of reactive hypoglycemia and chances are you will feel a lot better.

Hypoglycemia due to a serious medical problem is rare. Such conditions require in-depth investigation and treatment of the underlying cause.

An irregular eating pattern is the most common dietary habit that we see in people who have hypoglycemia. The following case study illustrates this very well.

To Prevent Reactive Hypoglycemia, Remember:

- Eat regular meals and snacks—plan to eat every 3 hours.
- Include low-GI carbohydrate foods at every meal and for snacks.
- Mix high-GI foods with low-GI foods in your meals— the combination will give an overall intermediate GI value.
- Avoid eating high-GI foods on their own for snacks— this can trigger reactive hypoglycemia.

▶ Case Study

Diane, with her hectic work schedule, often did not find time for proper meals. Finally, her body no longer accepted the strain it was under. Diane began to experience odd bouts of weakness and shakiness where she was unable to think clearly. A visit to the doctor and a glucose-tolerance test confirmed that she was suffering from hypoglycemia. The treatment was to change her habits—or at least her eating pattern. Diane needed to eat three regular meals a day with snacks in between. The thought of eating six times every day seemed an enormous task to Diane—and it took much thought and planning to organize her new diet. What kept her going was how much better she felt almost immediately. The following meal plan is a typical menu for Diane's day.

6 a.m.
Breakfast   Banana, milk, yogurt, honey, and vanilla blended into a smoothie for a quick start to the day

8:30 a.m.
At work   An oat-bran and apple muffin (homemade on the weekend and frozen individually)

12 noon
Lunch   A substantial sandwich, pita pocket, wrap, or foccacia; occasionally a Mexican dish with beans or a pasta meal if out

3 p.m.

At work   Handful of dried fruit (kept in a jar in her office)

5 p.m.

Still at work   Couple of small oatmeal cookies (kept in her office) for late days

7:30 p.m.

Dinner   Something quick, often pasta, chili, or meat and vegetables (always double-check for carbohydrate in the entreé)

9-10 p.m.

Late-night snack   Fruit or milkshake

12

The Glycemic Index and Heart Health: The Insulin-Resistance Syndrome

Did you know that heart disease is the single biggest killer of Americans? Every twenty-nine seconds, an American has a heart attack or goes into cardiac arrest. Most heart disease is caused by atherosclerosis, sometimes referred to as "hardening of the arteries."

Most people develop atherosclerosis gradually during their lifetime. If it occurs slowly it may not cause any problems at all, even into advanced old age. But if its development is accelerated by one or more of many processes (such as high cholesterol or high glucose levels), the condition may cause trouble much earlier in life.

Knowing your blood-glucose level is just as important as knowing your cholesterol level to ensure optimum heart health.

Atherosclerosis results in reduced blood flow through the affected arteries. In the heart this can mean that the heart muscle gets insufficient oxygen to provide the power for pumping blood, and it changes in such a way that pain is experienced (central chest pain or angina pectoris). Elsewhere in the body, atherosclerosis has a similar blood-flow-reducing effect: in the legs it can cause muscle pains during exercise; in the brain it can cause a variety of problems, from irregular gait to strokes.

An even more serious consequence of atherosclerosis occurs when a blood clot forms over the surface of a patch of atherosclerosis on an artery. This process of thrombosis can result in a complete blockage of the artery, with consequences ranging from sudden death to a small heart attack from which the patient recovers quickly.

The process of thrombosis can occur elsewhere in the arterial system with outcomes determined by the extent of the thrombosis. The probability of developing thrombosis is determined by the tendency of the blood to clot versus the natural ability of the blood to break down clots (fibrinolysis).

These two counteracting tendencies are influenced by a number of factors, including the level of glucose in the blood.

People who have gradually developed atherosclerosis of the arteries to the heart (the coronary arteries) may gradually develop reduced heart function. For a while the heart may be able to compensate for the problem, so there are no symptoms, but eventually it begins to fail. Shortness of breath may occur, initially on exercise, and there may sometimes be some swelling of the ankles.

Modern medicine has many effective drug treatments for heart failure, so this consequence of atherosclerosis does not now have quite the same serious implications it did in the past.

The Insulin-Resistance Syndrome

It is estimated that more than 60 million Americans have insulin resistance; one in four of them will go on to develop type 2 diabetes. The insulin-resistance syndrome (sometimes called the metabolic syndrome or syndrome X) is a collection of metabolic abnormalities that can silently increase your risk of heart attack.

If you have hypertension, impaired glucose tolerance, low HDL- cholesterol levels, and high triglycerides, then you probably have the insulin-resistance syndrome.

Chances are your total cholesterol levels are within the

normal range, giving you and your doctor a false impression of your coronary health.

You might also be of normal weight (or overweight), but your waist circumference is high (more than 35 inches in women, more than 40 inches in men), indicating excessive fat around the abdomen.

But the red flag is that your blood-glucose and insulin levels after a glucose load, or after eating, remain high. Resistance to the action of insulin is thought to underlie and unite all the features of this cluster of metabolic abnormalities.

It is often asked why insulin resistance is so common. We know that both genes and environment play a role. People of Native American, Hispanic, African American, or Asian origins appear to be more insulin resistant than those of European extraction, even when they are still young and lean.

But regardless of ethnic background, insulin resistance develops as we age. This has been attributed not to age per se, but to the fact that as we get older, we gain excessive fat around our middle, we become less physically active, and we lose some of our muscle mass. It's also likely that diet plays a role. Specifically, high-fat diets have been associated with insulin resistance, and high-carbohydrate diets with improving insulin sensitivity.

Insulin resistance as we age results in the insulin-resistance syndrome and gradually lays the foundations of a heart attack. To understand how and why this happens, we need to understand how heart disease develops.

Why Do People Get Heart Disease?

Atherosclerotic heart disease develops early in life when the many factors that cause it have a strong influence. Over many decades doctors and scientists have identified the processes in fine detail and now most of the factors that cause heart disease are well known.

Theoretically, this type of heart disease might be prevented if everyone's risks were assessed in youth and if all the right things were done throughout the rest of their lives. In practice there has been limited development of the ways to screen people for risk early in life, and the resources needed to achieve prevention are just not available.

A great deal is already being done, however, to identify risk factors (what we call red flags) in healthy people and those with established heart disease. A high cholesterol level is a well-established risk factor, as is a low level of HDL—the good cholesterol. More recently, high glucose levels after eating have been shown to be an important but underrecognized predictor of both cardiovascular disease and death from any cause. The good news is that those of us who take the necessary action will reduce our risk.

Risk Factors for Heart Disease

The chance of developing heart disease is increased if you smoke cigarettes or any other tobacco product, have high blood pressure, have diabetes or impaired glucose tolerance, have high blood cholesterol (which may be due to eating too much saturated fat in your diet), are overweight or obese, and/or do not do enough physical exercise.

- **Smoking** is now clearly established as a cause of atherosclerosis. Few authorities dispute the evidence. There are, however, some interesting dietary aspects: Smokers tend to eat fewer fruits and vegetables than nonsmokers (and thus eat less of the protective antioxidant plant compounds). Smokers tend to eat more fat and more salt than nonsmokers. These characteristics of the smoker's diet may be caused by a desire to seek stronger food flavors as a consequence of the taste-blunting effect of smoking. While these dietary differences may make the smoker at greater risk of heart disease, there is only one piece of advice for anyone who smokes: stop smoking!

- **High blood pressure** causes changes in the walls of arteries. The muscle layer (a muscular tube, which when healthy can change its size to control the flow of blood) becomes thickened, and atherosclerosis is more likely to develop. Treatments for blood pressure have become more effective over the last thirty years, but it is only now becoming clear which types of treatment for blood pressure are also effective at reducing heart disease risk.

- **Diabetes** and **impaired glucose tolerance** accelerate hardening of the arteries. When glucose levels are raised, even temporarily (such as after eating), oxidizing reactions are accelerated and antioxidants such as vitamins E and C are soaked up. In particular, the blood fats are oxidized, making them more damaging to artery walls. The walls become inflamed, thicken, and gradually lose their elasticity. The constriction of the arteries results in increased blood pressure. If that's not bad enough, high insulin levels increase the tendency for blood clots to form. The resulting increased risk of heart attack is a major reason why we put so much effort into helping people with diabetes achieve normal control of blood glucose.

  But you don't need to have diabetes to be at risk—raised blood-glucose levels hours after a meal have been associated with increased risk of heart disease in people without diabetes.

- **High blood cholesterol** increases the risk of heart disease. Your blood cholesterol is determined in part by genetic (inherited) factors, which you cannot change, and in part by lifestyle factors, which you can change.

There are some relatively rare conditions in which particularly high blood-cholesterol levels occur. People who have inherited these conditions need a thorough examination by a specialist doctor followed by lifelong drug treatment.

In most people, high blood cholesterol is partly determined by their genes, which have set the cholesterol slightly high, and lifestyle factors that push it up more.

The most important dietary factor is fat. The diets prescribed for blood-cholesterol lowering are low in fat (particularly saturated fat), high in carbohydrate, and high in fiber.

- **Body weight** also affects blood cholesterol. In some people, being overweight has a significant effect on their cholesterol levels, so attaining a reasonable weight can be helpful. The blood also contains triglycerides, another type of fat that is particularly high after meals. High triglycerides may be linked with increased risk of heart disease in some people.

Overweight and obese people are more likely to have high blood pressure and to have diabetes. They are also at increased risk of developing heart disease. Some of that increased risk is due to the high blood pressure, and the tendency to diabetes, but there is a separate independent effect of the obesity.

When increased fatness develops it can be distributed evenly all over the body or it may occur centrally—in and around the abdomen. This central form of obesity is particularly associated with heart disease. Thus, every effort should be made to get body weights nearer to normal—especially if the extra weight is middle-age spread.

- **Exercise,** on the other hand, has multiple benefits for the heart. Cardiovascular fitness is improved by regular strenuous exercise and the blood supply to the heart may be improved. Exercise is also important in maintaining body weight and has effects on metabolism and some factors related to blood clotting. Getting regular exercise is clearly important.

Treating Heart Disease and Secondary Prevention

When heart disease is detected, two types of treatment are given. First, the effects of the disease are treated (e.g., medical treatment with drugs and surgical treatment to bypass blocked arteries) and, second, the risk factors are treated to slow down the further progression of the disease.

Treatment of risk factors after the disease has already developed is *secondary prevention*. In people who have not yet developed the disease, treatment of risk factors is *primary prevention*. Obviously it would be better to give primary preventive treatment in all cases.

Preventing Heart Disease: Primary Prevention

More and more people now get regular checks of their blood pressure and tests to check for diabetes. Increasingly, blood-fat tests are done to check this risk factor as well.

All health professionals give lifestyle advice on stopping smoking, the benefits of exercise, and the nature of a good diet. When specific risk factors are discovered, diet and lifestyle advice is given, but may not be followed for long.

It is especially difficult to follow advice if the effect of not following it is likely not to matter for ten or more years, and if the changes needed are not seen as appealing. The changes must be wanted by the individual, who will be helped by encouragement from friends and relatives, and the changes must ideally be positive changes—"I want to do this," not "They've told me to do this." Any new dimension in heart-disease prevention must be seen as a great positive change rather than as a negative one.

The Glycemic Index and Heart Health

The glycemic index is vitally important for coronary health and the prevention of heart disease.

First, it has benefits for weight control, helping to curb appetite and preventing overeating and excessive body weight.

Second, it helps reduce post-meal blood-glucose levels in both normal and diabetic individuals. This improves the elasticity of the walls of the arteries, making dilation easier and improving blood flow. Third, blood fats and clotting factors can also be improved by low-GI diets. Specifically, population studies have shown that HDL levels are correlated with the GI values and glycemic load of the diet. Those of us who self-select the lowest-GI diets have the highest and best levels of HDL—the good cholesterol.

Furthermore, research studies in people with diabetes have shown that low-GI diets reduce triglycerides in the blood, a factor strongly linked to heart disease. Last, low-GI diets have been shown to improve insulin sensitivity in people at high risk of heart disease, thereby helping to reduce the rise in blood-glucose and insulin levels after normal meals.

By working on several fronts at one time, a low-GI diet has a distinct advantage over other types of diets or drugs that target only one risk factor at a time.

One study in particular has provided the best evidence in support of the role of the glycemic index in heart disease.

The study, conducted by Harvard University and known as the Nurses' Health Study, is an ongoing, long-term study of over 65,000 nurses who provide their personal health and diet information to researchers at the Harvard School of Public Health every few years. In this way, diet can be linked with the development of different diseases. Researchers with the Nurses' Health Study found that those who ate more *high*-GI foods had nearly twice the risk of having a heart attack over a ten-year period of follow-up than those eating low-GI diets. This association was independent of dietary fiber and other known risk factors, such as age and body mass index. In other words, even if fiber intake was high, there was still an adverse effect of high-GI diets on risk. Importantly, neither sugar nor total carbohydrate intake showed any association with risk of heart attack. Thus, there was no evidence that lower carbohydrate or sugar intake was helpful.

One of the most important findings of the Nurses' Health Study is that the increased risk associated with high-GI diets was largely seen in those with a body mass index (BMI) over 23 (to calculate your body mass, multiply your weight (lbs.) by 705 and then divide by the square of your height in inches (wt (lbs) × 705/ht (in)^2). (See Body Mass Index Table on page 384–385.) There was no increased risk in those with a BMI under 23. But the fact remains that the great majority of adults have a BMI greater than 23; indeed, a BMI of 23–25 is considered normal weight. The implication therefore is that the insulin resistance that comes with increasing weight is an integral part of the disease process. So, if you are very lean and insulin sensitive, high-GI diets won't make you more prone to heart attack. This might explain why traditional-living Asian populations, such as the Chinese, who eat high-GI rice as a staple food, do not show increased risk of heart disease. Their low BMI and their high level of physical activity conspire to keep them insulin sensitive and extremely carbohydrate tolerant.

The Glycemic Index and Insulin Resistance

In this condition the body is insensitive, or partially deaf, to insulin. The organs and tissues that ought to respond to even a small rise in insulin remain unresponsive. The body tries harder by secreting more insulin to achieve the same effect, just as you might raise your voice or shout for a hard-of-hearing person. Thus high insulin levels are part and parcel of insulin resistance. Tests on patients with heart disease and polycystic ovary syndrome (PCOS—see page 386.) show that insulin resistance is very common.

Can a low-GI diet help? In a recent study, patients with serious disease of the coronary arteries were given either low or high-GI diets before surgery for coronary-bypass grafts. They were given blood tests before their diets and just before surgery, and at surgery small pieces of fat tissue were removed

Body Mass Index Table

		Normal						Overweight					Obese					
BMI		19	20	21	22	23	24	25	26	27	28	29	30	31	32	33	34	35

Body Weight (pounds)

Height (inches)																		
58	91	96	100	105	110	115	119	124	129	134	138	143	148	153	158	162	167
59	94	99	104	109	114	119	124	128	133	138	143	148	153	158	163	168	173
60	97	102	107	112	118	123	128	133	138	143	148	153	158	163	168	174	179
61	100	106	111	116	122	127	132	137	143	148	153	158	164	169	174	180	185
62	104	109	115	120	126	131	136	142	147	153	158	164	169	175	180	186	191
63	107	113	118	124	130	135	141	146	152	158	163	169	175	180	186	191	197
64	110	116	122	128	134	140	145	151	157	163	169	174	180	186	192	197	204
65	114	120	126	132	138	144	150	156	162	168	174	180	186	192	198	204	210
66	118	124	130	136	142	148	155	161	167	173	179	186	192	198	204	210	216
67	121	127	134	140	146	153	159	166	172	178	185	191	198	204	211	217	223
68	125	131	138	144	151	158	164	171	177	184	190	197	203	210	216	223	230
69	128	135	142	149	155	162	169	176	182	189	196	203	209	216	223	230	236
70	132	139	146	153	160	167	174	181	188	195	202	209	216	222	229	236	243
71	136	143	150	157	165	172	179	186	193	200	208	215	222	229	236	243	250
72	140	147	154	162	169	177	184	191	199	206	213	221	228	235	242	250	258
73	144	151	159	166	174	182	189	197	204	212	219	227	235	242	250	257	265
74	148	155	163	171	179	186	194	202	210	218	225	233	241	249	256	264	272
75	152	160	168	176	184	192	200	208	216	224	232	240	248	256	264	272	279
76	156	164	172	180	189	197	205	213	221	230	238	246	254	263	271	279	287

Source: Adapted from Clinical Guidelines on the Identification, Evaluation, and Treatment of Overweight and Obesity in Adults: The Evidence Report.

Extreme Obesity																		
36	37	38	39	40	41	42	43	44	45	46	47	48	49	50	51	52	53	54
172	177	181	186	191	196	201	205	210	215	220	224	229	234	239	244	248	253	258
178	183	188	193	198	203	208	212	217	222	227	232	237	242	247	252	257	262	267
184	189	194	199	204	209	215	220	225	230	235	240	245	250	255	261	266	271	276
190	195	201	206	211	217	222	227	232	238	243	248	254	259	264	269	275	280	285
196	202	207	213	218	224	229	235	240	246	251	256	262	267	273	278	284	289	295
203	208	214	220	225	231	237	242	248	254	259	265	270	278	282	287	293	299	304
209	215	221	227	232	238	244	250	256	262	267	273	279	285	291	296	302	308	314
216	222	228	234	240	246	252	258	264	270	276	282	288	294	300	306	312	318	324
223	229	235	241	247	253	260	266	272	278	284	291	297	303	309	315	322	328	334
230	236	242	249	255	261	268	274	280	287	293	299	306	312	319	325	331	338	344
236	243	249	256	262	269	276	282	289	295	302	308	315	322	328	335	341	348	354
243	250	257	263	270	277	284	291	297	304	311	318	324	331	338	345	351	358	365
250	257	264	271	278	285	292	299	306	313	320	327	334	341	348	355	362	369	376
257	265	272	279	286	293	301	308	315	322	329	338	343	351	358	365	372	379	386
265	272	279	287	294	302	309	316	324	331	338	346	353	361	368	375	383	390	397
272	280	288	295	302	310	318	325	333	340	348	355	363	371	378	386	393	401	408
280	287	295	303	311	319	326	334	342	350	358	365	373	381	389	396	404	412	420
287	295	303	311	319	327	335	343	351	359	367	375	383	391	399	407	415	423	431
295	304	312	320	328	336	344	353	361	369	377	385	394	402	410	418	426	435	443

for testing. The tests on the fat showed that the low-GI diets made the tissues of these insulin insensitive patients more sensitive—in fact, they were back in the same range as normal control patients after just a few weeks on the diet.

If people with serious heart disease can be improved, would the same happen with younger people? Young women in their thirties were divided into those who did and those who did not have a family history of heart disease. They themselves had not yet developed the condition. They had blood tests followed by low or high-GI diets for four weeks, after which they had more blood tests, and then when they had surgery—for conditions unrelated to heart disease— pieces of fat were again removed and tested for insulin sensitivity. The young women with a family history of heart disease were insensitive to insulin (those without the family history of heart disease were normal). After four weeks on the low-GI diet, however, the insulin sensitivity of the young women with the family history of heart disease increased to within the normal range.

Polycystic Ovary Syndrome (PCOS)

Polycystic ovary syndrome occurs in women when multiple cysts form on the ovaries during the menstrual cycle and interfere with normal ovulation. It is often diagnosed when women have irregular periods or find it difficult to become pregnant. Excessive facial hair and acne are also present.

It is now known that insulin resistance is often severe in women with PCOS and that any means of improving insulin sensitivity (drugs, weight loss) will improve outcomes. Some physicians have found that low-GI diets are particularly useful for women with PCOS. At present, there is little research to back this up. However, since low-GI diets will help reduce weight and have been shown to improve insulin sensitivity in individuals at risk of coronary heart disease, it makes a lot of sense to try the low-GI approach.

───────

In both studies, the diets were designed to try to ensure that all the other variables (like total energy, total carbohydrates) were not different, so that the change in insulin sensitivity was likely to have been due to the low-GI diet rather than any other factor.

Work on these exciting findings continues, but what is known so far strongly suggests that a low-GI diet not only improves body weight and blood glucose in people with diabetes, but also improves the sensitivity of the body to insulin. It will take many years of further research to show that this simple dietary change to a low-GI diet will definitely slow the progress of atherosclerotic heart disease. In the mean-time, it is clear that risk factors for heart disease are improved by a low-GI diet. Low-GI diets are consistent with the other required dietary changes needed for prevention of heart disease.

**Low saturated fat and low GI values help
prevent heart disease.**

13

Children and the Glycemic Index

Helping our children eat well is one of the most important things we can do for them. In an environment where food is overly abundant and physical activity limited, the potential for energy imbalance is great—and the consequences are enormous. About 13 percent of children and 14 percent of adolescents in the United States are overweight. These numbers have tripled over the past twenty years.

Overweight children are at risk for sleep apnea, high blood pressure, and elevated blood fats. Many will also have elevated levels of circulating insulin, which is an early warning sign for the potential development of type 2 diabetes, a condition once seen only in adults. All in all, overweight children face adulthood with the prospect of cardiovascular disease and reduced longevity. As if this weren't enough, overweight children are commonly stigmatized as lazy, unhealthy, and less intelligent than children of normal weight. Loss of self-esteem and subsequent social isolation can make life a misery.

How Can the Glycemic Index Help?

The management of obesity in children is about altering energy balance. Energy intake has to decrease and energy expenditure has to increase. Today's American diet tends to be too high in fat and quickly digested carbohydrate foods with little fill-up value. Many of our starchy staples, like potato, white bread, breakfast cereals, and crackers, have very high GI values. So, too, do children's favorites such as mashed potatoes, Rice Krispies™, Gatorade™, and jelly beans. Because of their high GI values, it is easy to overconsume calories with these foods. In contrast, low-GI foods like pasta, yogurt, most fruits, and oatmeal cookies have been proven to be more filling and can reduce overeating.

In a study performed in twelve obese teenage boys in the United States, low-GI meals significantly reduced subsequent food intake compared to high-GI meals. The boys ate special breakfast and lunch meals that had either a low, medium, or high GI value, and then their food intake was measured during the remainder of the day. Researchers found that the boys ate twice as much food in the afternoon after a high-GI breakfast and lunch as they did after a low-GI breakfast and lunch. This difference in food intake corresponded with alterations in hormonal and metabolic changes thought to be responsible for stimulating excessive appetite.

There were higher levels of the hormones insulin, noradrenaline, and cortisol after the high-GI meals. The increased insulin response to high-GI carbohydrates may promote fat storage and obesity. Higher cortisol levels may result in increased appetite. Differences in these hormones are one possible explanation for significantly greater fat loss in a group of children prescribed a diet based on low-GI foods compared to those on a conventional low-fat diet. With the low-GI diet, the children were instructed to eat until they were full, to snack when hungry, and to eat low-GI carbohydrate, protein, and fat at every meal and snack. Body mass index and body weight decreased significantly more (over the four-month study period) in those on a low-GI diet.

The Importance of Physical Activity

An increase in physical activity is critical to weight management for children. This includes the reduction of sedentary behaviors (such as television viewing, time on the computer, and video games) and an increase in planned and incidental activity (such as helping with household tasks and dressing themselves).

It helps enormously if parents are involved in physical activity themselves, serving as a means of support and as role models. Family activities such as walks, swimming, bike rides, soccer or baseball games, etc., need to be planned. The number-one rule is to make it fun!

If children learn to combine regular physical activity with healthy low-GI eating, they will be in top condition throughout their lives.

───────

Some Dietary Guidelines for Childhood

A healthy diet for children:

- allows for good health and growth
- satisfies the appetite
- encourages good eating habits
- allows for varied and interesting meals and snacks
- accommodates the child's usual routines and activities
- maintains a healthy body weight

Children need to eat a wide variety of nutritious foods to grow and develop to their full potential. As a parent or guardian you can help by ensuring you:

- offer children whole-grain breads and cereals, vegetables, and fruits to eat

- include lean meats, fish, and dairy foods in their daily diet

- encourage children to drink plenty of water

- follow these guidelines yourself, so that children can imitate you

Incorporating Low-GI Foods into Your Child's Diet

The GI value of a diet can be lowered easily using a simple system of substitution, where at least half of high-GI carbohydrate choices are swapped for low-GI carbohydrate foods.

Keep the following characteristics of children's eating behavior in mind when attempting changes in their diet:

Children are naturally neophobic. That is, they dislike new foods. It is normal for children, especially young children, to refuse new foods. Repeated exposure to new foods in a positive environment increases their acceptance. But you have to persevere—at least five to ten tastes of the food may be needed before a child accepts it.

Most children are natural grazers. They usually like to have frequent meals and snacks throughout the day. It's not a good idea to make children eat everything on the plate, as this can encourage overconsumption.

It is preferable that they learn to stay in tune with their appetite and eat according to it.

Children have small stomachs with high nutrient requirements. Their food intake may vary considerably from meal to meal, but studies show it remains surprisingly constant from day to day. So long as the foods offered to children are nutritious, appetite is the best indicator of how much they need to eat.

Be clear on what your role is as the caregiver in relation to feeding your children. The American nutritionist Ellyn Satter expresses it well: "Parents are responsible for what is provided to eat. Children are responsible for how much, and even whether, they eat."

The Best Carbohydrate Choices

The following foods have low GI values, are high in micronutrients, and provide very little saturated fat. The recommended number of daily servings for children age four to eleven years is included.

Cereal Grains

This group includes whole-grain breads, oatmeal and barley, oats, popcorn, rice, rye, wheat, and anything made from them, such as bread, breakfast cereals, flour, noodles, pasta, polenta, ravioli, and semolina.

Servings per day: 3–6

Fruits

This includes apples, apricots, bananas, cherries, grapes, kiwi fruit, oranges, peaches, pears, plums, and raisins. Serve them whole, in salads, or as juices and smoothies.

Servings per day: 2–4

Vegetables and Legumes

Vegetables and legumes provide valuable amounts of vitamins, minerals, and fiber. You can eat most vegetables without thinking about their GI value because they are very low in carbohydrate. The higher-carbohydrate vegetables are potatoes, corn, peas, and sweet potatoes. Of these, corn and sweet potatoes are the lower-GI choices. All legumes—including baked beans, chickpeas, kidney beans, lentils, and split peas—are low-GI sources of carbohydrate.

Servings per day: 2–5

Milk and Milk Products

Low-fat milk and dairy foods such as pudding, ice cream, and yogurt are excellent sources of carbohydrate and calcium. Children under age two should be given full-fat milk, but low-fat varieties are quite suitable for older children.

Servings per day: 2–3

It isn't necessary to give children low-GI foods alone. On the contrary, balanced meals usually consist of a variety of foods, and we know that eating a low-GI food with a high-GI food produces an intermediate-GI meal.

To help yourself include low-GI foods in the family meals every day:

- become familiar with them

- have them available in the pantry and refrigerator

- experiment with them—try new foods and recipes and enjoy what you eat

Try to include a minimum of one low-GI food per meal to reap the benefits.

The Role of Sugar

Children naturally enjoy sweet foods. Sweetness is not a learned taste; in fact, it could be said that we're all born with a sweet tooth. Our first food, breast milk, is sweet. Infants smile when offered a sweet solution and reject sour and bitter tastes.

Today, scientists researching the glycemic index have shown that sugar is not the dietary demon that it once was made out to be. You and your children can enjoy sugar and foods containing sugar in moderation as part of a balanced, low-GI diet. In fact, studies show that diets containing moderate quantities of added sugars tend to be richest in micronutrients. As we explained in chapter 3, sugar itself has only a moderate GI value, and many foods containing sugar, such as yogurt and flavored milk, are excellent sources of low-GI nutrition.

What is a Moderate Intake of Sugar in a Child's Diet?

A moderate intake of refined sugar in a child's diet is between 7 and 12 teaspoons a day. This reflects average consumption in children and refers to the sugar found in foods such as soft drinks, breakfast cereals, candy, ice cream, cookies, and jams, as well as what we add—to breakfast cereal, for example. Adding sugar to a well-balanced, low-GI diet can make foods more palatable and acceptable to children without compromising their nutritional intake or the benefits of the low-GI foods.

Artificially Sweetened Products

While artificially sweetened products may sometimes be appropriate for some children, they are not necessary for the average child. Many of these products are simply flavored fillers such as diet sodas and candy and provide few, if any, nutrients. Often they are cited as useful in preventing tooth decay. This is not the case for low-calorie soft drinks, which are highly acidic and will dissolve dental enamel. Even their role in weight reduction is questionable, as individuals using diet products tend to compensate with extra calories at later meals.

A Moderate Quantity of Sugar in a 10-Year-Old Child's Diet

This child's menu provides 12 teaspoons of refined sugars. It provides 1,500 calories of energy, with 23 percent of energy from fat and 57 percent of energy from carbohydrate.

Breakfast	Lunch	Dinner
¾ cup of Cocoa Puffs™ with 4 oz 1% milk ½ banana 4 oz fruit juice	1 ham and cheese with lettuce and tomato sandwich (made from low-GI bread) 6–8 baby carrots 1 small apple 1 cup water	1 cup of spaghetti with tomato sauce and 3 small meatballs green salad, tossed with a little dressing if desired ½ cup steamed string beans ½ cup pudding and 2–3 strawberries water to drink
Snack: 1 Quaker chewy low-fat granola bar™ 1 cup 1% milk	**Snack:** 2 small chocolate-chip cookies 1 fruit smoothie (made with ½ cup 1% milk and ½ cup sliced fruit)	**Snack:** 1½ cups air-popped popcorn

Does Sugar Affect Children's Behavior?

Although some people believe sugar causes attention deficit disorder (ADD) or hyperactivity in children, results from many published studies have failed to provide any scientifically proven support for this. In situations where the investigator, the child, and the parent were unaware of the composition of the test food or capsule, refined sugar showed no effect on cognitive performance, nor did it cause or exacerbate ADD.

It is possible that a very small number of children may respond adversely to fluctuations in blood-glucose levels caused by sugar. But if this is the case, any carbohydrate, including bread and potatoes, will also be incriminated.

On the whole, there is more evidence that sugar might actually have a calming effect, if it has any effect at all. Glucose or sugar can reduce the distress associated with painful medical procedures in infants. In one study there was a reduction in crying and heart rate in infants subjected to heel pricks when they were given a sugar solution immediately prior to the procedure, compared to children who were given just water.

What about Fat in a Child's Diet?

Young children (under age two) rely on a certain amount of fat in their diet as a source of calories and should generally not be placed on a low-fat diet. A moderate amount of fat is also necessary as a source of essential fatty acids and fat-soluble vitamins. Kids need some fat—but don't go overboard. Children, like adults, should not regularly consume prepared foods that are high in saturated fat, such as cookies, cakes, pastries, ready-to-eat meals, candy, and snack foods.

A Low-GI 7-Day Sample Menu for Kids

MONDAY		
Breakfast	**Lunch**	**Dinner**
Bowl of Mini-Wheats™ cereal with milk. Half a banana.	Sandwich of natural peanut butter and jelly on sourdough bread. Bottle of water. ½ cup chocolate pudding.	Baby shrimp stir-fry with Asian vegetables over steamed long-grain rice.
Snack: Low-fat granola bar. Small carton orange juice.	**Snack:** Honey graham crackers.	**Snack:** 1–2 scoops frozen yogurt.

TUESDAY

Breakfast	Lunch	Dinner
Bowl of Cocoa Puffs™ with milk. Sliced apple quarters.	Tuna salad on multigrain bread. Small can of peaches.	Chicken, vegetable, sweet potato strata served with corn on the cob.
Snack: ½ cup fruit yogurt. Small bunch of grapes.	**Snack:** Cantaloupe chunks and light ice cream.	**Snack:** Fruit kebabs (fresh fruit wedges on a skewer).

WEDNESDAY

Breakfast	Lunch	Dinner
Low-fat granola with fruit yogurt and fruit.	Honey-roasted turkey breast on whole-grain sandwich bun. ½ baggie of grape tomatoes. Apricot nectar.	Baked Tex Mex potatoes (sweet potato baked with onion, bacon, taco seasoning, baked beans, grated cheese, sour cream, and tortilla chips).
Snack: Snap-lock bag of popcorn.	**Snack:** Oatmeal cookie and milk.	**Snack:** Nutella® on toast.

THURSDAY		
Breakfast	**Lunch**	**Dinner**
Scrambled egg on toast.	Grilled cheese sandwich. Apple. Bottle of water.	Grilled or barbecued sausages and grilled sweet potato slices with corn on the cob.
Snack: Apple cinnamon cookie bar.	**Snack:** Strawberry smoothie.	**Snack:** Fresh fruit salad.

FRIDAY		
Breakfast	**Lunch**	**Dinner**
Old-fashioned oatmeal made with milk. Raisins or sliced peaches.	A whole-wheat sandwich bun with egg salad. Yogurt drink.	Cheese pizza. Garden salad.
Snack: Small blueberry muffin.	**Snack:** Avocado or hummus dip served with fruit or vegetables.	**Snack:** Chocolate milk drink.

SATURDAY		
Breakfast	**Lunch**	**Dinner**
Banana-honey smoothie.	Vegetable soup with a crusty whole-grain roll.	Hamburger. Baked beans and coleslaw.
Snack: Sourdough pretzel nuggets.	**Snack:** Cheese wedges and dried fruit (apple, raisins, apricot, and pear).	**Snack:** Watermelon wedges.

SUNDAY		
Breakfast	**Lunch**	**Dinner**
French toast with fruit.	Baked ham. Green beans and tossed salad. Roasted new potatoes.	Macaroni and cheese. Poached pears.
Snack: Baked apple with cinnamon.	**Snack:** Ice cream in a cone.	**Snack:** Peanut butter on whole-grain toast.

Did you know that diets containing a moderate amount of sugar are associated with:

- the highest level of micronutrients
- a lower glycemic index
- lower intakes of saturated fat
- a lower body weight

14

The Glycemic Index and Peak Sports Performance

A s we have explained, the glycemic index ranks the carbohydrates in foods according to their glycemic impact. The rise in blood glucose affects the insulin response to that food and ultimately affects the fuel mix and carbohydrate stores available to the exercising muscles. For all athletes and those who exercise, there are times when low-GI foods provide an advantage (e.g., *before* the event) and times when high-GI foods are better (e.g., *during and after* the event). For best performance, a serious athlete needs to learn about which foods have high and low GI values and when to eat them.

But it's not only the type of carbohydrate that matters—
the amount of carbohydrate is equally important. Training
diets must be very high in carbohydrate if the glycemic index
is to make any difference at all.

**Manipulating the GI values of your diet can
give you the winning edge.**

A High-Carbohydrate Diet is Essential for Peak Athletic Performance

A high-carbohydrate training diet is a must for optimum
sports performance because it produces the biggest stores of
muscle glycogen. As we have previously described, the carbohydrate we eat is stored in the body in the form of glycogen
in the muscles and liver. A small amount of carbohydrate
(about 5 grams) circulates as glucose in the blood. When you
are exercising at a high intensity, your muscles rely on glycogen and glucose for fuel. Although the body can use fat when
exercising at lower intensities, fat cannot provide the fuel fast
enough when you are working very hard. The bigger your
stores of glycogen and glucose, the longer you can go before
fatigue sets in.

Unlike the fat stores in the body, which can release
almost unlimited amounts of fatty acids, the carbohydrate
stores are small. They are fully depleted after two or three

hours of strenuous exercise. This drying up of carbohydrate stores is often called "hitting the wall." The blood-glucose concentration begins to decline at this point. If exercise continues at the same rate, blood glucose may drop to levels that interfere with brain function and cause disorientation and unconsciousness. Some athletes refer to this as a *hypo,* and in cycling it is known as *bonking*.

All else being equal, the eventual winner is the person with the largest stores of muscle glycogen. Any good book on nutrition for athletes will tell you how to maximize your muscle glycogen stores by ingesting a high-carbohydrate training diet and by carbo loading in the days prior to the competition. In this chapter we provide instructions for increasing muscle glycogen as well as using the glycemic index to your advantage in any sports situation.

Low-GI Foods: Before the Event

Low-GI foods have been proven to extend endurance when eaten alone one to two hours before prolonged strenuous exercise. When a pre-event meal of lentils (low GI value) was compared with one of potatoes (high GI value), cyclists were able to continue cycling at high intensity (65 percent of their maximum capacity) for twenty minutes longer when the meal had a low GI value. Their blood-glucose and insulin levels were still above fasting levels at the end of exercise, indicating that carbohydrates were continuing to be absorbed from the small intestine even after ninety minutes of strenuous exercise. Figure 9 shows the blood-glucose levels during exercise after consumption of low and high-GI foods.

Figure 9. Comparison of the effect of low and high-GI foods on blood-glucose levels during prolonged strenuous exercise.

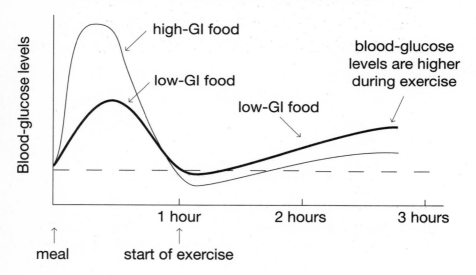

These findings were later confirmed by several other research groups in the United States. Some studies, however, have not been able to show a difference between high and low-GI foods. One explanation may be the use of different experimental protocols. Researchers who obtained a positive finding invariably used the "time to exhaustion" as the criterion for comparison, while those who showed no effect used a "time trial" (i.e., the amount of work done or distance traveled over a set time period). While the time trial may be more appropriate for some types of sports events (e.g., a marathon), the time to exhaustion may be closer to reality in other situations (e.g., a tennis match or firefighting).

Despite the fact that they were not able to show a difference in work output between high and low foods, *all of them* showed a difference in blood-glucose and insulin levels, and all of them showed differences in the ratio of carbohydrate and fat in the fuel mix. In the high-GI trials, more carbohydrate and less fat was burned over the course of the exercise. If this is taken to its logical conclusion, high-GI foods must lead to faster carbohydrate depletion and less time before "hitting the wall." Anecdotal evidence backs the use of low-GI foods before the event. Many elite athletes, including tennis players, have worked out for themselves that pasta gives them the staying power they need for prolonged strenuous events.

Before you read any further, it's important to appreciate the type of event where low-GI foods will help—specifically, it is one in which the athlete is undertaking a very strenuous form of exercise for longer than ninety minutes. Exercise physiologists define this by saying that the athlete is exercising at more than 65 percent of their maximum capacity for a prolonged period. Examples of such events include a running or swimming marathon, a triathlon, nonstop tennis competition, or a soccer game (depending on the player's position). In some forms of recreation, such as cross-country skiing and mountain climbing, an athlete may also benefit from low-GI foods. In some occupations that require prolonged strenuous activity for hours and hours (such as police rescue or forest firefighting), low-GI foods may also be beneficial.

Events Where the Glycemic Index Can Give You the Edge

- running marathon
- swimming marathon
- triathlon
- nonstop tennis competition
- soccer game (depending on the player's position)
- cross-country skiing
- mountain climbing
- prolonged strenuous aerobics
- gym workouts (longer than 90 minutes)

Low-GI foods are best eaten about two hours before the big event—so that the meal will have left the stomach but will remain in the small intestine, slowly releasing glucose energy, for hours afterwards. The slow rate of carbohydrate digestion in low-GI foods helps ensure that a small and steady stream of glucose trickles into the bloodstream during the event. Most importantly, the extra glucose will still be available toward the end of the exercise, when muscle stores are running close to empty. In this way, low-GI foods increase endurance and prolong the time before exhaustion hits.

The Pre-Event Meal

▶ *How much should I eat before the event?*

About 1 gram of carbohydrate for every 2 pounds of body weight (i.e., 55 grams of carbohydrate if you weigh 110 pounds or 90 grams of carbohydrate if you weigh 180 pounds).

▶ *How soon before?*

A good starting point is 1 to 2 hours before the event.

You should experiment to determine the timing that works best for you.

You will find the amounts of carbohydrate in a nominal serving of food (along with their GI values and glycemic load) in the tables in Part 4 of this book.

In any sports context, it's critical to select low-GI foods that do not cause gastrointestinal discomfort (stomach cramps and flatulence). Some low-GI foods, such as legumes that are high in fiber or indigestible sugars, may produce symptoms in people not used to eating large amounts of them. But there are plenty of low-fiber, low-GI choices, including pasta, noodles, and Basmati rice.

High-GI Foods: During and After the Event

While the pre-event meal should have a low GI value, scientific evidence indicates that there are times when high-GI foods are preferable. This includes during the event, after the event, and after normal training sessions. This is because high-GI foods are absorbed faster and stimulate more insulin, the hormone responsible for getting glucose back into the muscles for either immediate or future use.

During the Event

High-GI foods should be used during events lasting longer than ninety minutes. This form of carbohydrate is rapidly released into the bloodstream and ensures that glucose is available for oxidation in the muscle cells. Liquid foods are usually tolerated better than solid foods while racing because they are emptied more quickly from the stomach. Sports drinks are ideal during the race because they replace water and electrolytes as well. The old standby of bananas strapped to the bike doesn't have much scientific basis. The GI value of bananas is only 55 and some of their carbohydrate is completely resistant to digestion, which could give you gas and a pain in the belly. If you feel hungry for something solid during a cycling race, try jelly beans (GI value of 80) or another form of high-glucose candy.

Consume 30 to 60 grams of carbohydrate per hour during the event.

The GI Values of Sports Drinks and Sports Bars

Drinks	GI Value
GatorLode® (orange)	100
Gatorade™ (orange)	89
XLR8® (orange)	68
Poweraid® (orange)	65
Cytomax™ (orange)	62
AllSport™ (orange)	53
Bars	**GI Value**
Clif® bar (cookies & cream)	101
PowerBar® (chocolate)	83
METRx® bar (vanilla)	74

After the Event (Recovery)

In some competitive sports, athletes compete on consecutive days, and glycogen stores need to be at their maximum each time. Here it is important to restock the glycogen store in the muscles as quickly as possible after the event. High-GI foods are best in this situation. Muscles are more sensitive to glucose in the bloodstream in the first hour after exercise, so a concerted effort should be made to get as many high-GI foods in as soon as possible.

Suggested foods include most of the sports drinks on the market (which replace water and electrolyte losses, as well), or high-GI rice (e.g., jasmine), breads, and breakfast cereals such as cornflakes and Rice Krispies™. Potatoes cooked without fat are a good choice, too, but their high satiety means it is hard to eat lots of them. Soft drinks have an intermediate GI value, so they won't be ideal but they won't do any harm either. Alcohol is the worst choice.

A Word about Alcohol

Alcohol interferes with glycogen resynthesis and lowers blood-glucose levels, sometimes to dangerous levels. Keep alcohol intake moderate—no more than one or two drinks per day, and try to have two alcohol-free days a week. An average drink is equivalent to one glass of wine (5 ounces), one 12-ounce can of beer, or 1½ ounces of liquor.

Beer is not a good source of carbohydrate—there are only about 13 grams in a 12-ounce can.

Recovery Formula

Aim to ingest about 1 gram of carbohydrate per 2 pounds of body weight 2 hours after exercise.

A Word about Serving Size

Serious athletes need to choose large portions. At some times you may not feel like a big meal of rice or pasta, so at those times sports drinks and soft drinks can help. Choose what you can tolerate and what is easy and practical for you to bring or buy. The main point is to make sure you eat and drink carbohydrate soon after the exercise session.

To Maximize Glycogen Replenishment after the Competition

1. Ingest carbohydrate as soon as you can after the event and maintain a high carbohydrate intake for the next 24 hours.

2. Consume at least 5 grams of carbohydrate per pound of body weight over the 24 hours following prolonged exercise.
3. Choose high-GI foods in the replenishment phase.
4. Avoid alcohol (alcohol delays glycogen resynthesis).

The Training Diet and Carbohydrate Loading

It's not just your pre- and post-event meals that influence your performance. Consuming a high-carbohydrate diet every day will help you reach peak performance. The GI value of the carbohydrate is not the issue here, only the amount of carbohydrate. Science has proven over and over again—unlike the case for many dietary supplements—that eating lots of high-carbohydrate foods maximizes muscle glycogen stores and thereby increases endurance. Carbohydrate stores need to be replenished after each training session, not just after a race. If you train on a number of days per week, make sure you consume a high-carbohydrate diet throughout the week.

When athletes fail to consume adequate carbohydrate each day, muscle and liver glycogen stores eventually became depleted. Dr. Ted Costill at the University of Texas showed that the gradual and chronic depletion of stored glycogen may decrease endurance and exercise performance. Intense workouts two to three times a day draw heavily on the athlete's muscle glycogen stores. Athletes on a low-carbohydrate diet will not perform their best because muscle stores of fuel are low.

If the diet provides inadequate amounts of carbohydrate, the reduction in muscle glycogen will be critical. An athlete training heavily should consume about 500 to 800 grams of carbohydrate a day (about two to three times normal) to help prevent carbohydrate depletion. Typically, American adults consume between 200 and 250 grams of carbohydrate each day.

How to Choose a High-Carbohydrate Diet

In this section we give some extra pointers because very active people need to eat much larger amounts of carbohydrate than inactive people.

You may feel that you already know a lot about diet. But athletes, like everyone else, can have their facts wrong. Many foods that you might believe are good sources of carbohydrate are even better sources of fat. For example, chocolate is 55 percent carbohydrate, but also 30 percent fat. And fat won't help you win the race.

Dietary advice aimed at the general public needs to be modified for the serious athlete. Athletes have far greater energy needs, perhaps double that of the average office worker. Many high-carbohydrate and low-fat foods that are recommended for the average person are too bulky and satiating for athletes. It is their bulk that makes it difficult to consume the required amount of food. For example, a 75-gram-carbohydrate portion of potatoes is equal to more than a pound of potatoes—about four normal servings. Most people can't eat that much at a time. On the other hand, white bread is easy to eat in large amounts. A 75-gram-carbohydrate portion of white bread is only five slices. Other foods that you might have believed were not so good for you, like soft drinks, candy, honey, sugar, flavored milk, and ice cream, are actually very concentrated sources of carbohydrate that can be used to supplement your diet.

Could a High-GI Diet Be Harmful to Athletes?

No. By virtue of their high activity levels, athletes have optimal insulin sensitivity. When they eat high-carbohydrate, high-GI foods, blood-glucose and insulin levels rise far less in them than in the average person. Hence their bodies are not exposed to the dangerous levels that produce disease in sedentary, insulin-resistant individuals.

▶ Case Study

Ian was manager of an under-18 men's hockey team. In addition to his role as manager, he was also in charge of the team's fitness and nutrition programs. He had done quite a lot of reading about the glycemic index and decided to base the team's diet on it.

Despite some early grumbling and moaning, the players stuck to the diet almost 100 percent during the whole two weeks of the championship matches. Ian planned the diet very carefully so that they got all the right foods at the right time— low-GI foods before the game and high-GI foods immediately after, along with jelly beans at halftime!

He noticed that the benefits became very apparent early in the championship. The players themselves were noticing that they were not running out of energy during the game and were recovering a lot more quickly than they had in the past.

About halfway through the tournament other people started to wonder just where this team was getting all its energy from!

"At first they thought it was amusing and perhaps a little strange that we were eating Cocoa Puffs™ and Rice Krispies™ at the team bus in the parking lot immediately after each game, but soon their amusement turned to curiosity," Ian said. "People kept commenting on how fit the team was. But I knew that it wasn't just their fitness. I had not had as much time as I would have liked to work on their fitness, and in fact I remember being concerned just before we went away that their fitness levels may not have been high enough. I knew that what I was seeing was not just their fitness—it was the combination of fitness and a sustained energy supply. It clearly demonstrated to me that you cannot have one without the other.

"We ended up winning the championship by a relatively easy margin, and our fitness and energy levels were certainly a major contributing factor.

"One of the things I liked about using the glycemic index as the basis of the diet was that the players were able to very quickly understand the basic principles, and by the end of the first week they knew exactly what to eat.

"I gave the players a questionnaire to complete at the conclusion of the tournament, and I thought you would be interested to hear some of their comments."

- "I felt that when I played each game I was at my peak. I believe the diet played a major part in this."

- "I found I had more energy coming into and during the game."

- "Energy and glycogen levels were at perfect level."

- "I never felt flat or without energy."

- "Felt really good after every game, never felt run down during the game."

- "Everything made me feel good before, during, and after the game."

- "Diet was major reason we did do well in the champi-onships."

- "Feel better after games, recovery is better, better energy in the game."

- "I was never short of energy. My glycogen levels were constantly maintained and replenished at the necessary points. I always felt fit and healthy."
- "Kept my energy level high in the game and also after the game."
- "After the game, recovery is far more rapid."

Is Your Diet Fit for Peak Performance?

Take the diet-fitness quiz below and see how well you score. It's a good idea to use this quiz regularly to pick up on areas where you may need to improve your diet.

1. Circle your answer.

- I eat at least 3 meals a day with no longer
  than 5 hours in between   Yes/No

▶ Eating patterns

Carbohydrate checker

- I eat at least 4 slices of bread each day
  (1 roll = 2 slices of bread)   Yes/No
- I eat at least 1 cup of breakfast cereal
  each day or an extra slice of bread   Yes/No
- I usually eat 2 or more pieces of fruit
  each day   Yes/No

- I eat at least 3 different vegetables or
  have a salad most days   Yes/No
- I include carbohydrate like pasta, rice,
  and potatoes in my diet each day   Yes/No

Protein checker

- I eat at least 1 and usually 2 servings of
  meat or meat alternatives (poultry, seafood,
  eggs, dried peas/beans, or nuts) each day   Yes/No

Fat checker

- I spread butter or margarine thinly on
  bread or use none at all   Yes/No
- I eat fried food no more than once per week   Yes/No
- I use polyunsaturated or monounsaturated
  oil (canola or olive) for cooking (circle
  yes if you never fry in oil or fat)   Yes/No
- I avoid oil-based dressings on salads   Yes/No
- I use reduced-fat or low-fat dairy products   Yes/No
- I cut the fat off meat and take the skin off
  chicken   Yes/No
- I eat fatty snacks such as chocolate, chips,
  cookies, or rich desserts/cakes etc.
  no more than twice a week   Yes/No
- I eat fast or take-out food no more than
  once per week   Yes/No

Iron checker

- ■ I eat lean red meat at least 3 times per week or 2 servings of white meat daily or, for vegetarians, include at least 1–2 cups of dried peas and beans (e.g., lentils, soy beans, chickpeas) daily   Yes/No
- ■ I include a vitamin C source with meals based on bread, cereals, fruits, and vegetables to assist the iron absorption in these "plant" sources of iron   Yes/No

Calcium checker

- ■ I eat at least 3 servings of dairy food or soy milk alternative each day (1 serving = 8 oz milk or fortified soy milk; 1 slice (1½ oz) hard cheese; 8 oz yogurt)   Yes/No

Fluids

- ■ I drink fluids regularly before, during, and after exercise   Yes/No

Alcohol

- ■ When I drink alcohol, I would mostly drink no more than is recommended for the safe drunk-driving limit (circle yes if you don't drink alcohol)   Yes/No

2. Score 1 point for every "yes" answer

Scoring scale

18–20 Excellent 15–17 Room for improvement

12–14 Just made it 0–12 Poor

Note: Very active people will need to eat more breads, cereals, and fruit than on this quiz, but to stay healthy no one should be eating less.

Part

4

The Glycemic Index Tables

The Tables

An Introduction and How to Use Them

In **this part** we, provide *two* sets of tables: a *condensed* list of approximately 400 of the most popular foods and a *comprehensive* list, which is a complete listing of all the foods that have ever been tested for their GI value. Approximately 1,500 individual foods and mixed meals are included in the expanded, comprehensive list.

The condensed list of tables is arranged in alphabetical order for easy access. Consult this list when you want to locate the GI value of a popular food quickly.

In the comprehensive table, we have listed foods not in exact alphabetical order, but in food categories:

- bakery products
- beverages
- breads

427

- breakfast cereals and bars
- cereal grains
- cookies
- crackers
- dairy products
- fruit and fruit products
- legumes and nuts
- meal-replacement products
- mixed meals and convenience foods
- nutritional- support products
- pasta and noodles
- protein foods
- snack foods and candy
- sports bars
- soups
- sugars
- vegetables
- indigenous and ethnic foods

Within food categories, foods are grouped in alphabetical order to help you choose the low-GI versions within each food group ("this for that") and also to mix and match. If your favorite food has a high GI value, check out its glycemic load. If that's relatively low compared to other foods in that group, then you don't have to worry unduly about its high GI value. If it has both a high GI value and a high GL, try to cut down the serving size or team it with a very low-GI food (e.g., short-grain rice and lentils).

In both tables, you'll find not only the GI but also the glycemic load (GL = carbohydrate content × GI/100). The glycemic load has been calculated using an average serving size and the carbohydrate content of that serving, both of which are also listed in the tables. In this way, you can choose foods with either a low GI value and/or a low GL. Where there are no carbohydrate or GL values supplied, refer to the mean figures shown.

In the condensed tables, we provide the *average* result for a particular food. The average may be the mean of ten studies of that food worldwide or of only two to four studies. In a few instances data from the United States differ from that of the rest of the world, and in those cases we present the American data rather than the average.

In a significant change from the previous edition, the comprehensive tables now present *all* the data available—not simply average figures. Included are GI values from all over the world, including the United States, Canada, Australia, New Zealand, Italy, Sweden, Japan, and China, among others. Ethnic and indigenous foods and dishes have also been included. Quite simply, these are the most comprehensive lists available anywhere. We continue to be amazed and impressed by how many readers ask for more detailed information on GI—and increasingly, glycemic load—data and we include this comprehensive international GI and glycemic load data to acknowledge and meet this interest.

In these new editions of the tables, we also include foods that have very little carbohydrate and have therefore been automatically omitted from previous editions. However, since so many people ask us for the GI values of these foods, we decided to include them and show their GI value as zero, indicated by [0]. Many vegetables, such as avocados and broccoli, and protein foods such as chicken, cheese, and tuna, fall into the low- or no-carbohydrate category.

A Word about Glycemic Load

Some readers will undoubtedly want to know what total glycemic load they should aim for. This depends on many factors—your total energy intake and the carbohydrate intake you are aiming for (moderate or high, as discussed on pages 27 to 28). If you are aiming for 250 grams of carbohydrate per day from low-GI sources alone (foods 55), then the total glycemic load for the whole day should be less than 250 × 55/100 = 138 (rounded up).

Remember, however, that you don't need to eat all your

carbohydrate from low-GI sources. If half of your carbohydrate is from low-GI sources, you are doing well. In this case, you should aim for a glycemic load of about 250 × 65/100 = 163 (rounded up).

Remember, too, that the average serving size is just that—and it may not be yours. If in doubt, weigh out your actual serving size and adjust the carbohydrate per serving and glycemic load proportionately.

We urge you not to make the mistake of using the glycemic load alone. If you do, you might find yourself eating a diet with very little carbohydrate but a lot of fat, especially saturated fat, and excessive amounts of protein. That's a mistake for the reasons outlined on pages 25 to 26. For your overall health, the fat, fiber, and micronutrient content of your diet is also important. A dietitian can guide you further with healthy food choices.

As we have mentioned, foods are continually being tested for their GI values. But we have a long way to go before we know the GI value of every food. If you can't find a GI value for a food you eat on many occasions, please write, call, or e-mail the manufacturer and encourage them to have the glycemic index of the food tested by an accredited laboratory, such as the Sydney University Glycemic Index Research Service (SUGiRS), reachable at www.glycemicindex.com.

Finally, the GI values in these tables are correct at the time of publication. However, the formulation of commercial foods can change, and the GI values may subsequently change. We continually update our website, www.glycemicindex.com, with revised and new data.

Acknowledgment

These tables would not be as comprehensive as they are without the efforts of Dr. Susanna Holt of the Human Nutrition Unit, University of Sydney. Dr. Holt is the research manager of Sydney University Glycemic Index Research Service (SUGiRS) and particularly responsible for the high quality and large quantity of the Australian data included in the tables.

Condensed Tables

FOOD	GI VALUE GLUCOSE = 100	NOMINAL SERVING SIZE	AVAILABLE CARB PER SERVING	GL PER SERVING
All-Bran®, breakfast cereal	30	½ cup	15	4
All Sport™ (orange) sports drink	53	8 oz	15	8
Almonds	[0]	1.75 oz	0	0
Angel food cake, 1 slice	67	¹⁄₁₂ cake	29	19
Apple, 1 medium	38 (avg)	4 oz	15	6
Apple, dried	29	9 rings	34	10
Apple juice, pure, unsweetened, reconstituted	40	8 oz	29	12
Apple muffin, small	44	3.5 oz	41	18
Apricots, fresh, 3 medium	57	4 oz	9	5
Apricots, canned in light syrup	64	4 halves	19	12
Apricots, dried	30	17 halves	27	8
Arborio, risotto rice, boiled	69	¾ cup	53	36
Artichokes (Jerusalem)	[0]	½ cup	0	0
Avocado	[0]	¼	0	0
Bagel, white	72	½	35	25
Baked beans	38 (avg)	⅔ cup	31	12
Baked beans, canned in tomato sauce	48 (avg)	⅔ cup	15	7
Banana, raw, 1 medium	52 (avg)	4 oz	24	12
Banana cake, 1 slice	47	⅛ cake	38	18
Barley, pearled, boiled	25 (avg)	1 cup	42	11

[0] indicates that the food has so little carbohydrate that the GI value cannot be tested. The GL is therefore 0.

FOOD	GI VALUE GLUCOSE = 100	NOMINAL SERVING SIZE	AVAILABLE CARB PER SERVING	GL PER SERVING
Basmati rice, white, boiled	58	1 cup	38	22
Beef		[0]	4 oz	0
Beets, canned	64	½ cup	7	5
Bengal gram dhal, chickpea	11	5 oz	36	4
Black bean soup	64	1 cup	27	17
Black beans, boiled	30	⅘ cup	23	7
Black-eyed peas, canned	42	⅔ cup	17	7
Blueberry muffin, small	59	3.5 oz	47	28
Bok choy, raw	[0]	1 cup	0	0
Bran Flakes™, breakfast cereal	74	½ cup	18	13
Bran muffin, small	60	3.5 oz	41	25
Brazil nuts	[0]	1.75 oz	0	0
Breton wheat crackers	67	6 crackers	14	10
Broad beans	79	½ cup	11	9
Broad beans (Canada)	79	⅓ cup	11	9
Broccoli, raw	[0]	1 cup	0	0
Broken rice, white, cooked in rice cooker	86	1 cup	43	37
Buckwheat	54 (avg)	¾ cup	30	16
Bulgur, boiled 20 min	48 (avg)	¾ cup	26	12
Bun, hamburger	61	1.5 oz	22	13
Butter beans, canned	31	⅔ cup	20	6
Cabbage, raw	[0]	1 cup	0	0

[0] indicates that the food has so little carbohydrate that the GI value cannot be tested. The GL is therefore 0.

FOOD	GI VALUE GLUCOSE = 100	NOMINAL SERVING SIZE	AVAILABLE CARB PER SERVING	GL PER SERVING
Cactus Nectar, Organic Agave, light, 90% fructose (Western Commerce, USA)	11	1 Tbsp	8	1
Cactus Nectar, Organic Agave, light, 97% fructose (Western Commerce, USA)	10	1 Tbsp	8	1
Cantaloupe, raw	65	4 oz	6	4
Capellini pasta, boiled	45	1½ cups	45	20
Carrots, mean of four studies, raw	47	1 medium	6	3
Carrots, peeled, boiled	49	½ cup	5	2
Cauliflower	[0]	¾ cup	0	0
Cashew nuts, salted (Coles Supermarkets, Australia)	22	1.75 oz	13	3
Celery	[0]	2 stalks	0	0
Cheese	[0]	4 oz	0	0
Cherries, raw	22	18	12	3
Chickpeas, canned	42	⅔ cup	22	9
Chickpeas, dried, boiled	28 (avg)	⅔ cup	30	8
Chicken nuggets, frozen, reheated in microwave oven 5 min	46	4 oz	16	7
Chocolate, milk	42	8 oz	31	13
Chocolate, white, Milky Bar®	44	1.75 oz	29	13
Chocolate cake made from mix with chocolate frosting	38	4 oz	52	20
Chocolate mousse, 2% fat	31	½ cup	22	7

[0] indicates that the food has so little carbohydrate that the GI value cannot be tested. The GL is therefore 0.

FOOD	GI VALUE GLUCOSE = 100	NOMINAL SERVING SIZE	AVAILABLE CARB PER SERVING	GL PER SERVING
Chocolate powder, dissolved in water	55	8 oz	16	9
Chocolate pudding, made from powder and whole milk	47	½ cup	24	11
Choice dm™, nutrional support product, vanilla (Mead Johnson, USA)	23	8 oz	24	6
Clif® Bar (cookies & cream)	101	2.4 oz	34	34
Coca-Cola®, soft drink	53	8 oz	26	14
Cocoa Puffs™, breakfast cereal	77	1 cup	26	20
Complete™, breakfast cereal	48	1 cup	21	10
Condensed milk, sweetened	61	2½ Tbsp	27	17
Corn Flakes™, breakfast cereal	92	1 cup	26	24
Corn Flakes™, Honey Crunch, breakfast cereal	72	1 cup	24	17
Cornmeal, boiled in salted water 2 min	68	1 cup	13	9
Corn pasta, gluten-free	78	1¼ cups	42	32
Corn Pops™, breakfast cereal	80	1 cup	26	21
Corn, sweet, boiled (USA)	60	½ cup	18	11
Corn Thins, puffed corn cakes, gluten-free	87	1 oz	20	18
Couscous, boiled 5 min	65 (avg)	¾ cup	35	23
Cranberry juice cocktail	52	8 oz	31	16
Crispix™, breakfast cereal	87	1 cup	25	22

[0] indicates that the food has so little carbohydrate that the GI value cannot be tested. The GL is therefore 0.

FOOD	GI VALUE GLUCOSE = 100	NOMINAL SERVING SIZE	AVAILABLE CARB PER SERVING	GL PER SERVING
Croissant, medium	67	2 oz	26	17
Crumpet	69	2 oz	19	13
Cucumber	[0]	¾ cup	0	0
Cupcake, strawberry-iced, small	73	1.5 oz	26	19
Custard, homemade from milk, wheat starch, and sugar	43	½ cup	26	11
Custard, prepared from powder with whole milk, no bake	35	½ cup	26	9
Custard apple, raw, flesh only	54	4 oz	19	10
Cytomax™ (orange) sports drink	62	8 oz	15	9
Dates, dried, bahri	50	7	40	20
Desiree potato, peeled, boiled 35 min	101	5 oz	17	17
Doughnut, cake type	76	1.75 oz	23	17
Egg custard, prepared from powder with whole milk, no bake	35	½ cup	26	9
Eggs, large	[0]	2	0	0
Enercal Plus™ (Wyeth-Ayerst, USA)	61	8 oz	40	24
English Muffin™ bread	77	1 oz	14	11
Ensure™, vanilla drink	48	8 oz	34	16

[0] indicates that the food has so little carbohydrate that the GI value cannot be tested. The GL is therefore 0.

FOOD	GI VALUE GLUCOSE = 100	NOMINAL SERVING SIZE	AVAILABLE CARB PER SERVING	GL PER SERVING
Ensure™ bar, chocolate fudge brownie	43	1.4 oz	20	8
Ensure Plus™, vanilla drink	40	8 oz	47	19
Ensure Pudding™, old-fashioned vanilla	36	4 oz	26	9
Fanta®, orange soft drink	68	8 oz	34	23
Fettuccine, egg, cooked	32	1½ cups	46	15
Figs, dried	61	3	26	16
Fish		[0]	4 oz	0
Fish sticks	38	3.5 oz	19	7
Flan/crème caramel	65	½ cup	73	47
French baguette, white, plain	95	1 oz	15	15
French beans (runner beans), boiled	[0]	½ cup	0	0
French fries, frozen, reheated in microwave	75	30 pcs	29	22
French vanilla cake made from mix with vanilla frosting	42	4 oz	58	24
French vanilla ice cream, premium, 16% fat	38	½ cup	14	5
Froot Loops™, breakfast cereal	69	1 cup	26	18
Frosted Flakes™, breakfast cereal	55	1 cup	26	15
Fructose, pure	19 (avg)	1 Tbsp	10	2
Fruit cocktail, canned	55	½ cup	16	9

[0] indicates that the food has so little carbohydrate that the GI value cannot be tested. The GL is therefore 0.

FOOD	GI VALUE GLUCOSE = 100	NOMINAL SERVING SIZE	AVAILABLE CARB PER SERVING	GL PER SERVING
Fruit Fingers, Heinz Kidz™, banana	61	30	20	12
Fruit leather	61	2 pcs	24	15
GatorLode® (orange) sports drink	100	8 oz	15	15
Gatorade™ (orange) sports drink	89	8 oz	15	13
Glucerna™, vanilla (Abbott, USA)	31	8 oz	23	7
Glucose tablets	102	3 pcs	15	15
Glucose (dextrose), mean of 11 studies	99	1 Tbsp	10	10
Gluten-free white bread, sliced	80	1 oz	15	12
Gluten-free multigrain bread	79	1 oz	13	10
Gluten-free muesli, with 1.5% fat milk	39	1 oz	19	7
Gluten-free corn pasta	78	1½ cups	42	32
Gluten-free rice and corn pasta	76	1½ cups	49	37
Gluten-free split pea and soy pasta shells	29	1½ cups	31	9
Gluten-free spaghetti, rice and split pea, canned in tomato sauce	68	8 oz	27	19
Glutinous rice, white, cooked in rice cooker	92 (avg)	⅔ cup	48	44

[0] indicates that the food has so little carbohydrate that the GI value cannot be tested. The GL is therefore 0.

FOOD	GI VALUE GLUCOSE = 100	NOMINAL SERVING SIZE	AVAILABLE CARB PER SERVING	GL PER SERVING
Gnocchi	68	6 oz	48	33
Grapefruit, raw, medium	25	½	11	3
Grapefruit juice, unsweetened	48	8 oz	20	9
Grapenuts™ (Kraft, USA)	75	¼ cup	22	16
Grapes, green	46 (avg)	¾ cup	18	8
Green peas, mean of three studies	48	⅓ cup	7	3
Green pea soup, canned	66	8 oz	41	27
Hamburger bun	61	1.5 oz	22	13
Happiness™ (cinnamon, raisin, pecan bread) (Natural Ovens, USA)	63	1 oz	14	9
Hazelnuts	[0]	1.75 oz	0	0
Healthy Choice™ Hearty 7 Grain (Con Agra Inc., USA)	55	1 oz	14	8
Healthy Choice™ Hearty 100% Whole Grain (Con Agra Inc., USA)	62	1 oz	14	9
Honey	55 (avg)	1 Tbsp	18	10
Hot cereal, apple & cinnamon (Con Agra Inc., USA)	37	1.2 oz dry	22	8
Hot cereal, unflavored (Con Agra Inc., USA)	25	1.2 oz dry	19	5
Hunger Filler™, whole-grain bread (Natural Ovens, USA)	59	1 oz	13	7
Ice cream, regular fat	61 (avg)	½ cup	20	12

[0] indicates that the food has so little carbohydrate that the GI value cannot be tested. The GL is therefore 0.

FOOD	GI VALUE GLUCOSE = 100	NOMINAL SERVING SIZE	AVAILABLE CARB PER SERVING	GL PER SERVING
Ice cream, low fat, vanilla, "light"	50	½ cup	9	5
Ice cream, premium, French vanilla, 16% fat	38	½ cup	14	5
Ice cream, premium, "ultra chocolate," 15% fat	37	½ cup	14	5
Instant potato, prepared	85 (avg)	¾ cup	20	17
Instant rice, white, cooked 6 min	74	¾ cup	42	36
Ironman PR bar®, chocolate	39	2.3 oz	26	10
Jam, apricot fruit spread, reduced sugar	55	1½ Tbsp	13	7
Jam, strawberry	51	1½ Tbsp	20	10
Jasmine rice, white, cooked in rice cooker	109	1 cup	42	46
Jelly beans	78 (avg)	10 large	28	22
Kaiser roll	73	½	16	12
Kavli™ Norwegian crispbread	71	5 pcs	16	12
Kidney beans, canned	52	⅔ cup	17	9
Kidney beans	46	¾ cup	18	8
Kidney beans, boiled	23 (avg)	⅔ cup	25	6
Kiwi fruit	53	4 oz	12	7
Kudos® Whole Grain Bars, chocolate chip	62	1.8 oz	32	20
Lactose, pure	46 (avg)	1 Tbsp	10	5

[0] indicates that the food has so little carbohydrate that the GI value cannot be tested. The GL is therefore 0.

FOOD	GI VALUE GLUCOSE = 100	NOMINAL SERVING SIZE	AVAILABLE CARB PER SERVING	GL PER SERVING
Lamb		[0]	4 oz	0
Leafy vegetables (spinach, rocket, etc.), raw	[0]	1½ cup	0	0
L.E.A.N Fibergy™ bar, Harvest Oat	45	1.75 oz	29	13
L.E.A.N Life long Nutribar™, Peanut Crunch	30	1.5 oz	19	6
L.E.A.N Life long Nutribar™, Chocolate Crunch	32	1.5 oz	19	6
L.E.A.N Nutrimeal™, drink powder, Dutch Chocolate	26	8 oz	13	3
Lemonade, reconstituted	66	8 oz	20	13
Lentils, canned	44	9 oz	21	9
Lentils, green, boiled	30 (avg)	¾ cup	17	5
Lentils	29 (avg)	¾ cup	18	5
Lentils, red, boiled	26	¾ cup	18	5
Lettuce	[0]	4 leaves	0	0
Life Savers®, peppermint candy	70	18 pcs	30	21
Light rye bread	68	1 oz	14	10
Lima beans, baby, frozen, reheated in microwave oven	32	¾ cup	30	10
Linguine pasta, thick, cooked	46	1½ cups	48	22
Linguine pasta, thin, cooked	52	1½ cups	45	23
Lychees, canned in syrup, drained	79	4 oz	20	16

[0] indicates that the food has so little carbohydrate that the GI value cannot be tested. The GL is therefore 0.

FOOD	GI VALUE GLUCOSE = 100	NOMINAL SERVING SIZE	AVAILABLE CARB PER SERVING	GL PER SERVING
M & M's®, peanut	33	15 pcs	17	6
Macadamia nuts	[0]	1.75 oz	0	0
Macaroni, cooked	47 (avg)	1¼ cups	48	23
Macaroni and cheese, boxed	64	1 cup	51	32
Maltose	105	1 Tbsp	10	11
Mango	51	4 oz	15	8
Marmalade, orange (Australia)	48	1½ Tbsp	20	9
Mars Bar®	68	2 oz	40	27
Melba toast, Old London	70	6 pcs	23	16
METRx® Bar (vanilla)	74	3.6 oz	50	37
Milk, full fat cow's milk, fresh	31	8 oz	12	4
Milk, skim	32	8 oz	13	4
Milk, low fat, chocolate, with sugar	34	8 oz	26	9
Milk, condensed, sweetened	61	2½ Tbsp	27	17
Milk Arrowroot™ cookies	69	5	18	12
Milky Bar®, chocolate, white	44	1.75 oz	29	13
Millet, boiled	71	⅔ cup	36	25
Mini Wheats™, whole-wheat breakfast cereal	58	12 pcs	21	12
Mini Wheats™, black currant whole-wheat breakfast cereal	72	1 cup	21	15
Mousse, butterscotch, 1.9% fat	36	1.75 oz	10	4
Mousse, chocolate, 2% fat	31	1.75 oz	11	3
Mousse, hazelnut, 2.4% fat	36	1.75 oz	10	4

[0] indicates that the food has so little carbohydrate that the GI value cannot be tested. The GL is therefore 0.

FOOD	GI VALUE GLUCOSE = 100	NOMINAL SERVING SIZE	AVAILABLE CARB PER SERVING	GL PER SERVING
Mousse, mango, 1.8% fat	33	1.75 oz	11	4
Mousse, mixed berry, 2.2% fat	36	1.75 oz	10	4
Mousse, strawberry, 2.3% fat	32	1.75 oz	10	3
Muesli bar containing dried fruit	61	1 oz	21	13
Muesli bread, made from mix in bread oven (Con Agra Inc., USA)	54	1 oz	12	7
Muesli, gluten-free with 1.5% fat milk	39	1 oz	19	7
Muesli, toasted	43	1 oz	17	7
Muesli, Swiss Formula	56	1 oz	16	9
Multi-Grain 9-Grain bread	43	1 oz	14	6
Nesquik™, chocolate dissolved in 1.5% fat milk, no-sugar-added	41	8 oz	11	5
Nesquik™, strawberry dissolved in 1.5% fat milk, no-sugar-added	35	8 oz	12	4
New potato, unpeeled and boiled 20 min	78	5 oz	21	16
New potato, canned, heated in microwave 3 min	65	5 oz	18	12
Noodles, instant "two-minute" Maggi®	46	1½ cups	40	19
Noodles, mung bean (Lungkow beanthread), dried, boiled	39	1½ cups	45	18

[0] indicates that the food has so little carbohydrate that the GI value cannot be tested. The GL is therefore 0.

FOOD	GI VALUE GLUCOSE = 100	NOMINAL SERVING SIZE	AVAILABLE CARB PER SERVING	GL PER SERVING
Noodles, rice, freshly made, boiled	40	1½ cups	39	15
Nutella®, chocolate hazelnut spread	33	1 Tbsp	12	4
Nutrigrain™, breakfast cereal	66	1 cup	15	10
Nutty Natural™, whole-grain bread (Natural Ovens, USA)	59	1 oz	12	7
Oat bran, raw	55 (avg)	2 Tbsp	5	3
Oatmeal	42	1 cup	21	9
Oatmeal cookies	55	4 small	21	12
Orange, medium	42 (avg)	4 oz	11	5
Orange juice, unsweetened, reconstituted	53	8 oz	18	9
Pancakes, prepared from mix	67	2–4"	58	39
Pancakes, buckwheat, gluten-free	102	2–4"	22	22 made from mix
Papaya	56	4 oz	8	5
Parsnips	97	½ cup	12	12
Pastry	59	2 oz	26	15
Peach, fresh, large	42 (avg)	4 oz	11	5
Peach, canned in heavy syrup	58	½ cup	15	9
Peach, canned in light syrup	52	½ cup	18	9
Peanuts, mean of three studies	14	1.75 oz	6	1
Peanuts, roasted, salted	14 (avg)	1.75 oz	6	1
Pear, raw	38 (avg)	4 oz	11	4

[0] indicates that the food has so little carbohydrate that the GI value cannot be tested. The GL is therefore 0.

FOOD	GI VALUE GLUCOSE = 100	NOMINAL SERVING SIZE	AVAILABLE CARB PER SERVING	GL PER SERVING
Pear halves, canned in natural juice	43	½ cup	13	5
Peas, green, frozen, boiled	48 (avg)	½ cup	7	3
Pecans	[0]	1.75 oz	0	0
Pepper, green or red	[0]	3 oz	0	0
Pineapple, raw	66	4 oz	10	6
Pineapple juice, unsweetened	46	8 oz	34	15
Pinto beans, canned	45	⅔ cup	22	10
Pinto beans, dried, boiled	39	¾ cup	26	10
Pita bread, white	57	1 oz	17	10
Pizza, cheese	60	1 slice	27	16
Pizza, Super Supreme, pan (11.4% fat)	36	1 slice	24	9
Pizza, Super Supreme, thin and crispy (13.2% fat)	30	1 slice	22	7
Plums, raw	39	2 med	12	5
Pop Tarts™, double chocolate	70	1.8 oz pastry	36	25
Popcorn, plain, cooked in microwave oven	72	1½ cups	11	8
Pork		[0]	4 oz	0
Potato, baked	85 (avg)	5 oz	30	26
Potato, type NS ▲, microwaved (USA)	82	5 oz	33	27
Potato chips, plain, salted	57	2 oz	18	10
Pound cake	54	2 oz	28	15
Pound cake (Sara Lee)	54	2 oz	28	15

[0] indicates that the food has so little carbohydrate that the GI value cannot be tested. The GL is therefore 0.

▲ indicates brand not specified

FOOD	GI VALUE GLUCOSE = 100	NOMINAL SERVING SIZE	AVAILABLE CARB PER SERVING	GL PER SERVING
Poweraid® (orange) sports drink	65	8 oz	15	10
PowerBar® (chocolate)	83	2.6 oz	42	35
PR*Bar® (cookies & cream)	81	4.2 oz		
Premium soda crackers	74	5 crackers	17	12
Pretzels, oven-baked, traditional wheat flavor	83	1 oz	20	16
Prunes, pitted	29	6	33	10
Pudding, instant, chocolate, made from powder and whole milk	47	½ cup	24	11
Pudding, instant, vanilla, made from powder and whole milk	40	½ cup	24	10
Puffed crispbread	81	1 oz	19	15
Puffed rice cakes, white	82	3 cakes	21	17
Puffed Wheat, breakfast cereal	80	2 cups	21	17
Pumpernickel rye kernel bread	41	1 oz	12	5
Pumpkin	75	3 oz	4	3
Quik™, chocolate (Nestlé, Australia), dissolved in 1.5% fat milk	41	8 oz	11	5
Quik™, strawberry (Nestlé, Australia), dissolved in 1.5% fat milk	35	8 oz	12	4

[0] indicates that the food has so little carbohydrate that the GI value cannot be tested. The GL is therefore 0.

FOOD	GI VALUE GLUCOSE = 100	NOMINAL SERVING SIZE	AVAILABLE CARB PER SERVING	GL PER SERVING
Raisin Bran™, breakfast cereal	61	½ cup	19	12
Raisins	64	½ cup	44	28
Ravioli, durum wheat flour, meat filled, boiled	39	6.5 oz	38	15
Real Fruit Bars, strawberry processed fruit bars	90	1 oz	26	23
Red-skinned potato, peeled, boiled 35 min	88	5 oz	18	16
Red-skinned potato, peeled and microwaved on high for 6–7.5 min	79	5 oz	18	14
Red-skinned potato, peeled, cubed, boiled 15 min, mashed	91	5 oz	20	18
Resource Diabetic™, nutritional support product, vanilla (Novartis, USA)	34	8 oz	23	8
Rice, brown, steamed (USA)	50	1 cup	33	16
Rice, parboiled (USA)	72	1 cup	36	26
Rice, Converted®, white, boiled 20–30 min, Uncle Ben's® (USA)	38	1 cup	36	14
Rice, Converted®, white, long grain, boiled 20–30 min, Uncle Ben's® (USA)	50	1 cup	36	18
Rice, long grain, boiled, 10 min (USA)	61	1 cup	36	22

[0] indicates that the food has so little carbohydrate that the GI value cannot be tested. The GL is therefore 0.

FOOD	GI VALUE GLUCOSE = 100	NOMINAL SERVING SIZE	AVAILABLE CARB PER SERVING	GL PER SERVING
Rice and corn pasta, gluten-free	76	1½ cups	49	37
Rice bran, extruded	19	1 oz	14	3
Rice cakes, white	78	3 cakes	21	17
Rice Krispies™, breakfast cereal	87	1¼ cups	26	21
Rice Krispies Treat™ bar	63	1 oz	24	15
Rice noodles, freshly made, boiled	40	1½ cups	39	15
Rice pasta, brown, boiled 16 min	92	1½ cups	38	35
Rice vermicelli	58	1½ cups	39	22
Risotto rice, arborio, boiled	69	¾ cup	53	36
Roll (bread), kaiser	73	½	16	12
Rolled oats	42	1 cup	21	9
Roll-Ups®, processed fruit snack	99	1 oz	25	24
Russet, baked potato, mean of four studies	85	5 oz	30	26
Rye bread	58 (avg)	1 oz	14	8
Ryvita® crackers	69	3 slices	16	11
Salami	[0]	4 oz	0	0
Sausages, fried	28	3.5 oz	3	1
Scones, plain	92	1 oz	9	8
Sebago potato, peeled, boiled 35 min	87	5 oz	17	14

[0] indicates that the food has so little carbohydrate that the GI value cannot be tested. The GL is therefore 0.

FOOD	GI VALUE GLUCOSE = 100	NOMINAL SERVING SIZE	AVAILABLE CARB PER SERVING	GL PER SERVING
Seeded rye bread	55	1 oz	13	7
Semolina, steamed	55	⅓ cup (dry)	50	28
Shellfish (shrimp, crab, lobster etc.)	[0]	4 oz	0	0
Shortbread cookies	64	1 oz	16	10
Shredded Wheat, breakfast cereal	75 (avg)	⅔ cup	20	15
Shredded Wheat™ biscuits	62	1 oz	18	11
Skittles®	70	45 pcs	45	32
Smacks™, breakfast cereal	71	¾ cup	23	11
Smoothie, raspberry (Con Agra Inc., USA)	33	8 oz	41	14
Snack bar, Apple Cinnamon (Con Agra Inc., USA)	40	1.75 oz	29	12
Snack bar, Peanut Butter & Choc-Chip (Con Agra Inc. USA)	37	1.75 oz	27	10
Snickers Bar®	68	2.2 oz	35	23
Social Tea Biscuits	55	6 cookies	19	10
Soda Crackers, Premium	74	5 crackers	17	12
Soft drink, Coca-Cola®	53	8 oz	26	14
Soft drink, Fanta®, orange	68	8 oz	34	23
Sourdough rye	48	1 oz	12	6
Sourdough wheat	54	1 oz	14	8

[0] indicates that the food has so little carbohydrate that the GI value cannot be tested. The GL is therefore 0.

FOOD	GI VALUE GLUCOSE = 100	NOMINAL SERVING SIZE	AVAILABLE CARB PER SERVING	GL PER SERVING
Soy & Flaxseed bread (mix in bread oven) (Con Agra Inc., USA)	50	1 oz	10	5
Soybeans, dried, boiled	20	1 cup	6	1
Soybeans, canned	14	1 cup	6	1
Spaghetti, durum wheat, boiled 20 min (USA)	64	1½ cups	43	27
Spaghetti, gluten-free, rice and split pea, canned in tomato sauce	68	8 oz	27	19
Spaghetti, white, boiled 5 min	38 (avg)	1½ cups	48	18
Spaghetti, whole wheat, boiled 5 min	32	1½ cups	44	14
Special K™, breakfast cereal	69	1 cup	21	14
Spirali pasta, durum wheat, white, boiled to al dente texture	43	1½ cups	44	19
Split pea and soy pasta shells, gluten-free	29	1½ cups	31	9
Split pea soup	60	1 cup	27	16
Split peas, yellow, boiled 20 min	32	¾ cup	19	6
Sponge cake, plain	46	2 oz	36	17
Squash, raw	[0]	⅔ cup	0	0
Star pastina, white, boiled 5 min	38	1½ cups	48	18

[0] indicates that the food has so little carbohydrate that the GI value cannot be tested. The GL is therefore 0.

FOOD	GI VALUE GLUCOSE = 100	NOMINAL SERVING SIZE	AVAILABLE CARB PER SERVING	GL PER SERVING
Stay Trim™, whole-grain bread (Natural Ovens, USA)	70	1 oz	15	10
Stoned Wheat Thins	67	14 crackers	17	12
100% stone-ground whole-wheat bread	53	1 slice	13	7
Strawberry jam	51	1½ Tbsp	20	10
Strawberry shortcake	42	8 oz	1	1
Stuffing, bread	74	1 oz	21	16
Sucrose	68 (avg)	1 Tbsp	10	7
Super Supreme pizza, pan (11.4% fat)	36	1 slice	24	9
Super Supreme pizza, thin and crispy (13.2% fat)	30	1 slice	22	7
Sushi, salmon	48	3.5 oz	36	17
Sweet corn, whole kernel, canned, diet-pack, drained	46	1 cup	28	13
Sweet potato	44	5 oz	25	11
Sweetened condensed milk	61	8 oz	136	83
Taco shells, cornmeal-based, baked	68	2 shells	12	8
Tapioca, boiled with milk	81	¾ cup	18	14
Tofu-based frozen dessert, chocolate with high-fructose (24%) corn syrup	115	1.75 oz	9	10
Tomato soup	38	1 cup	17	6
Tortellini, cheese	50	6.5 oz	21	10

[0] indicates that the food has so little carbohydrate that the GI value cannot be tested. The GL is therefore 0.

FOOD	GI VALUE GLUCOSE = 100	NOMINAL SERVING SIZE	AVAILABLE CARB PER SERVING	GL PER SERVING
Tortilla chips, plain, salted	63	1.75 oz	26	17
Total™, breakfast cereal	76	¾ cup	22	17
Tuna		[0]	4 oz	0
Twix® Cookie Bar, caramel	44	2 cookies	39	17
Ultracal™ with fiber (Mead Johnson, USA)	40	8 oz	29	12
Ultra chocolate ice cream, premium, 15% fat	37	½ cup	14	5
Vanilla cake made from mix with vanilla frosting	42	4 oz	58	24
Vanilla pudding, instant, made from powder and whole milk	40	½ cup	24	10
Vanilla wafers	77	6 cookies	18	14
Veal	[0]	4 oz	0	0
Vermicelli, white, boiled	35	1½ cups	44	16
Waffles	76	1	13	10
Waffles, Aunt Jemima®	76	½ waffle	13	10
Walnuts	[0]	1.75 oz	0	0
Water crackers	78	7 crackers	18	14
Watermelon, raw	72	4 oz	6	4
Weet-Bix™, breakfast cereal	69	2 biscuits	17	12
Wheaties™, breakfast cereal	82	1 cup	21	17

[0] indicates that the food has so little carbohydrate that the GI value cannot be tested. The GL is therefore 0.

FOOD	GI VALUE GLUCOSE = 100	NOMINAL SERVING SIZE	AVAILABLE CARB PER SERVING	GL PER SERVING
White bread	70	1 oz	14	10
100% Whole Grain™ bread	51	1 oz	13	7 (Natural Ovens, USA)
Whole-wheat bread, wheat flour	77	1 oz	12	9
Wonder™ white bread	80	1 oz	14	11
XLR8® (orange) sports drink	68	8 oz	15	10
Xylitol, mean of two studies	8	1 Tbsp	10	1
Yam, peeled, boiled	37 (avg)	5 oz	36	13
Yogurt, low fat, fruit, with artificial sweetener	14	8 oz	15	2
Yogurt, low fat, fruit, with sugar	33	8 oz	35	12
Yogurt, low fat (0.9%), wild strawberry	31	8 oz	34	11

[0] indicates that the food has so little carbohydrate that the GI value cannot be tested. The GL is therefore 0.

Comprehensive Tables

FOOD	GI VALUE GLUCOSE = 100	NOMINAL SERVING SIZE	AVAILABLE CARB PER SERVING	GL PER SERVING
BAKERY PRODUCTS				
Cakes				
Angel food cake (Loblaw's, Toronto, Canada)	67	50	29	19
Banana cake, made with sugar	47	80	38	18
Banana cake, made without sugar	55	80	29	16
Chocolate cake, made from packet mix with chocolate frosting (Betty Crocker)	38	111	52	20
Cupcake, strawberry-iced	73	38	26	19
Lamingtons (sponge dipped in chocolate and coconut)	87	50	29	25
Pound cake (Sara Lee)	54	53	28	15
Sponge cake, plain	46	63	36	17
Vanilla cake, made from packet mix with vanilla frosting (Betty Crocker)	42	111	58	24
Croissant	67	57	26	17
Crumpet	69	50	19	13
Doughnut, cake type	76	47	23	17
Flan cake	65	70	48	31

FOOD	GI VALUE GLUCOSE = 100	NOMINAL SERVING SIZE	AVAILABLE CARB PER SERVING	GL PER SERVING
Muffins				
Apple, made with sugar	44	60	29	13
Apple, made without sugar	48	60	19	9
Apple, oat, raisin, made from packet mix	54	50	26	14
Apricot, coconut and honey, made from packet mix	60	50	26	16
Banana, oat and honey, made from packet mix	65	50	26	17
Bran	60	57	24	15
Blueberry	59	57	29	17
Carrot	62	57	32	20
Chocolate butterscotch, made from packet mix	53	50	28	15
Corn muffin, low-amylose	102	57	29	30
Corn muffin, high-amylose	49	57	29	14
Oatmeal, muffin, made from mix (Quaker Oats)	69	50	35	24
Pancakes, prepared from shake mix	67	80	58	39
Pancakes, buckwheat, gluten-free, made from packet mix (Orgran)	102	77	22	22
Pastry	59	57	26	15
Pikelets, Golden brand (Tip Top)	85	40	21	18

[0] indicates that the food has so little carbohydrate that the GI value cannot be tested. The GL is therefore 0.

▲ indicates brand not specified

FOOD	GI VALUE GLUCOSE = 100	NOMINAL SERVING SIZE	AVAILABLE CARB PER SERVING	GL PER SERVING
Scones, plain, made from packet mix	92	25	9	8
Waffles, Aunt Jemima	76	35	13	10
BEVERAGES				
Coca-Cola®, soft drink (Australia)	53	250	26	14
Coca-Cola®, soft drink/soda (USA)	63	250	26	16
Cordial, orange, reconstituted (Berri)	66	250	20	13
Fanta®, orange soft drink (Australia)	68	250	34	23
Lucozade®, original (sparkling glucose drink)	95	250	42	40
Smoothie, raspberry (Con Agra)	33	250	41	14
Smoothie drink, soy, banana (So Natural)	30	250	22	7
Smoothie drink, soy, chocolate hazelnut (So Natural)	34	250	25	8
Solo™, lemon squash, soft drink (Australia)	58	250	29	17
Up & Go, cocoa malt flavor (Sanitarium)	43	250	26	11
Up & Go, original malt flavor (Sanitarium)	46	250	24	11

[0] indicates that the food has so little carbohydrate that the GI value cannot be tested. The GL is therefore 0.

▲ indicates brand not specified

FOOD	GI VALUE GLUCOSE = 100	NOMINAL SERVING SIZE	AVAILABLE CARB PER SERVING	GL PER SERVING
Xpress, chocolate (So Natural, Australia)	39	250	34	13
Yakult® (Yakult, Australia)	46	65	12	6

Juices
APPLE JUICE

FOOD	GI VALUE GLUCOSE = 100	NOMINAL SERVING SIZE	AVAILABLE CARB PER SERVING	GL PER SERVING
Apple juice, pure, unsweetened, reconstituted (Australia)	39			
Apple juice, unsweetened	40			
Apple juice, unsweetened (Canada)	41			
■ mean of three studies	40	250	29	12
Apple juice, pure, clear, unsweetened (Wild About Fruit, Australia)	44	250	30	13
Apple juice, pure, cloudy, unsweetened (Wild About Fruit, Australia)	37	250	28	10
Carrot juice, freshly made (Sydney, Australia)	43	250	23	10
Cranberry juice cocktail (Ocean Spray®, Australia)	52	250	31	16
Cranberry juice cocktail (Ocean Spray®, USA)	68	250	36	24
Cranberry juice drink (Ocean Spray®, UK)	56	250	29	16

[0] indicates that the food has so little carbohydrate that the GI value cannot be tested. The GL is therefore 0.

▲ indicates brand not specified

FOOD	GI VALUE GLUCOSE = 100	NOMINAL SERVING SIZE	AVAILABLE CARB PER SERVING	GL PER SERVING
Grapefruit juice, unsweetened (Sunpac, Canada)	48	250	22	11
ORANGE JUICE				
Orange juice (Canada)	46	250	26	12
Orange juice, unsweetened, (Quelch®, Australia)	53	250	18	9
Pineapple juice, unsweetened (Dole, Canada)	46	250	34	16
Tomato juice, canned, no added sugar (Berri, Australia)	38	250	9	4
Sports drinks				
Gatorade® (Australia)	78	250	15	12
Isostar® (Switzerland)	70	250	18	13
Sports Plus® (Australia)	74	250	17	13
Sustagen Sport® (Australia)	43	250	49	21
Drinks made from drinking-mix powders				
Build-Up™ with fiber (Nestlé)	41	250	33	14
Complete Hot Chocolate mix with hot water (Nestlé)	51	250	23	11
Hi-Pro energy drink mix, vanilla (Harrod)	36	250	19	7
Malted milk in full-fat cow's milk (Nestlé, Australia)	45	250	26	12
Milo™ (chocolate nutrient-fortified drink powder)				
Milo™ (Nestlé, Australia), in water	55	250	16	9

[0] indicates that the food has so little carbohydrate that the GI value cannot be tested. The GL is therefore 0.

▲ indicates brand not specified

FOOD	GI VALUE GLUCOSE = 100	NOMINAL SERVING SIZE	AVAILABLE CARB PER SERVING	GL PER SERVING
Milo™ (Nestlé, Auckland, New Zealand), in water	52	250	16	9
Milo™ (Nestlé, Australia), in full-fat cow's milk	35	250	25	9
Milo™ (Nestlé, New Zealand), in full-fat cow's milk	36	250	26	9
Nutrimeal™, meal replacement drink, Dutch Chocolate (Usana)	26	250	17	4
Quik™, chocolate (Nestlé, Australia), in water	53	250	7	4
Quik™, chocolate (Nestlé, Australia), in 1.5% milk	41	250	11	5
Quik™, strawberry (Nestlé, Australia), in water	64	250	8	5
Quik™, strawberry (Nestlé, Australia), in 1.5% milk	35	250	12	4
BREADS				
Bagel, white, frozen (Canada)	72	70	35	25
Baguette, white, plain (France)	95	30	15	15
French baguette with chocolate spread (France)	72	70	37	27
French baguette with butter and strawberry jam (France)	62	70	41	26
Pain au lait (Pasquier, France)	63	60	32	20
Bread stuffing, Paxo (Canada)	74	30	21	16

[0] indicates that the food has so little carbohydrate that the GI value cannot be tested. The GL is therefore 0.

▲ indicates brand not specified

Barley breads

FOOD	GI VALUE GLUCOSE = 100	NOMINAL SERVING SIZE	AVAILABLE CARB PER SERVING	GL PER SERVING
COARSE BARLEY KERNEL BREAD				
75% kernels	27	30	20	5
80% scalded intact kernels (20% white wheat flour)	34	30	20	7
80% intact kernels (20% white wheat flour)	40	30	20	8
BARLEY KERNEL BREAD, 50% KERNELS				
50% kernels (Canada)	43	30	20	9
50% kibbled barley (Australia)	48	30	20	10
Sunflower and barley bread (Riga, Sydney, Australia)	57	30	11	6
BARLEY FLOUR BREADS				
100% barley flour (Canada)	67	30	13	9
Whole-wheat barley flour (80%) bread (Sweden)	67	30	20	13
Whole-wheat barley bread, flat, thin, soft	50	30	15	7
Whole-wheat barley bread, flat, thin, soft, high fiber (Sweden)	43	30	11	5
Whole-wheat barley flour bread	70	30	20	14
Whole-wheat barley flour bread with sourdough (lactic acid)	53	30	20	10
Whole-wheat barley flour bread with lactic acid	66	30	19	12

[0] indicates that the food has so little carbohydrate that the GI value cannot be tested. The GL is therefore 0.

▲ indicates brand not specified

FOOD	GI VALUE GLUCOSE = 100	NOMINAL SERVING SIZE	AVAILABLE CARB PER SERVING	GL PER SERVING
Whole-wheat barley flour bread with calcium lactate	59	30	20	12
Whole-wheat barley flour bread with sodium propionate	65	30	20	13
Whole-wheat barley flour bread with higher dose sodium propionate	57	30	19	11
Buckwheat bread				
Buckwheat bread with 50% white wheat flour (Sweden)	47	30	21	10
Fruit breads				
Bürgen™ Fruit loaf (Tip Top, Australia)	44	30	13	6
Fruit and Spice Loaf, thick sliced (Buttercup, Australia)	54	30	15	8
Continental fruit loaf, wheat bread with dried fruit (Australia)	47	30	15	7
Happiness™ (cinnamon, raisin, pecan bread) (Natural Ovens, USA)	63	30	14	9
Muesli bread, made from packet mix in bread oven (Con Agra Inc., USA)	54	30	12	7
Hamburger bun (Loblaw's, Toronto, Canada)	61	30	15	9
Kaiser rolls (Loblaw's, Canada)	73	30	16	12

[0] indicates that the food has so little carbohydrate that the GI value cannot be tested. The GL is therefore 0.

▲ indicates brand not specified

FOOD	GI VALUE GLUCOSE = 100	NOMINAL SERVING SIZE	AVAILABLE CARB PER SERVING	GL PER SERVING
Melba toast, Old London (Best Foods Canada Inc.)	70	30	23	16
Gluten-free breads				
Gluten-free multigrain bread (Country Life Bakeries, Australia)	79	30	13	10
Gluten-free white bread, unsliced (gluten-free wheat starch) (UK)	71	30	15	11
Gluten-free white bread, sliced (gluten-free wheat starch) (UK)	80	30	15	12
■ *mean of two studies*	76	30	15	11
Gluten-free fiber-enriched, unsliced (gluten-free wheat starch, soya bran) (UK)	69	30	13	9
Gluten-free fiber-enriched, sliced (gluten-free wheat starch, soya bran) (UK)	76	30	13	10
■ *mean of two studies*	73	30	13	9
Oat bread				
Coarse oat kernel bread, 80% intact oat kernels (Sweden)	65	30	19	12
Oat bran bread				
50% oat bran (Australia)	44	30	18	8

[0] indicates that the food has so little carbohydrate that the GI value cannot be tested. The GL is therefore 0.

▲ indicates brand not specified

FOOD	GI VALUE GLUCOSE = 100	NOMINAL SERVING SIZE	AVAILABLE CARB PER SERVING	GL PER SERVING
45% oat bran and 50% wheat flour (Sweden)	50	30	18	9
■ *mean of two studies*	47	30	18	9
Rice bread				
Rice bread, low-amylose Calrose rice (Pav's, Australia)	72	30	12	8
Rice bread, high-amylose Doongara rice (Pav's, Australia)	61	30	12	7
Rye bread				
RYE KERNEL (PUMPERNICKEL) BREAD				
Coarse rye kernel bread, 80% intact kernels (Sweden)	41	30	12	5
Rye kernel bread (Pumpernickel) (Canada)	41	30	12	5
Whole grain pumpernickel (Holtzheuser Brothers Ltd., Toronto, Canada)	46	30	11	5
Rye kernel bread, pumpernickel (80% kernels) (Canada)	55	30	12	7
Cocktail, sliced (Kasselar Food Products, Toronto, Canada)	55	30	12	7
Cocktail, sliced (Kasselar Food Products, Canada)	62	30	12	8
■ *mean of six studies*	50	30	12	6

[0] indicates that the food has so little carbohydrate that the GI value cannot be tested. The GL is therefore 0.

▲ indicates brand not specified

FOOD	GI VALUE GLUCOSE = 100	NOMINAL SERVING SIZE	AVAILABLE CARB PER SERVING	GL PER SERVING
WHOLE-WHEAT RYE BREAD				
Whole-wheat rye bread (Canada)	41			
Whole-wheat rye bread (Canada)	62			
Whole-wheat rye bread (Canada)	63			
Whole-wheat rye bread (Canada)	66			
■ *mean of four studies*	58	30	14	8
SPECIALTY RYE BREADS				
Blackbread, Riga (Berzin's, Sydney, Australia)	76	30	13	10
Bürgen™ Dark/Swiss rye (Tip Top Bakeries, Australia)	55			
Bürgen™ Dark/Swiss rye (Tip Top Bakeries, Australia)	74			
■ *mean of two studies*	65	30	10	7
Klosterbrot whole-wheat rye bread (Dimpflmeier, Canada)	67	30	13	9
Light rye (Silverstein's, Canada)	68	30	14	10
Linseed rye (Rudolph's, Canada)	55	30	13	7
Roggenbrot, Vogel's (Stevns & Co, Sydney, Australia)	59	30	14	8

[0] indicates that the food has so little carbohydrate that the GI value cannot be tested. The GL is therefore 0.

▲ indicates brand not specified

FOOD	GI VALUE GLUCOSE = 100	NOMINAL SERVING SIZE	AVAILABLE CARB PER SERVING	GL PER SERVING
Schinkenbrot, Riga (Berzin's, Sydney, Australia)	86	30	14	12
Sourdough rye (Canada)	57			
Sourdough rye (Australia)	48			
■ *mean of two studies*	53	30	12	6
Volkornbrot, whole-wheat rye bread (Dimpflmeier, Canada)	56	30	13	7
Wheat breads				
Coarse wheat kernel bread, 80% intact kernels (Sweden)	52	30	20	10
Cracked wheat kernel (bulgur) bread				
50% cracked wheat kernel (Canada)	58	30	20	12
75% cracked wheat kernels (Canada)	48	30	20	10
■ *mean of two studies*	53	30	20	11
Spelt wheat breads				
White spelt wheat bread (Slovenia)	74	30	23	17
Whole-wheat spelt wheat bread (Slovenia)	63	30	19	12
Scalded spelt wheat kernel bread (Slovenia)	67	30	22	15
Spelt multigrain bread® (Pav's, Australia)	54	30	12	7

[0] indicates that the food has so little carbohydrate that the GI value cannot be tested. The GL is therefore 0.

▲ indicates brand not specified

FOOD	GI VALUE GLUCOSE = 100	NOMINAL SERVING SIZE	AVAILABLE CARB PER SERVING	GL PER SERVING
White wheat flour bread				
White flour (Canada)	69	30	14	10
White flour (USA)	70	30	14	10
White flour, Sunblest™ (Tip Top, Australia)	70	30	14	10
White flour (Dempster's Corporate Foods Ltd., Canada)	71	30	14	10
White flour (South Africa)	71	30	13	9
White flour (Canada)	71	30	14	10
■ *mean of six studies*	70	30	14	10
White wheat flour bread, hard, toasted (Italian)	73	30	15	11
Wonder™, enriched white bread (USA)	71			
Wonder™, enriched white bread (USA)	72			
Wonder™, enriched white bread (USA)	77			
■ *mean of three studies*	73	30	14	10
White Turkish bread (Turkey)	87	30	17	15
White bread with enzyme inhibitors				
White bread + acarbose (200 mg) (Mexico)	18	30	17	3
White bread + acarbose (200 mg) (Mexico)	50	30	17	8
■ *mean in two groups of subjects*	34	30	17	6

[0] indicates that the food has so little carbohydrate that the GI value cannot be tested. The GL is therefore 0.

▲ indicates brand not specified

FOOD	GI VALUE GLUCOSE = 100	NOMINAL SERVING SIZE	AVAILABLE CARB PER SERVING	GL PER SERVING
White bread roll + 3 mg trestatin (pancreatic alpha-amylase inhibitor)	48	30	12	6
White bread roll + 6 mg trestatin	29	30	12	4
White bread with soluble fiber				
White bread + 15 g psyllium fiber	41	30	17	7
White bread + 15 g psyllium fiber	65	30	17	11
■ *mean in two groups of subjects*	53	30	17	9
White bread eaten with vinegar as vinaigrette (Sweden)	45	30	15	7
White bread eaten with powdered dried seaweed	48	30	15	7
White bread containing Eurylon® high-amylose maize starch (France)	42	30	19	8
White fiber-enriched bread				
White, high-fiber bread (Dempster's, Canada)	67			
White, high-fiber bread (Weston's Bakery, Toronto, Canada)	69			
■ *mean of two studies*	68	30	13	9

[0] indicates that the food has so little carbohydrate that the GI value cannot be tested. The GL is therefore 0.

▲ indicates brand not specified

FOOD	GI VALUE GLUCOSE = 100	NOMINAL SERVING SIZE	AVAILABLE CARB PER SERVING	GL PER SERVING
White resistant-starch–enriched bread				
Fiber White™ (Nature's Fresh, New Zealand)	77	30	15	11
Wonderwhite™ (Buttercup, Australia)	80	30	14	11
Whole-wheat wheat flour bread				
Whole-wheat flour (Canada)	52	30	12	6
Whole-wheat flour (Canada)	64	30	12	8
Whole-wheat flour (Canada)	65	30	12	8
Whole-wheat flour (Canada)	67	30	12	8
Whole-wheat flour (Canada)	67	30	12	8
Whole-wheat flour (Canada)	69	30	12	8
Whole-wheat flour (Canada)	71	30	12	8
Whole-wheat flour (Canada)	72	30	12	8
Whole-wheat flour (USA)	73	30	14	10
Whole-wheat flour (South Africa)	75	30	13	9
Whole-wheat flour (Tip Top Bakeries, Australia)	77	30	12	9
Whole-wheat flour (Tip Top Bakeries, Australia)	78	30	12	9
Whole-wheat flour (Kenya)	87	30	13	11
■ *mean of thirteen studies*	71	30	13	9
Whole-wheat Turkish bread	49	30	16	8

[0] indicates that the food has so little carbohydrate that the GI value cannot be tested. The GL is therefore 0.

▲ indicates brand not specified

FOOD	GI VALUE GLUCOSE = 100	NOMINAL SERVING SIZE	AVAILABLE CARB PER SERVING	GL PER SERVING
Specialty wheat breads				
BÜRGEN® MIXED GRAIN BREAD (AUSTRALIA)				
Bürgen® Mixed Grain (Tip Top, Australia)	34			
Bürgen® Mixed Grain	45			
Bürgen® Mixed Grain	69			
■ *mean of three studies*	49	30	11	6
Bürgen® Oat Bran & Honey Loaf with Barley (Tip Top, Australia)	31	30	10	3
Bürgen® Soy-Lin, kibbled soy (8%) and linseed (8%) loaf (Tip Top)	36	30	9	3
English Muffin™ bread (Natural Ovens, USA)	77	30	14	11
Healthy Choice™ Hearty 7 Grain (Con Agra Inc., USA)	55	30	14	8
Healthy Choice™ Hearty 100% Whole Grain (Con Agra Inc., USA)	62	30	14	9
Helga's™ Classic Seed Loaf (Quality Bakers, Australia)	68	30	14	9
Helga's™ traditional whole-wheat bread (Quality Bakers, Australia)	70	30	13	9
Hunger Filler™, whole-grain bread (Natural Ovens, USA)	59	30	13	7

[0] indicates that the food has so little carbohydrate that the GI value cannot be tested. The GL is therefore 0.

▲ indicates brand not specified

FOOD	GI VALUE GLUCOSE = 100	NOMINAL SERVING SIZE	AVAILABLE CARB PER SERVING	GL PER SERVING
Molenberg™ (Goodman Fielder, Auckland, New Zealand)	75			
Molenberg™ (Goodman Fielder, New Zealand)	84			
■ *mean of two studies*	80	30	14	11
9-Grain Multi-Grain (Tip Top, Australia)	43	30	14	6
Multigrain Loaf, spelt wheat flour (Australia)	54	30	15	8
Multigrain (50% kibbled wheat grain) (Australia)	43	30	14	6
Nutty Natural™, whole grain bread (Natural Ovens, USA)	59	30	12	7
Performax™ (Country Life Bakeries, Australia)	38	30	13	5
Ploughman's™ Whole grain, original recipe (Quality Bakers, Australia)	47	30	14	7
Ploughman's™ Whole wheat, smooth milled (Quality Bakers, Australia)	64	30	13	9
Semolina Bread (Kenya)	64			
Sourdough wheat (Australia)	54	30	14	8
Soy & Linseed bread (packet mix in bread oven) (Con Agra Inc., USA)	50	30	10	5

[0] indicates that the food has so little carbohydrate that the GI value cannot be tested. The GL is therefore 0.

▲ indicates brand not specified

FOOD	GI VALUE GLUCOSE = 100	NOMINAL SERVING SIZE	AVAILABLE CARB PER SERVING	GL PER SERVING
Stay Trim™, whole-grain bread (Natural Ovens, USA)	70	30	15	10
Sunflower & Barley bread, Riga brand (Berzin's, Australia)	57	30	13	7
Vogel's Honey & Oats (Stevns & Co., Australia)	55	30	14	7
Vogel's Roggenbrot (Stevns & Co., Australia)	59	30	14	8
Whole-wheat snack bread (Ryvita Co Ltd., UK)	74	30	22	16
100% Whole Grain™ bread (Natural Ovens, USA)	51	30	13	7
White wheat flour flatbread (Sweden)	79	30	16	13
Unleavened breads				
Lebanese bread, white (Seda Bakery, Australia)	75	30	16	12
Middle Eastern flatbread	97	30	16	15
Pita bread, white (Canada)	57	30	17	10
Wheat flour flatbread (India)	66	30	16	10
Amaranth: wheat (25:75) composite flour flatbread (India)	66	30	15	10
Amaranth: wheat (50:50) composite flour flatbread (India)	76	30	15	11

[0] indicates that the food has so little carbohydrate that the GI value cannot be tested. The GL is therefore 0.

▲ indicates brand not specified

FOOD	GI VALUE GLUCOSE = 100	NOMINAL SERVING SIZE	AVAILABLE CARB PER SERVING	GL PER SERVING
BREAKFAST CEREALS AND RELATED PRODUCTS				
ALL-BRAN				
All-Bran™ (Kellogg's, Australia)	30	30	15	4
All-Bran® (Kellogg's, USA)	38	30	23	9
All-Bran™ (Kellogg's Inc., Canada)	50	30	23	9
All-Bran™ (Kellogg's Inc., Canada)	51	30	23	9
■ *mean of four studies*	42	30	21	9
All-Bran Fruit 'n' Oats™ (Kellogg's, Australia)	39	30	17	7
All-Bran Soy 'n' Fiber™ (Kellogg's, Australia)	33	30	14	4
Amaranth, popped, with milk (India)	97	30	19	18
BARLEY PORRIDGE				
Whole-wheat barley flour porridge (100% regular barley) (Sweden)	68	50 (dry)	34	23
Whole-wheat high-fiber barley flour porridge (Sweden)	55	50 (dry)	15	8
Barley porridge made from thin dehulled flakes (Sweden)	62	50 (dry)	28	17
Barley porridge made from thick dehulled flakes (Sweden)	65	50 (dry)	28	18

[0] indicates that the food has so little carbohydrate that the GI value cannot be tested. The GL is therefore 0.

▲ indicates brand not specified

FOOD	GI VALUE GLUCOSE = 100	NOMINAL SERVING SIZE	AVAILABLE CARB PER SERVING	GL PER SERVING
Bran Buds™ (Kellogg's, Canada)	58	30	12	7
Bran Buds with psyllium (Kellogg's, Canada)	47	30	12	6
Bran Chex™ (Nabisco, Canada)	58	30	19	11
Bran Flakes™ (Kellogg's, Australia)	74	30	18	13
Cheerios™ (General Mills, Canada)	74	30	20	15
Chocapic™ (Nestlé, France)	84	30	25	21
Coco Pops™ (Kellogg's, Australia)	77	30	26	20
Corn Bran™ (Quaker Oats, Canada)	75	30	20	15
Corn Chex™ (Nabisco, Canada)	83	30	25	21
CORN FLAKES™				
Cornflakes™ (Kellogg's, New Zealand)	72	30	25	18
Cornflakes™ (Kellogg's, Australia)	77	30	25	20
Cornflakes™ (Kellogg's, Canada)	80	30	26	21
Cornflakes™ (Kellogg's, Canada)	86	30	26	22
Corn Flakes™ (Kellogg's, USA)	92	30	26	24
■ *mean of five studies*	81	30	26	21

[0] indicates that the food has so little carbohydrate that the GI value cannot be tested. The GL is therefore 0.

▲ indicates brand not specified

FOOD	GI VALUE GLUCOSE = 100	NOMINAL SERVING SIZE	AVAILABLE CARB PER SERVING	GL PER SERVING
Cornflakes, high fiber (Presidents Choice, Canada)	74	30	23	17
Cornflakes, Crunchy Nut™ (Kellogg's, Australia)	72	30	24	17
Corn Pops™ (Kellogg's, Australia)	80	30	26	21
Cream of Wheat™ (Nabisco, Canada)	66	250	26	17
Cream of Wheat™, Instant (Nabisco, Canada)	74	250	30	22
Crispix™ (Kellogg's, Canada)	87	30	25	22
Energy Mix™ (Quaker, France)	80	30	24	19
Froot Loops™ (Kellogg's, Australia)	69	30	26	18
Frosties™, sugar-coated cornflakes (Kellogg's, Australia)	55	30	26	15
Fruitful Lite™ (Hubbards, New Zealand)	61	30	20	12
Fruity-Bix™, berry (Sanitarium, New Zealand)	113	30	22	25
Golden Grahams™ (General Mills, Canada)	71	30	25	18
Golden Wheats™ (Kellogg's, Australia)	71	30	23	16
GRAPENUTS™				
Grapenuts™ (Post, Kraft, Canada)	67	30	19	13

[0] indicates that the food has so little carbohydrate that the GI value cannot be tested. The GL is therefore 0.

▲ indicates brand not specified

FOOD	GI VALUE GLUCOSE = 100	NOMINAL SERVING SIZE	AVAILABLE CARB PER SERVING	GL PER SERVING
Grapenuts™ (Kraft, USA)	75	30	22	16
■ mean of two studies	71	30	21	15
Grapenuts™ Flakes (Post, Canada)	80	30	22	17
Guardian™ (Kellogg's, Australia)	37	30	12	5
Healthwise™ for bowel health (Uncle Toby's, Australia)	66	30	18	12
Healthwise™ for heart health (Uncle Toby's, Australia)	48	30	19	9
Honey Rice Bubbles™ (Kellogg's, Australia)	77	30	27	20
Honey Smacks™ (Kellogg's, Australia)	71	30	23	16
Hot cereal, apple & cinnamon (Con Agra Inc., USA)	37	30	22	8
Hot cereal, unflavored (Con Agra Inc., USA)	25	30	19	5
Just Right™ (Kellogg's, Australia)	60	30	22	13
Just Right Just Grains™ (Kellogg's, Australia)	62	30	23	14
Komplete™ (Kellogg's, Australia)	48	30	21	10
Life™ (Quaker Oats Co., Canada)	66	30	25	16

[0] indicates that the food has so little carbohydrate that the GI value cannot be tested. The GL is therefore 0.

▲ indicates brand not specified

FOOD	GI VALUE GLUCOSE = 100	NOMINAL SERVING SIZE	AVAILABLE CARB PER SERVING	GL PER SERVING
Mini Wheats™, whole wheat (Kellogg's, Australia)	58	30	21	12
Mini Wheats™, black currant (Kellogg's, Australia)	72	30	21	15
MUESLI				
Muesli (Canada)	66	30	24	16
Alpen Muesli (Wheetabix, France)	55	30	19	10
Muesli, gluten-free (Freedom Foods, Australia)	39	30	19	7
Muesli, Lite (Sanitarium, New Zealand)	54	30	18	10
Muesli, Natural (Sanitarium, New Zealand)	57	30	19	11
Muesli, Natural (Sanitarium, Australia)	40	30	19	8
■ *mean of two studies*	49	30	20	10
Muesli, No Name (Sunfresh, Canada)	60	30	18	11
Muesli, Swiss Formula (Uncle Toby's, Australia)	56	30	16	9
Muesli, toasted (Purina, Australia)	43	30	17	7
Nutrigrain™ (Kellogg's, Australia)	66	30	15	10
Oat 'n' Honey Bake™ (Kellogg's, Australia)	77	30	17	13

[0] indicates that the food has so little carbohydrate that the GI value cannot be tested. The GL is therefore 0.

▲ indicates brand not specified

FOOD	GI VALUE GLUCOSE = 100	NOMINAL SERVING SIZE	AVAILABLE CARB PER SERVING	GL PER SERVING
OAT BRAN				
Oat bran, raw (Quaker Oats, Canada)	50	10	5	2
Oat bran, raw	59	10	5	3
■ *mean of two studies*	55	10	5	3
PORRIDGE MADE FROM ROLLED OATS				
Porridge (Uncle Toby's, Australia)	42	250	21	9
Porridge (Canada)	49	250	23	11
Traditional porridge oats (Lowan, Australia)	51	250	21	11
Porridge (Hubbards, New Zealand)	58	250	21	12
Porridge (Australia)	58	250	21	12
Porridge (Canada)	62	250	23	14
Porridge (Canada)	69	250	23	16
Porridge (USA)	75	250	23	17
■ *mean of eight studies*	58	250	22	13
Whole-wheat oat flour porridge (Sweden)	74	50 (dry)	32	24
Oat porridge made from thick flakes (Sweden)	55	250	27	15
Oat porridge made from roasted thin flakes (Sweden)	69	250	27	19
Oat porridge made from roasted thick flakes (Sweden)	50	250	27	14

[0] indicates that the food has so little carbohydrate that the GI value cannot be tested. The GL is therefore 0.

▲ indicates brand not specified

FOOD	GI VALUE GLUCOSE = 100	NOMINAL SERVING SIZE	AVAILABLE CARB PER SERVING	GL PER SERVING
Oat porridge made from roasted and steamed thin oat flakes (Sweden)	80	250	27	22
Oat porridge made from steamed thick (1.0 mm) dehulled oat flakes (Sweden)	53	250	27	14
INSTANT PORRIDGE				
Quick Oats (Quaker Oats, Canada)	65			
One Minute Oats (Quaker Oats, Canada)	66			
■ *mean of two studies*	66	250	26	17
Pop Tarts™, Double Chocolate (Kellogg's, Australia)	70	50	36	25
Pro Stars™ (General Mills, Canada)	71	30	24	17
PUFFED WHEAT				
Puffed Wheat (Quaker Oats, Canada)	67	30	20	13
Puffed Wheat (Sanitarium, Australia)	80	30	21	17
■ *mean of two studies*	74	30	21	16
Raisin Bran™ (Kellogg's, USA)	61	30	19	12
Red River Cereal (Maple Leaf Mills, Canada)	49	30	22	11
Rice Bran, extruded (Rice Growers, Australia)	19	30	14	3

[0] indicates that the food has so little carbohydrate that the GI value cannot be tested. The GL is therefore 0.

▲ indicates brand not specified

FOOD	GI VALUE GLUCOSE = 100	NOMINAL SERVING SIZE	AVAILABLE CARB PER SERVING	GL PER SERVING
RICE BUBBLES™ (PUFFED RICE)				
Rice Bubbles™ (Kellogg's, Australia)	81			
Rice Bubbles™ (Kellogg's, Australia)	85			
Rice Bubbles™ (Kellogg's, Australia)	95			
■ *mean of three studies*	87	30	26	22
Rice Chex™ (Nabisco, Canada)	89	30	26	23
Rice Krispies™ (Kellogg's, Canada)	82	30	26	21
SHREDDED WHEAT				
Shredded Wheat (Canada)	67	30	20	13
Shredded Wheat™ (Nabisco, Canada)	83	30	20	17
■ *mean of two studies*	75	30	20	15
SPECIAL K™—*FORMULATION OF THIS CEREAL VARIES IN DIFFERENT COUNTRIES*				
Special K™ (Kellogg's, Australia)	54	30	21	11
Special K™ (Kellogg's, USA)	69	30	21	14
Special K™ (Kellogg's, France)	84	30	24	20
Soy Tasty™ (Sanitarium, Australia)	60	30	20	12
Soytana™ (Vogel's, Australia)	49	45	25	12

[0] indicates that the food has so little carbohydrate that the GI value cannot be tested. The GL is therefore 0.

▲ indicates brand not specified

FOOD	GI VALUE GLUCOSE = 100	NOMINAL SERVING SIZE	AVAILABLE CARB PER SERVING	GL PER SERVING
Raisin Bran™ (Kellogg's, Australia)	73	30	19	14
Sustain™ (Kellogg's, Australia)	68	30	22	15
Team™ (Nabisco, Canada)	82	30	22	17
Thank Goodness™ (Hubbards, New Zealand)	65	30	23	15
Total™ (General Mills, Canada)	76	30	22	17
Ultra-bran™ (Vogel's, Australia)	41	30	13	5
Wheat-bites™ (Uncle Toby's, Australia)	72	30	25	18
WHEAT BISCUITS (PLAIN FLAKED WHEAT)				
Vita-Brits™ (Uncle Toby's, Australia)	61	30	20	12
Vita-Brits™ (Uncle Toby's, Australia)	68	30	20	13
Weet-Bix™ (Sanitarium, Australia)	69	30	17	12
Weet-Bix™ (Sanitarium, Australia)	69	30	17	12
Weetabix™ (Weetabix, Canada)	74	30	22	16
Weetabix™ (Weetabix, Canada)	75	30	22	16

[0] indicates that the food has so little carbohydrate that the GI value cannot be tested. The GL is therefore 0.

▲ indicates brand not specified

FOOD	GI VALUE GLUCOSE = 100	NOMINAL SERVING SIZE	AVAILABLE CARB PER SERVING	GL PER SERVING
Whole wheat Goldies™ (Kellogg's, Australia)	70	30	20	14
■ *mean of seven studies*	70	30	19	13
WHEAT BISCUITS (FLAKED WHEAT) WITH ADDITIONAL INGREDIENTS				
Good Start™, muesli wheat biscuits (Sanitarium, Australia)	68	30	20	14
Hi-Bran Weet-Bix™, wheat biscuits (Sanitarium, Australia)	61	30	17	10
Hi-Bran Weet-Bix™ with soy and linseed (Sanitarium, Australia)	57	30	16	9
Honey Goldies™ (Kellogg's Australia)	72	30	21	15
Lite-Bix™, plain, no added sugar (Sanitarium, Australia)	70	30	20	14
Oat bran Weet-Bix™ (Sanitarium, Australia)	57	30	20	11
Raisin Goldies™ (Kellogg's Australia)	65	30	21	13
BREAKFAST CEREAL BARS				
Crunchy Nut Cornflakes™ bar (Kellogg's, Australia)	72	30	26	19
Fiber Plus™ bar (Uncle Toby's, Australia)	78	30	23	18
Fruity-Bix™ bar, fruit and nut (Sanitarium, Australia)	56	30	19	10

[0] indicates that the food has so little carbohydrate that the GI value cannot be tested. The GL is therefore 0.

▲ indicates brand not specified

FOOD	GI VALUE GLUCOSE = 100	NOMINAL SERVING SIZE	AVAILABLE CARB PER SERVING	GL PER SERVING
Fruity-Bix™ bar, wild berry (Sanitarium, Australia)	51	30	19	9
K-Time Just Right™ bar (Kellogg's, Australia)	72	30	24	17
K-Time Strawberry Crunch™ bar (Kellogg's, Australia)	77	30	25	19
Rice Bubble Treat™ bar (Kellogg's, Australia)	63	30	24	15
Sustain™ bar (Kellogg's, Australia)	57	30	25	14
CEREAL GRAINS				
Amaranth				
Amaranth (*Amaranthus esculentum*) popped, with milk	97	30	22	21
Barley				
PEARL BARLEY				
Barley, pearled (Canada)	22			
Barley (Canada)	22			
Barley, pot, boiled in salted water 20 min	25			
Barley (Canada)	27			
Barley, pearled (Canada)	29			
■ *mean of five studies*	25	150	42	11
Barley (*Hordeum vulgare*) (India)	37			

[0] indicates that the food has so little carbohydrate that the GI value cannot be tested. The GL is therefore 0.

▲ indicates brand not specified

FOOD	GI VALUE GLUCOSE = 100	NOMINAL SERVING SIZE	AVAILABLE CARB PER SERVING	GL PER SERVING
Barley (*Hordeum vulgare*) (India)	48			
■ *mean of two groups of subjects*	43	150	42	26
Barley, cracked (Malthouth, Tunisia)	50	150	42	21
Barley, rolled (Australia)	66	50 (dry)	38	25
Buckwheat				
Buckwheat (Canada)	49			
Buckwheat (Canada)	51			
Buckwheat (Canada)	63			
■ *mean of three studies*	54	150	30	16
Buckwheat groats, boiled 12 min (Sweden)	45	150	30	13
Corn				
CORN/MAIZE				
Maize (*Zea mays*), flour made into chapatti (India)	59	–	–	–
Maize meal porridge/gruel (Kenya)	109	–	–	–
CORNMEAL				
Cornmeal, boiled in salted water 2 min (Canada)	68	150	13	9
Cornmeal + margarine (Canada)	69	150	12	9

[0] indicates that the food has so little carbohydrate that the GI value cannot be tested. The GL is therefore 0.

▲ indicates brand not specified

FOOD	GI VALUE GLUCOSE = 100	NOMINAL SERVING SIZE	AVAILABLE CARB PER SERVING	GL PER SERVING
■ *mean of two studies*	69	150	13	9
SWEET CORN				
Sweet corn, "Honey & Pearl" variety (New Zealand)	37	150	30	11
Sweet corn, on the cob, boiled 20 min (Australia)	48	150	30	14
Sweet corn (Canada)	59	150	33	20
Sweet corn (USA)	60	150	33	20
Sweet corn (South Africa)	62	150	33	20
■ *mean of six studies*	53	150	32	17
Sweet corn, canned, diet-pack (USA)	46	150	28	13
Sweet corn, frozen, reheated in microwave (Canada)	47	150	33	16
Taco shells, cornmeal-based, baked (Old El Paso, Canada)	68	20	12	8
Couscous				
Couscous, boiled 5 min (USA)	61			
Couscous, boiled 5 min (Tunisia)	69			
■ *mean of two studies*	65	150	35	23
Millet				
Millet, boiled (Canada)	71	150	36	25
Millet flour porridge (Kenya)	107	–	–	–

[0] indicates that the food has so little carbohydrate that the GI value cannot be tested. The GL is therefore 0.

▲ indicates brand not specified

FOOD	GI VALUE GLUCOSE = 100	NOMINAL SERVING SIZE	AVAILABLE CARB PER SERVING	GL PER SERVING
Rice				
WHITE RICE				
Arborio, risotto rice, boiled (Sun Rice, Australia)	69	150	53	36
White (*Oryza sativa*), boiled (India)	69	150	43	30
BOILED WHITE RICE				
Type NS ▲ (France)	45	150	30	14
Type NS ▲ (India)	48	150	38	18
Type NS ▲ (Canada)	51	150	42	21
Type NS ▲ (France)	52	150	36	19
Type NS ▲ (Canada)	56	150	42	23
Type NS ▲ (Pakistan)	69	150	38	26
Type NS ▲ (Canada)	72	150	42	30
Type NS ▲, boiled in salted water (India)	72	150	38	27
Type NS ▲, boiled 13 min (Italy)	102	150	30	31
Type NS ▲ (Kenya)	112	150	42	47
Type NS ▲, boiled (France)	43	150	30	13
Type NS ▲, boiled (France)	47	150	30	14
Type NS ▲, boiled in salted water, refrigerated 16–20h, reheated (India)	53	150	38	20
Type NS ▲, boiled 13 min, then baked 10 min (Italy)	104	150	30	31

[0] indicates that the food has so little carbohydrate that the GI value cannot be tested. The GL is therefore 0.

▲ indicates brand not specified

FOOD	GI VALUE GLUCOSE = 100	NOMINAL SERVING SIZE	AVAILABLE CARB PER SERVING	GL PER SERVING
LONG GRAIN, BOILED RICE				
Long grain, boiled 5 min (Canada)	41	150	40	16
Long grain, boiled 15 min (Mahatma, Australia)	50	150	43	21
Gem long grain (Dainty Food, Canada)	55	150	40	22
Long grain (Uncle Ben's, New Zealand)	56	150	43	24
Long grain, boiled 25 min (Surinam)	56	150	43	24
Gem long grain (Dainty, Canada)	57	150	40	23
Long grain, boiled 15 min	58	150	40	23
Gem long grain (Dainty, Canada)	60	150	40	24
Gem long grain (Dainty, Canada)	60	150	40	24
Long grain, boiled 7 min (Star, Canada)	64	150	40	26
■ *mean of 10 studies*	56	150	41	23
LONG GRAIN, QUICK-COOKING RICE VARIETIES				
Long grain, parboiled 10 min cooking time (Uncle Ben's, Belgium)	68	150	37	25

[0] indicates that the food has so little carbohydrate that the GI value cannot be tested. The GL is therefore 0.

▲ indicates brand not specified

FOOD	GI VALUE GLUCOSE = 100	NOMINAL SERVING SIZE	AVAILABLE CARB PER SERVING	GL PER SERVING
Long grain, parboiled, 20 min cooking time (Uncle Ben's, Belgium)	75	150	37	28
Long grain, microwaved 2 min (Express Rice, Masterfoods, UK)	52	150	37	19
SPECIALTY RICES				
Cajun Style, Uncle Ben's® (Effem Foods, Canada)	51	150	37	19
Garden Style, Uncle Ben's® (Effem Foods, Canada)	55	150	37	21
Long Grain and Wild, Uncle Ben's® (Effem Foods, Canada)	54	150	37	20
Mexican Fast and Fancy, Uncle Ben's® (Effem Foods, Canada)	58	150	37	22
Saskatchewan wild rice (Canada)	57	150	32	18
Broken rice (Lion Foods, Thailand)	86	150	43	37
Glutinous rice (Thailand)	98	150	32	31
Jasmine rice (Thailand)	109	150	42	46
WHITE, LOW-AMYLOSE RICE				
Calrose, white, medium grain, boiled (Rice Growers, Australia)	83	150	43	36
Sungold, Pelde, parboiled (Rice Growers, Australia)	87	150	43	37

[0] indicates that the food has so little carbohydrate that the GI value cannot be tested. The GL is therefore 0.

▲ indicates brand not specified

FOOD	GI VALUE GLUCOSE = 100	NOMINAL SERVING SIZE	AVAILABLE CARB PER SERVING	GL PER SERVING
Waxy (0–2% amylose) (Rice Growers, Australia)	88	150	43	38
Pelde, white (Rice Growers, Australia)	93	150	43	40
White, low-amylose, boiled (Turkey)	139	150	43	60
WHITE, HIGH-AMYLOSE RICE				
Bangladeshi rice variety BR16 (28% amylose)	37	150	39	14
Bangladeshi rice variety BR16, long-grain (27% amylose)	39	150	39	15
■ *mean of two studies*	38	150	39	15
Doongara, white (Rice Growers, Australia)	50			
Doongara, white (Rice Growers, Australia)	64			
Doongara, white (Rice Growers, Australia)	54			
■ *mean of three studies*	56	150	39	22
Koshikari (Japonica), short-grain (Japan)	48	150	38	18
BASMATI RICE				
Basmati, boiled (Mahatma, Australia)	58	150	38	22
Precooked basmati rice, Uncle Ben's Express® (UK)	57	150	41	24
Quick-cooking basmati, Uncle Ben's® Superior (Belgium)	60	150	38	23

[0] indicates that the food has so little carbohydrate that the GI value cannot be tested. The GL is therefore 0.

▲ indicates brand not specified

FOOD	GI VALUE GLUCOSE = 100	NOMINAL SERVING SIZE	AVAILABLE CARB PER SERVING	GL PER SERVING
BROWN RICE				
Brown (Canada)	66	150	33	21
Brown, steamed (USA)	50	150	33	16
Brown (*Oriza Sativa*), boiled (South India)	50	150	33	16
■ *mean of three studies*	55	150	33	18
Calrose brown (Rice Growers, Australia)	87	150	38	33
Doongara brown, high-amylose (Rice Growers, Australia)	66	150	37	24
Pelde brown (Rice Growers, Australia)	76	150	38	29
Parboiled, cooked 20 min, Uncle Ben's Natur-reis® (Belgium)	64	150	36	23
Sunbrown Quick™ (Rice Growers, Australia)	80	150	38	31
INSTANT/PUFFED RICE				
Instant rice, white, boiled 1 min (Canada)	46	150	42	19
Instant rice, white, cooked 6 min (Trice brand, Australia)	87	150	42	36
Puffed, white, cooked 5 min, Uncle Ben's Snabbris® (Belgium)	74	150	42	31
■ *mean of three studies*	69	150	42	29

[0] indicates that the food has so little carbohydrate that the GI value cannot be tested. The GL is therefore 0.

▲ indicates brand not specified

FOOD	GI VALUE GLUCOSE = 100	NOMINAL SERVING SIZE	AVAILABLE CARB PER SERVING	GL PER SERVING
Instant Doongara, white, cooked 5 min (Rice Growers, Australia)	94	150	42	35
PARBOILED RICE				
Parboiled rice (Canada)	48	150	36	18
Parboiled rice (USA)	72	150	36	26
Converted, white, Uncle Ben's® (Canada)	45	150	36	16
Converted, white, boiled 20–30 min, Uncle Ben's® (USA)	38	150	36	14
Converted, white, long grain, boiled 20–30 min, Uncle Ben's® (USA)	50	150	36	18
Boiled, 12 min (Denmark)	39	150	36	14
Boiled, 12 min (Denmark)	42	150	36	15
Boiled, 12 min (Denmark)	43	150	36	16
Boiled, 12 min (Denmark)	46	150	36	17
Long grain, boiled 5 min (Canada)	38	150	36	14
Long grain, boiled, 10 min (USA)	61	150	36	22
Long grain, boiled 15 min (Canada)	47	150	36	17
Long grain, boiled 25 min (Canada)	46	150	36	17
■ *mean of thirteen studies*	47	150	36	17

[0] indicates that the food has so little carbohydrate that the GI value cannot be tested. The GL is therefore 0.

▲ indicates brand not specified

FOOD	GI VALUE GLUCOSE = 100	NOMINAL SERVING SIZE	AVAILABLE CARB PER SERVING	GL PER SERVING
PARBOILED, LOW-AMYLOSE RICE				
Bangladeshi rice variety BR2, parboiled (12% amylose)	51	150	38	19
Parboiled, Sungold (Rice Growers, Australia)	87	150	39	34
PARBOILED, HIGH-AMYLOSE RICE				
Parboiled, high-amylose (28%), Doongara (Rice Growers, Australia)	50	150	39	19
Bangladeshi rice variety BR16 (28% amylose)	35	150	37	13
Bangladeshi rice variety BR16, traditional method (27% amylose)	32	150	38	12
Bangladeshi rice variety BR16, pressure parboiled (27% amylose)	27	150	41	11
Bangladeshi rice variety BR4 (27% amylose)	33	150	38	13
■ *mean of 5 studies*	35	150	39	14
Rye				
Rye, whole kernels (Canada)	29	50 (dry)	38	11
Rye, whole kernels, pressure cooked (Canada)	34	50 (dry)	38	13
Rye, whole kernels (Canada)	39	50 (dry)	38	15
■ *mean of three studies*	34	50 (dry)	38	13

[0] indicates that the food has so little carbohydrate that the GI value cannot be tested. The GL is therefore 0.

▲ indicates brand not specified

FOOD	GI VALUE GLUCOSE = 100	NOMINAL SERVING SIZE	AVAILABLE CARB PER SERVING	GL PER SERVING
Wheat				
WHEAT, WHOLE KERNELS				
Wheat, whole kernels (*Triticum aestivum*) (India)	30	50 (dry)	38	11
Wheat, whole kernels (Canada)	42	50 (dry)	33	14
Wheat, whole kernels, pressure cooked (Canada)	44	50 (dry)	33	14
Wheat, whole kernels (Canada)	48	50 (dry)	33	16
■ *mean of four studies*	41	50 (dry)	34	14
Wheat, type NS ▲ (India)	90	50 (dry)	38	34
WHEAT, PRECOOKED KERNELS				
Durum wheat, precooked, cooked 20 min (France)	52	50 (dry)	37	19
Durum wheat, precooked, cooked 10 min (France)	50	50 (dry)	33	17
Durum wheat, precooked in pouch, reheated (France)	40	125	39	16
Quick-cooking (White Wings, Australia)	54	150	47	25
SEMOLINA				
Semolina, roasted at 105°C then gelatinized with water (India)	55			
Semolina, steamed and gelatinized (India)	54			
■ *mean of two studies*	55	150	11	6

[0] indicates that the food has so little carbohydrate that the GI value cannot be tested. The GL is therefore 0.

▲ indicates brand not specified

FOOD	GI VALUE GLUCOSE = 100	NOMINAL SERVING SIZE	AVAILABLE CARB PER SERVING	GL PER SERVING
CRACKED WHEAT (BULGUR)				
Bulgur, boiled (Canada)	46			
Bulgur, boiled in 800 mL water 20 min (Canada)	46			
Bulgur, boiled 20 min (Canada)	46			
Bulgur, boiled 20 min (Canada)	53			
■ *mean of four studies*	48	150	26	12
COOKIES				
Arrowroot (McCormick's, Canada)	63	25	20	13
Arrowroot plus (McCormick's, Canada)	62	25	18	11
Milk Arrowroot™ (Arnotts, Australia)	69	25	18	12
■ *mean of three studies*	65	25	19	12
Barquette Abricot (LU, France)	71	40	32	23
Bebe Dobre Rano Chocolate (LU, Czech Republic)	57	50	33	19
Bebe Dobre Rano Honey and Hazelnuts (LU, Czech Republic)	51	50	34	17
Bebe Jemne Susenky (LU, Czech Republic)	67	25	20	14
Digestives (Canada)	55			
Digestives (Canada)	59			
Digestives, Peak Freans (Nabisco, Canada)	62			

[0] indicates that the food has so little carbohydrate that the GI value cannot be tested. The GL is therefore 0.

▲ indicates brand not specified

FOOD	GI VALUE GLUCOSE = 100	NOMINAL SERVING SIZE	AVAILABLE CARB PER SERVING	GL PER SERVING
■ *mean of three studies*	59	25	16	10
Digestives, gluten-free (Nutricia, UK)	58	25	17	10
Evergreen met Krenten (LU, Netherlands)	66	38	21	14
Golden Fruit (Griffin's, New Zealand)	77	25	17	13
Graham Wafers (Christie Brown, Canada)	74	25	18	14
Gran'Dia Banana, Oats and Honey (LU, Brazil)	28	30	23	6
Grany en-cas Abricot (LU, France)	55	30	16	9
Grany en-cas Fruits des bois (LU, France)	50	30	14	7
Grany Rush Apricot (LU, Netherlands)	62	30	20	12
Highland Oatmeal™ (Westons, Australia)	55	25	18	10
Highland Oatcakes (Walker's, Scotland)	57	25	15	8
LU P'tit Déjeuner Chocolat (LU, France)	42	50	34	14
LU P'tit Déjeuner Miel et Pépites Chocolat (LU, France)	45	50	35	16
LU P'tit Déjeuner Miel et Pépites Chocolat (LU, France)	52	50	35	18

[0] indicates that the food has so little carbohydrate that the GI value cannot be tested. The GL is therefore 0.

▲ indicates brand not specified

FOOD	GI VALUE GLUCOSE = 100	NOMINAL SERVING SIZE	AVAILABLE CARB PER SERVING	GL PER SERVING
LU P'tit Déjeuner Miel et Pépites Chocolat (LU, France)	49	50	35	18
■ *mean of three studies*	49	50	35	17
Maltmeal wafer (Griffin's, New Zealand)	50	25	17	9
Morning Coffee™ (Arnotts, Australia)	79	25	19	15
Nutrigrain Fruits des bois (Kellogg's, France)	57	35	23	13
Oatmeal (Canada)	54	25	17	9
Oro (Saiwa, Italy)	61	40	32	20
Oro (Saiwa, Italy)	67	40	32	21
■ *mean of two studies*	64	40	32	20
Petit LU Normand (LU, France)	51	25	19	10
Petit LU Roussillon (LU, France)	48	25	18	9
Prince Energie+ (LU, France)	73	25	17	13
Prince fourré chocolat (LU, France)	53			
Prince fourré chocolat (LU, France)	50			
■ *mean of two studies*	52	45	30	16
Prince Meganana Chocolate (LU, Spain)	49	50	36	18
Prince Petit Déjeuner Vanille (LU, France and Spain)	45	50	36	16

[0] indicates that the food has so little carbohydrate that the GI value cannot be tested. The GL is therefore 0.

▲ indicates brand not specified

FOOD	GI VALUE GLUCOSE = 100	NOMINAL SERVING SIZE	AVAILABLE CARB PER SERVING	GL PER SERVING
Rich Tea (Canada)	55	25	19	10
Sablé des Flandres (LU, France)	57	20	15	8
Shortbread (Arnotts, Australia)	64	25	16	10
Shredded Wheatmeal™ (Arnotts, Australia)	62	25	18	11
Snack Right Fruit Slice (97% fat-free) (Arnott's, Australia)	45	25	19	9
Thé (LU, France)	41	20	16	6
Vanilla Wafers (Christie Brown, Canada)	77	25	18	14
Véritable Petit Beurre (LU, France)	51	25	18	9
CRACKERS				
Breton wheat crackers (Dare Foods, Canada)	67	25	14	10
Corn Thins, puffed corn cakes, gluten-free (Real Foods, Australia)	87	25	20	18
Cream Cracker (LU, Brazil)	65	25	17	11
High-calcium cracker (Danone, Malaysia)	52	25	17	9
Jatz™, plain salted cracker biscuits (Arnotts, Australia)	55	25	17	10
Puffed Crispbread (Westons, Australia)	81	25	19	15

[0] indicates that the food has so little carbohydrate that the GI value cannot be tested. The GL is therefore 0.

▲ indicates brand not specified

FOOD	GI VALUE GLUCOSE = 100	NOMINAL SERVING SIZE	AVAILABLE CARB PER SERVING	GL PER SERVING
Puffed rice cakes				
Puffed rice cakes (Rice Growers, Australia)	82	25	21	17
Rice cakes, Calrose (low-amylose) (Rice Growers, Australia)	91	25	21	19
Rice cakes, Doongara (high-amylose) (Rice Growers, Australia)	61	25	21	13
■ *mean of three studies*	78	25	21	17
Rye crispbread				
Rye crispbread (Canada)	63	25	16	10
Ryvita™ (Canada)	69	25	16	11
High-fiber rye crispbread (Ryvita, UK)	59	25	15	9
Rye crispbread (Ryvita, UK)	63	25	18	11
■ *mean of four studies*	64	25	16	11
Kavli™ Norwegian Crispbread (Players, Australia)	71	25	16	12
Sao™, plain square crackers (Arnotts, Australia)	70	25	17	12
Stoned Wheat Thins (Christie Brown, Canada)	67	25	17	12
Water cracker				
Water cracker (Canada)	63	25	18	11

[0] indicates that the food has so little carbohydrate that the GI value cannot be tested. The GL is therefore 0.

▲ indicates brand not specified

FOOD	GI VALUE GLUCOSE = 100	NOMINAL SERVING SIZE	AVAILABLE CARB PER SERVING	GL PER SERVING
Water cracker (Arnotts, Australia)	78	25	18	14
■ *mean of two studies*	71	25	18	13
Premium Soda Crackers (Christie Brown, Canada)	74	25	17	12
Vita-wheat™, original, crispbread (Arnott's, Australia)	55	25	19	10
DAIRY PRODUCTS AND ALTERNATIVES				
Custard				
No Bake Egg Custard (Nestlé, Australia)	35	100	17	6
Custard, homemade (Australia)	43	100	17	7
TRIM™, reduced-fat custard (Pauls, Australia)	37	100	15	6
■ *mean of three studies*	38	100	16	6
Ice cream, regular/NS ▲				
Ice cream, NS ▲ (Canada)	36			
Ice cream (half vanilla, half chocolate) (Italy)	57			
Ice cream, NS ▲ (USA)	62			
Ice cream, chocolate flavored (USA)	68			
Ice cream (half vanilla, half chocolate) (Italy)	80			

[0] indicates that the food has so little carbohydrate that the GI value cannot be tested. The GL is therefore 0.

▲ indicates brand not specified

FOOD	GI VALUE GLUCOSE = 100	NOMINAL SERVING SIZE	AVAILABLE CARB PER SERVING	GL PER SERVING
■ *mean of five studies*	61	50	13	8
Ice cream, reduced or low fat				
Ice cream, vanilla (Peter's, Australia)	50	50	6	3
Ice cream (1.2 % fat), Prestige Light vanilla (Norco, Australia)	47	50	10	5
Ice cream (1.4% fat), Prestige Light toffee (Norco, Australia)	37	50	14	5
Ice cream (7.1 % fat), Prestige macadamia (Norco, Australia)	39	50	12	5
Ice cream, premium				
Ice cream, Ultra chocolate, 15% fat (Sara Lee, Australia)	37	50	9	4
Ice cream, French vanilla, 16% fat (Sara Lee, Australia)	38	50	9	3
Milk, full fat				
Full fat (Italy)	11			
Full fat (3% fat, Sweden)	21			
Full fat (Italy)	24			
Full fat (Australia)	31			
Full fat (Canada)	34			
Full fat (USA)	40			
■ *mean of five studies*	27	250	12	3
Fermented cow's milk (ropy milk, Sweden)	11			

[0] indicates that the food has so little carbohydrate that the GI value cannot be tested. The GL is therefore 0.

▲ indicates brand not specified

FOOD	GI VALUE GLUCOSE = 100	NOMINAL SERVING SIZE	AVAILABLE CARB PER SERVING	GL PER SERVING
Fermented cow's milk (filmjölk, Sweden)	11			
■ *mean of two foods*	11	–	–	–
Milk, full fat, plus bran				
Full fat + 20 g wheat bran (Italy)	25			
Full fat + 20 g wheat bran (Italy)	28			
■ *mean of two studies*	27	250	12	3
Milk, skim (Canada)	32	250	13	4
Milk, condensed, sweetened (Nestlé, Australia)	61	50	136	33
Milk, low fat, chocolate, with aspartame, Lite White™ (Australia)	24	250	15	3
Milk, low fat, chocolate, with sugar, Lite White™ (Australia)	34	250	26	9
Mousse, reduced fat, mix with water				
Butterscotch, 1.9% fat (Nestlé, Australia)	36	50	10	4
Chocolate, 2% fat (Nestlé, Australia)	31	50	11	3
Hazelnut, 2.4% fat (Nestlé, Australia)	36	50	10	4
Mango, 1.8% fat (Nestlé, Australia)	33	50	11	4

[0] indicates that the food has so little carbohydrate that the GI value cannot be tested. The GL is therefore 0.

▲ indicates brand not specified

FOOD	GI VALUE GLUCOSE = 100	NOMINAL SERVING SIZE	AVAILABLE CARB PER SERVING	GL PER SERVING
Mixed berry, 2.2% fat (Nestlé, Australia)	36	50	10	4
Strawberry, 2.3% fat (Nestlé, Australia)	32	50	10	3
■ *mean of six foods*	34	50	10	4
Pudding				
Instant, chocolate, made from powder and milk (White Wings, Australia)	47	100	16	7
Instant, vanilla, made from powder and milk (White Wings, Australia)	40	100	16	6
■ *mean of two foods*	44	100	16	7
Yogurt				
Yogurt, type ▲ (Canada)	36	200	9	3
LOW-FAT YOGURT				
Low fat, fruit, aspartame, Ski™ (Dairy Farmers, Australia)	14	200	13	2
Low fat, fruit, sugar, Ski™ (Dairy Farmers, Australia)	33	200	31	10
Low fat (0.9%), fruit, wild strawberry (Ski d'lite™, Dairy Farmers, Australia)	31	200	30	9
NON-FAT YOGURT, SWEETENED WITH ACESULFAME K AND SPLENDA				
Diet Vaalia™, exotic fruits (Pauls, Australia)	23	200	16	4

[0] indicates that the food has so little carbohydrate that the GI value cannot be tested. The GL is therefore 0.

▲ indicates brand not specified

FOOD	GI VALUE GLUCOSE = 100	NOMINAL SERVING SIZE	AVAILABLE CARB PER SERVING	GL PER SERVING
Diet Vaalia™, mango (Pauls, Australia)	23	200	14	3
Diet Vaalia™, mixed berry (Pauls, Australia)	25	200	13	3
Diet Vaalia™, strawberry (Pauls, Australia)	23	200	13	3
Diet Vaalia™, vanilla (Pauls, Australia)	23	200	13	3
■ *mean of five foods*	24	200	14	3
REDUCED-FAT YOGURT				
Reduced fat, Vaalia™, apricot & mango (Pauls, Australia)	26	200	30	8
Reduced fat, Vaalia™, French vanilla (Pauls, Australia)	26	200	10	3
Reduced fat, Extra-Lite™, strawberry (Pauls, Australia)	28	200	33	9
■ *mean of three foods*	27	200	24	7
Yogurt drink, reduced fat, Vaalia™, passionfruit (Pauls, Australia)	38	200	29	11
Soy milks				
Soy milk, full fat, Original (So Natural, Australia)	44	250	17	8
Soy milk, full fat, Calciforte (So Natural, Australia)	36	250	18	6
Soy milk, reduced fat, Light (So Natural, Australia)	44	250	17	8

[0] indicates that the food has so little carbohydrate that the GI value cannot be tested. The GL is therefore 0.

▲ indicates brand not specified

FOOD	GI VALUE GLUCOSE = 100	NOMINAL SERVING SIZE	AVAILABLE CARB PER SERVING	GL PER SERVING
Soy smoothie drink, banana, 1% fat (So Natural, Australia)	30	250	22	7
Soy smoothie drink, chocolate hazelnut, 1% fat (So Natural, Australia)	34	250	25	8
■ *mean of two drinks*	32	250	23	7
Up & Go™, cocoa malt flavor (Sanitarium, Australia)	43	250	26	11
Up & Go™, original malt flavor (Sanitarium, Australia)	46	250	24	11
■ *mean of two drinks*	45	250	25	11
Xpress™, chocolate (So Natural, Australia)	39	250	34	13
Soy yogurt				
Soy yogurt, peach and mango, 2% fat, sugar (So Natural, Australia)	50	200	26	13
Tofu-based frozen dessert, chocolate (USA)	115	50	9	10
FRUIT AND FRUIT PRODUCTS				
Apples, raw				
Apple, ▲ (Denmark)	28	120	13	4
Apple, Braeburn (New Zealand)	32	120	13	4
Apple, ▲ (Canada)	34	120	16	5

[0] indicates that the food has so little carbohydrate that the GI value cannot be tested. The GL is therefore 0.

▲ indicates brand not specified

FOOD	GI VALUE GLUCOSE = 100	NOMINAL SERVING SIZE	AVAILABLE CARB PER SERVING	GL PER SERVING
Apple, Golden Delicious (Canada)	39	120	16	6
Apple, ▲ (USA)	40	120	16	6
Apple, ▲ (Italy)	44	120	13	6
■ *mean of six studies*	38	120	15	6
Apple, dried (Australia)	29	60	34	10
Apple juice				
Apple juice, unsweetened, reconstituted (Berri, Australia)	39	250	25	10
Apple juice, unsweetened (USA)	40	250	29	12
Apple juice, unsweetened (Allens, Canada)	41	250	30	12
■ *mean of three studies*	40	250	28	11
Apricots				
Apricots, raw (Italy)	57	120	9	5
Apricots, canned in light syrup (Riviera, Canada)	64	120	19	12
Apricots, dried (Australia)	30	60	27	8
Apricots, dried (Wasco, Canada)	32	60	30	10
■ *mean of two studies*	31	60	28	9
Apricot fruit bar (Mother Earth, New Zealand)	50	50	34	17
Apricot fruit spread (Glen Ewin, Australia)	55	30	13	7

[0] indicates that the food has so little carbohydrate that the GI value cannot be tested. The GL is therefore 0.

▲ indicates brand not specified

FOOD	GI VALUE GLUCOSE = 100	NOMINAL SERVING SIZE	AVAILABLE CARB PER SERVING	GL PER SERVING
Apricot Fruity Bitz™ (Blackmores, Australia)	42	15	12	5
Banana, raw				
Banana (Canada)	46	120	25	12
Banana (Italy)	58	120	23	13
Banana (Canada)	58	120	25	15
Banana (Canada)	62	120	25	16
Banana (South Africa)	70	120	23	16
Banana, ripe (all yellow) (USA)	51	120	25	13
Banana, under-ripe (Denmark)	30	120	21	6
Banana, slightly under-ripe (yellow with green sections) (USA)	42	120	25	11
Banana, over-ripe (yellow flecked with brown) (USA)	48	120	25	12
Banana, over-ripe (Denmark)	52	120	20	11
■ *mean of 10 studies*	52	120	24	12
Banana, processed fruit fingers, Heinz Kidz™ (Australia)	61	30	20	12
Breadfruit (*Artocarpus altilis*), raw (Australia)	68	120	27	18
Cherries, raw, NS[8] (Canada)	22	120	12	3
Chico (*Zapota zapotilla coville*), raw (Philippines)	40	120	29	12

[0] indicates that the food has so little carbohydrate that the GI value cannot be tested. The GL is therefore 0.

▲ indicates brand not specified

FOOD	GI VALUE GLUCOSE = 100	NOMINAL SERVING SIZE	AVAILABLE CARB PER SERVING	GL PER SERVING
Cranberry juice cocktail (Ocean Spray, Australia)	52	250	31	16
Cranberry juice cocktail (Ocean Spray, USA)	68	250	35	24
Cranberry juice drink (Ocean Spray®, UK)	56	250	29	16
Custard apple, raw, flesh only (Australia)	54	120	19	10
Dates, dried, bahri	50	60	40	20
Dates, dried, kahlas	36	60	40	14
Dates, dried, bo ma'an	31	60	40	12
Dates, dried (Australia)	103	60	40	42
Figs, dried, tenderised (Dessert Maid, Australia)	61	60	26	16
Fruit Cocktail, canned (Delmonte, Canada)	55	120	16	9
Grapefruit, raw (Canada)	25	120	11	3
Grapefruit juice, unsweetened (Sunpac, Canada)	48	250	20	9
Grapes, raw				
Grapes, NS ▲ (Canada)	43	120	17	7
Grapes, NS ▲ (Italy)	49	120	19	9
■ *mean of two studies*	46	120	18	8
Grapes, black, Waltham Cross (Australia)	59	120	18	11

[0] indicates that the food has so little carbohydrate that the GI value cannot be tested. The GL is therefore 0.

▲ indicates brand not specified

FOOD	GI VALUE GLUCOSE = 100	NOMINAL SERVING SIZE	AVAILABLE CARB PER SERVING	GL PER SERVING
Kiwi fruit, raw				
Kiwi fruit, Hayward (New Zealand)	47	120	12	5
Kiwi fruit (Australia)	58	120	12	7
■ *mean of two studies*	53	120	12	6
Lychee, canned in syrup and drained, Narcissus brand (China)	79	120	20	16
Mango, raw				
Mango (*Mangifera indica*) (Philippines)	41	120	20	8
Mango (*Mangifera indica*) (Australia)	51	120	15	8
Mango, ripe (*Mangifera indica*) (India)	60	120	15	9
mean of three studies	51	120	17	8
Mango, Frutia™ (Weis, Australia)	42	100	23	10
Marmalade, orange (Australia)	48	30	20	9
Oranges, raw				
Oranges, NS ▲ (Denmark)	31	120	11	3
Oranges, NS ▲ (South Africa)	33	120	10	3
Oranges, NS ▲ (Canada)	40	120	11	4
Oranges, NS ▲ (Italy)	48	120	11	5
Oranges (Sunkist, USA)	48	120	11	5

[0] indicates that the food has so little carbohydrate that the GI value cannot be tested. The GL is therefore 0.

▲ indicates brand not specified

FOOD	GI VALUE GLUCOSE = 100	NOMINAL SERVING SIZE	AVAILABLE CARB PER SERVING	GL PER SERVING
Oranges, NS ▲ (Canada)	51	120	11	6
■ *mean of six studies*	42	120	11	5
Orange juice				
Orange juice (Canada)	46	250	26	12
Orange juice, reconstituted (Quelch, Australia)	53	250	18	9
Orange juice, reconstituted from frozen concentrate (USA)	57	250	26	15
■ *mean of three studies*	52	250	23	12
Paw paw/papaya, raw				
Paw paw (*Carica papaya*) (Australia)	56	120	8	5
Paw paw, ripe (India)	60	120	29	17
Papaya (*Carica papaya*) (Philippines)	60	120	15	9
■ *mean of three studies*	59	120	17	10
Peaches				
Peach, raw (Canada)	28	120	13	4
Peach, raw (Italy)	56	120	8	5
■ *mean of two studies*	42	120	11	5
Peach, canned in natural juice (Ardmona, Australia)	30	120	11	3
Peach, canned in natural juice (SPC, Australia)	45	120	11	5
■ *mean of two studies*	38	120	11	4

[0] indicates that the food has so little carbohydrate that the GI value cannot be tested. The GL is therefore 0.

▲ indicates brand not specified

FOOD	GI VALUE GLUCOSE = 100	NOMINAL SERVING SIZE	AVAILABLE CARB PER SERVING	GL PER SERVING
Peach, canned in heavy syrup (Letona, Australia)	58	120	15	9
Peach, canned in light syrup (Delmonte, Canada)	52	120	18	9
Peach, canned in reduced-sugar syrup (SPC, Australia)	62	120	17	11
Pears				
Pear, raw, NS ▲ (Canada)	33	120	13	4
Pear, Winter Nellis, raw (New Zealand)	34	120	12	4
Pear, Bartlett, raw (Canada)	41	120	8	3
Pear, raw NS ▲ (Italy)	42	120	11	4
■ *mean of four studies*	38	120	11	4
Pear halves, canned in reduced-sugar syrup, SPC Lite (Australia)	25	120	14	4
Pear halves, canned in natural juice (SPC, Australia)	43	120	13	5
Pear, canned in pear juice, Bartlett (Delmonte, Canada)	44	120	11	5
Pineapple				
Pineapple, raw (Australia)	66	120	10	6
Pineapple (Ananas comosus), raw (Philippines)	51	120	16	8
■ *mean of two studies*	59	120	13	7

[0] indicates that the food has so little carbohydrate that the GI value cannot be tested. The GL is therefore 0.

▲ indicates brand not specified

FOOD	GI VALUE GLUCOSE = 100	NOMINAL SERVING SIZE	AVAILABLE CARB PER SERVING	GL PER SERVING
Pineapple juice, unsweetened (Dole, Canada)	46	250	34	15
Plums				
Plum, raw, NS ▲ (Canada)	24	120	14	3
Plum, raw, NS ▲ (Italy)	53	120	11	6
■ *mean of two studies*	39	120	12	5
Prunes, pitted (Sunsweet, USA)	29	60	33	10
Raisins (Canada)	64	60	44	28
Rockmelon/Cantaloupe, raw (Australia)	65	120	6	4
Strawberries, fresh, raw (Australia)	40	120	3	1
Strawberry jam	51	30	20	10
Strawberry Real Fruit Bars (Uncle Toby's, Australia)	90	30	26	23
Raisins	56	60	45	25
Tomato juice, no added sugar (Berri, Australia)	38	250	9	4
Tropical Fruity Bitz™, (Blackmores, Australia)	41	15	11	5
Vitari, wild berry, non-dairy, frozen dessert (Nestlé, Australia)	59	100	21	12
Watermelon, raw (Australia)	72	120	6	4
Wild Berry Fruity Bitz™ (Blackmores, Australia)	35	15	12	4

[0] indicates that the food has so little carbohydrate that the GI value cannot be tested. The GL is therefore 0.

▲ indicates brand not specified

FOOD	GI VALUE GLUCOSE = 100	NOMINAL SERVING SIZE	AVAILABLE CARB PER SERVING	GL PER SERVING
INFANT FORMULA AND WEANING FOODS				
Formula				
Infasoy™, soy-based, milk-free (Wyeth, Australia)	55	100 mL	7	4
Karicare™ formula with omega oils (Nutricia, New Zealand)	35	100 mL	7	2
Nan-1™ infant formula with iron (Nestlé, Australia)	30	100 mL	8	2
S-26™ infant formula (Wyeth, Australia)	36	100 mL	7	3
Weaning Foods				
Farex™ baby rice (Heinz, Australia)	95	87	6	6
Robinsons First Tastes from 4 months (Nutricia, UK)				
Apple, apricot and banana cereal	56	75	13	7
Creamed porridge	59	75	9	5
Rice pudding	59	75	11	6
Heinz for Baby from 4 months (Heinz, Australia)				
Chicken and noodles with vegetables, strained	67	120	7	5
Sweetcorn and rice	65	120	15	10
LEGUMES AND NUTS				
Baked beans				
Baked Beans, canned (Canada)	40			

[0] indicates that the food has so little carbohydrate that the GI value cannot be tested. The GL is therefore 0.

▲ indicates brand not specified

FOOD	GI VALUE GLUCOSE = 100	NOMINAL SERVING SIZE	AVAILABLE CARB PER SERVING	GL PER SERVING
Baked Beans, canned beans in tomato sauce (Libby, Canada)	56			
■ *mean of two studies*	48	150	15	7
Beans, dried, boiled				
Beans, dried, type NS ▲ (Italy)	36	150	30	11
Beans, dried, type NS ▲ (Italy)	20	150	30	6
■ *mean of two studies*	29	150	30	9
Black-eyed beans/peas (cowpeas), boiled				
Black-eyed beans (Canada)	50	150	30	15
Black-eyed beans (Canada)	33	150	30	10
■ *mean of two studies*	42	150	30	13
Butter beans				
Butter beans (South Africa)	28	150	20	5
Butter beans, dried, cooked (South Africa)	29	150	20	6
Butter beans (Canada)	36	150	20	7
■ *mean of three studies*	31	150	20	6
Butter beans, dried, boiled + 5 g sucrose (South Africa)	30	150	20	6
Butter beans, dried, boiled + 10 g sucrose (South Africa)	31	150	20	6
Butter beans, dried, boiled + 15 g sucrose (South Africa)	54	150	20	11

[0] indicates that the food has so little carbohydrate that the GI value cannot be tested. The GL is therefore 0.

▲ indicates brand not specified

FOOD	GI VALUE GLUCOSE = 100	NOMINAL SERVING SIZE	AVAILABLE CARB PER SERVING	GL PER SERVING
Chickpeas (garbanzo beans, Bengal gram), boiled				
Chickpeas (*Cicer arietinum Linn*), boiled (Philippines)	10	150	30	3
Chickpeas, dried, boiled (Canada)	31	150	30	9
Chickpeas (Canada)	33	150	30	10
Chickpeas (Canada)	36	150	30	11
■ *mean of four studies*	28	150	30	8
Chickpeas, canned in brine (Lancia-Bravo, Canada)	42	150	22	9
Chickpeas, curry, canned (Canasia, Canada)	41	150	16	7
Haricot/navy beans				
Haricot/navy beans, pressure cooked (King Grains, Canada)	29	150	33	9
Haricot/navy beans, dried, boiled (Canada)	30	150	30	9
Haricot/navy beans, boiled (Canada)	31	150	30	9
Haricot/navy beans (King Grains, Canada)	39	150	30	12
Haricot/navy beans, pressure cooked (King Grains, Canada)	59	150	33	19
■ *mean of five studies*	38	150	31	12

[0] indicates that the food has so little carbohydrate that the GI value cannot be tested. The GL is therefore 0.

▲ indicates brand not specified

FOOD	GI VALUE GLUCOSE = 100	NOMINAL SERVING SIZE	AVAILABLE CARB PER SERVING	GL PER SERVING
Kidney beans				
Kidney/white bean (*Phaseolus vulgaris Linn*), boiled (Philippines)	13	150	25	3
Kidney beans (*Phaseolus vulgaris*) (India)	19	150	25	5
Kidney beans (USA)	23	150	25	6
Kidney beans, dried, boiled (France)	23	150	25	6
Kidney beans (*Phaseolus vulgaris* L.), red, boiled (Sweden)	25	150	25	6
Kidney beans (Canada)	29	150	25	7
Kidney beans, dried, boiled (Canada)	42	150	25	10
Kidney beans (Canada)	46	150	25	11
■ *mean of eight studies*	28	150	25	7
Kidney beans (*Phaseolus vulgaris* L.)—autoclaved	34	150	25	8
Kidney beans, canned (Lancia-Bravo, Canada)	52	150	17	9
Kidney beans, soaked 12 h, stored moist 24 h, steamed 1 h (India)	70	150	25	17
Black bean (*Phaseolus vulgaris* Linn), cooked (Philippines)	20	150	25	5

[0] indicates that the food has so little carbohydrate that the GI value cannot be tested. The GL is therefore 0.

▲ indicates brand not specified

FOOD	GI VALUE GLUCOSE = 100	NOMINAL SERVING SIZE	AVAILABLE CARB PER SERVING	GL PER SERVING
Lentils, type NS				
Lentils, type NS ▲ (USA)	28			
Lentils, type NS ▲ (Canada)	29			
■ *mean of two studies*	29	150	18	5
Lentils, green				
Lentils, green, dried, boiled (Canada)	22	150	18	4
Lentils, green, dried, boiled (France)	30	150	18	6
Lentils, green, dried, boiled (Australia)	37	150	14	5
■ *mean of three studies*	30	150	17	5
Lentils, green, canned in brine (Lancia-Bravo Foods Ltd., Canada)	52	150	17	9
Lentils, red				
Lentils, red, dried, boiled (Canada)	18	150	18	3
Lentils, red, dried, boiled (Canada)	21	150	18	4
Lentils, red, dried, boiled (Canada)	31	150	18	6
Lentils, red, dried, boiled (Canada)	32	150	18	6
■ *mean of four studies*	26	150	18	5

[0] indicates that the food has so little carbohydrate that the GI value cannot be tested. The GL is therefore 0.

▲ indicates brand not specified

FOOD	GI VALUE GLUCOSE = 100	NOMINAL SERVING SIZE	AVAILABLE CARB PER SERVING	GL PER SERVING
Lima beans, baby, frozen (York, Canada)	32	150	30	10
Marrowfat peas				
Marrowfat peas, dried, boiled (USA)	31			
Marrowfat peas, dried, boiled (Canada)	47			
■ *mean of two studies*	39	150	19	7
Mung beans				
Mung bean (*Phaseolus areus* Roxb), boiled (Philippines)	31	150	17	5
Mung bean, fried (Australia)	53			
Mung bean, germinated (Australia)	25	150	17	4
Mung bean, pressure cooked (Australia)	42	150	17	7
Peas, dried, boiled (Australia)	22	150	9	2
Pigeon pea (*Cajanus cajan* Linn Huth), boiled (Philippines)	22	150	20	4
Pinto beans				
Pinto beans, boiled (Canada)	39	150	26	10
Pinto beans, canned in brine (Lancia-Bravo, Canada)	45	150	22	10
Romano beans (Canada)	46	150	18	8

[0] indicates that the food has so little carbohydrate that the GI value cannot be tested. The GL is therefore 0.

▲ indicates brand not specified

FOOD	GI VALUE GLUCOSE = 100	NOMINAL SERVING SIZE	AVAILABLE CARB PER SERVING	GL PER SERVING
Soy beans				
Soy beans, boiled (Canada)	15	150	6	1
Soy beans, boiled (Australia)	20	150	6	1
■ *mean of two studies*	18	150	6	1
Soy beans, canned (Canada)	14	150	6	1
Split peas, yellow, boiled (Nupack, Canada)	32	150	19	6
MEAL-REPLACEMENT PRODUCTS				
Hazelnut and Apricot bar (Dietworks, Australia)	42	50	22	9
L.E.A.N™ products (Usana, USA)				
L.E.A.N Fibergy™ bar, Harvest Oat	45	50	29	13
Nutrimeal™, drink powder, Dutch Chocolate	26	250	13	3
L.E.A.N (Life long) Nutribar™, Peanut Crunch	30	40	19	6
L.E.A.N (Life long) Nutribar™, Chocolate Crunch	32	40	19	6
■ *mean of two Nutribars*	31	40	19	6
Worldwide Sport Nutrition low-carbohydrate products (USA)				
Designer chocolate, sugar-free	14	35	22	3
Burn-it™ bars				
Chocolate deluxe	29	50	8	2

[0] indicates that the food has so little carbohydrate that the GI value cannot be tested. The GL is therefore 0.

▲ indicates brand not specified

FOOD	GI VALUE GLUCOSE = 100	NOMINAL SERVING SIZE	AVAILABLE CARB PER SERVING	GL PER SERVING
Peanut butter	23	50	6	1
Pure-protein™ bars				
Chewy choc-chip	30	80	14	4
Chocolate deluxe	38	80	13	5
Peanut butter	22	80	9	2
Strawberry shortcake	43	80	13	6
White chocolate mousse	40	80	15	6
Pure-protein™ cookies				
Choc-chip cookie dough	25	55	11	3
Coconut	42	55	9	4
Peanut butter	37	55	9	3
Ultra pure-protein™ shakes				
Cappuccino	47	250	1	1
Frosty chocolate	37	250	3	1
Strawberry shortcake	42	250	1	1
Vanilla ice cream	32	250	3	1
MIXED MEALS AND CONVENIENCE FOODS				
Chicken nuggets, frozen, reheated (Australia)	46	100	16	7
Fish fingers (Canada)	38	100	19	7
Greek lentil stew with a bread roll, homemade (Australia)	40	360	37	15

[0] indicates that the food has so little carbohydrate that the GI value cannot be tested. The GL is therefore 0.

▲ indicates brand not specified

FOOD	GI VALUE GLUCOSE = 100	NOMINAL SERVING SIZE	AVAILABLE CARB PER SERVING	GL PER SERVING
Kugel (Polish dish containing egg noodles, sugar, cheese and raisins) (Israel)	65	150	48	31
Lean Cuisine™, chicken with rice (Nestlé, Australia)	36	400	68	24
Pies, beef, party size (Farmland, Australia)	45	100	27	12
Pizza				
Pizza, cheese (Pillsbury, Canada)	60	100	27	16
Pizza, plain (Italy)	80	100	27	22
Pizza, Super Supreme, pan (Pizza Hut, Australia)	36	100	24	9
Pizza, Super Supreme, thin and crispy (Pizza Hut, Australia)	30	100	22	7
Pizza, Vegetarian Supreme, thin and crispy (Pizza Hut, Australia)	49	100	25	12
Sausages NS ▲ (Canada)	28	100	3	1
Sirloin chop with mixed vegetables and mashed potato (Australia)	66	360	53	35
Spaghetti bolognaise, homemade (Australia)	52	360	48	25
Stir-fried vegetables with chicken and rice, homemade (Australia)	73	360	75	55

[0] indicates that the food has so little carbohydrate that the GI value cannot be tested. The GL is therefore 0.

▲ indicates brand not specified

FOOD	GI VALUE GLUCOSE = 100	NOMINAL SERVING SIZE	AVAILABLE CARB PER SERVING	GL PER SERVING
Sushi				
Sushi, salmon (Australia)	48	100	36	17
Sushi, roasted sea algae, vinegar, and rice (Japan)	55	100	37	20
■ *mean of two studies*	52	100	37	19
White boiled rice, grilled beefburger, cheese, and butter (France)	27	440	50	14
White boiled rice, grilled beefburger, cheese and butter (France)	22	440	50	11
■ *mean in two groups of subjects*	25	440	50	13
White bread with toppings				
White bread, butter, regular cow's milk cheese and fresh cucumber (Sweden)	55	200	68	38
White bread, butter, yogurt and pickled cucumber (Sweden)	39	200	28	11
White bread with butter (Canada)	59	100	48	29
White bread with skim-milk cheese (Canada)	55	100	47	26
White bread with butter and skim-milk cheese (Canada)	62	100	38	23

[0] indicates that the food has so little carbohydrate that the GI value cannot be tested. The GL is therefore 0.

▲ indicates brand not specified

FOOD	GI VALUE GLUCOSE = 100	NOMINAL SERVING SIZE	AVAILABLE CARB PER SERVING	GL PER SERVING
White/whole-wheat bread with peanut butter (Canada)	51	100	44	23
White/whole-wheat bread with peanut butter (Canada)	67	100	44	30
■ *mean of two studies*	59	100	44	26
NUTS				
Almonds	[0]	50	0	0
Brazil nuts	[0]	50	0	0
Cashew nuts, salted (Coles Supermarkets, Australia)	22	50	13	3
Hazelnuts	[0]	50	0	0
Macadamia	[0]	50	0	0
Pecan	[0]	50	0	0
PEANUTS				
Peanuts, crushed (South Africa)	7	50	4	0
Peanuts (Canada)	13	50	7	1
Peanuts (Mexico)	23	50	7	2
■ *mean of three studies*	14	50	6	1
Walnuts	[0]	50	0	0
NUTRITIONAL-SUPPORT PRODUCTS				
Choice dm™, vanilla (Mead Johnson, USA)	23	237mL	24	6
Enercal Plus™ (Wyeth-Ayerst, USA)	61	237mL	40	24
Ensure™ (Abbott, Australia)	50	237mL	40	19

[0] indicates that the food has so little carbohydrate that the GI value cannot be tested. The GL is therefore 0.

▲ indicates brand not specified

FOOD	GI VALUE GLUCOSE = 100	NOMINAL SERVING SIZE	AVAILABLE CARB PER SERVING	GL PER SERVING
Ensure™, vanilla (Abbott, Australia)	48	250mL	34	16
Ensure™ bar, chocolate fudge brownie (Abbott, Australia)	43	38	20	8
Ensure Plus™, vanilla (Abbott, Australia)	40	237mL	47	19
Ensure Pudding™, vanilla (Abbott, USA)	36	113	26	9
Glucerna™, vanilla (Abbott, USA)	31	237mL	23	7
Jevity™ (Abbott, Australia)	48	237mL	36	17
Resource Diabetic™, vanilla (Novartis, USA)	34	237mL	23	8
Resource Diabetic™, chocolate (Novartis, New Zealand)	16	237mL	41	7
Resource™ thickened orange juice (Novartis, New Zealand)	47	237mL	39	18
Resource™ thickened orange juice (Novartis, New Zealand)	54	237mL	36	19
Resource™ fruit beverage, peach flavor (Novartis, New Zealand)	40	237mL	41	16
Sustagen™, Dutch Chocolate (Mead Johnson, Australia)	31	250mL	41	13
Sustagen™ Hospital with extra fiber (Mead Johnson, Australia)	33	250mL	44	15

[0] indicates that the food has so little carbohydrate that the GI value cannot be tested. The GL is therefore 0.

▲ indicates brand not specified

FOOD	GI VALUE GLUCOSE = 100	NOMINAL SERVING SIZE	AVAILABLE CARB PER SERVING	GL PER SERVING
Sustagen™ Instant Pudding, vanilla (Mead Johnson, Australia)	27	250	47	13
Ultracal™ with fiber (Mead Johnson, USA)	40	237mL	29	12
PASTA AND NOODLES				
Capellini (Primo, Canada)	45	180	45	20
Corn pasta, gluten-free (Orgran, Australia)	78	180	42	32
Fettucine, egg				
Fettucine, egg	32	180	46	15
Fettucine, egg (Mother Earth, Australia)	47	180	46	22
■ *mean of two studies*	40	180	46	18
Gluten-free pasta, maize starch, boiled (UK)	54	180	42	22
Gnocchi, NS ▲ (Latina, Australia)	68	180	48	33
Instant noodles				
Instant "two-minute" noodles, Maggi® (Australia)	46			
Instant "two-minute" noodles, Maggi® (New Zealand)	48			
Instant noodles (Mr Noodle, Canada)	47			

[0] indicates that the food has so little carbohydrate that the GI value cannot be tested. The GL is therefore 0.

▲ indicates brand not specified

FOOD	GI VALUE GLUCOSE = 100	NOMINAL SERVING SIZE	AVAILABLE CARB PER SERVING	GL PER SERVING
■ *mean of three studies*	47	180	40	19
Linguine				
Thick, durum wheat, white, fresh (Sweden)	43	180	48	21
Thick, fresh, durum wheat flour (Sweden)	48	180	48	23
mean of two studies	46	180	48	22
Thin, durum wheat (Sweden)	49	180	48	23
Thin, fresh, durum wheat flour (Sweden)	61	180	48	29
Thin, fresh, durum wheat with 39% w/w egg (Sweden)	45	180	41	18
Thin, fresh, 30% w/w egg (Sweden)	53	180	41	22
■ *mean of four studies*	52	180	45	23
Mung bean noodles				
Lungkow beanthread noodles (National Cereals, China)	26	180	45	12
Mung bean noodles (Longkou beanthread) (Yantai, China)	39	180	45	18
■ *mean of two studies*	33			
Macaroni				
Macaroni, plain, boiled 5 min (Lancia-Bravo, Canada)	45	180	49	22
Macaroni, plain, boiled (Turkey)	48	180	49	23

[0] indicates that the food has so little carbohydrate that the GI value cannot be tested. The GL is therefore 0.

▲ indicates brand not specified

FOOD	GI VALUE GLUCOSE = 100	NOMINAL SERVING SIZE	AVAILABLE CARB PER SERVING	GL PER SERVING
■ *mean of two studies*	47	180	48	23
Macaroni and cheese, boxed (Kraft, Canada)	64	180	51	32
Ravioli (Australia)	39	180	38	15
Rice noodles/pasta				
Rice noodles, dried, boiled (Thai World, Thailand)	61	180	39	23
Rice noodles, freshly made, boiled (Sydney, Australia)	40	180	39	15
Rice pasta, brown, boiled 16 min (Rice Growers, Australia)	92	180	38	35
Rice and maize pasta, gluten-free, Ris'O'Mais (Orgran, Australia)	76	180	49	37
Rice vermicelli, Kongmoon (China)	58	180	39	22
Spaghetti				
Spaghetti, gluten-free, canned in tomato sauce (Orgran, Australia)	68	220	27	19
Spaghetti, protein enriched, boiled 7 min (Catelli, Canada)	27	180	52	14
Spaghetti, white, boiled 5 min				
Boiled 5 min (Lancia-Bravo, Canada)	32	180	48	15
Boiled 5 min (Canada)	34	180	48	16

[0] indicates that the food has so little carbohydrate that the GI value cannot be tested. The GL is therefore 0.

▲ indicates brand not specified

FOOD	GI VALUE GLUCOSE = 100	NOMINAL SERVING SIZE	AVAILABLE CARB PER SERVING	GL PER SERVING
Boiled 5 min (Canada)	40	180	48	19
Boiled 5 min (Middle East)	44	180	48	21
■ mean of four studies	38	180	48	18

Spaghetti, white or type NS ▲, boiled 10-15 min

FOOD	GI VALUE GLUCOSE = 100	NOMINAL SERVING SIZE	AVAILABLE CARB PER SERVING	GL PER SERVING
White, durum wheat, boiled 10 min (Barilla, Italy)	58	180	48	28
White, durum wheat flour, boiled 12 min (Starhushålls, Sweden)	47	180	48	23
White, durum wheat flour, boiled 12 min (Sweden)	53	180	48	25
Boiled 15 min (Lancia-Bravo, Canada)	32	180	48	15
Boiled 15 min (Lancia-Bravo, Canada)	36	180	48	17
Boiled 15 min (Canada)	41	180	48	20
White, boiled 15 min in salted water (Unico, Canada)	44	180	48	21
■ mean of seven studies	44	180	48	21

Spaghetti, white or type NS ▲, boiled 20 min

FOOD	GI VALUE GLUCOSE = 100	NOMINAL SERVING SIZE	AVAILABLE CARB PER SERVING	GL PER SERVING
White, durum wheat, boiled 20 min (Australia)	58	180	44	26
Durum wheat, boiled 20 min (USA)	64	180	43	27
■ mean of two studies	61	180	44	27

[0] indicates that the food has so little carbohydrate that the GI value cannot be tested. The GL is therefore 0.

▲ indicates brand not specified

FOOD	GI VALUE GLUCOSE = 100	NOMINAL SERVING SIZE	AVAILABLE CARB PER SERVING	GL PER SERVING
Spaghetti, white, boiled				
White (Denmark)	33	180	48	16
White, durum wheat (Catelli, Canada)	34	180	48	16
White (Australia)	38	180	44	17
White (Canada)	42	180	48	20
White (Canada)	48	180	48	23
White (Vetta, Australia)	49	180	44	22
White (Canada)	50	180	48	24
■ *mean of seven studies*	42	180	47	20
Spaghetti, white, durum wheat semolina (Panzani, France)				
Boiled for 11 min	59	180	48	28
Boiled for 16.5 min	65	180	48	31
Boiled for 22 min	46	180	48	22
■ *mean of three cooking times*	57	180	48	27
Spaghetti, whole wheat, boiled				
Whole wheat (USA)	32	180	44	14
Whole wheat (Canada)	42	180	40	17
■ *mean of two studies*	37	180	42	16
Spirali, durum wheat, white, boiled (Vetta, Australia)	43	180	44	19
Split pea and soy pasta shells, gluten-free (Orgran, Australia)	29	180	31	9

[0] indicates that the food has so little carbohydrate that the GI value cannot be tested. The GL is therefore 0.

▲ indicates brand not specified

FOOD	GI VALUE GLUCOSE = 100	NOMINAL SERVING SIZE	AVAILABLE CARB PER SERVING	GL PER SERVING
Star pastina, white, boiled 5 minutes (Lancia-Bravo, Canada)	38	180	48	18
Tortellini, cheese (Stouffer, Canada)	50	180	21	10
Udon noodles, plain, reheated 5 min (Australia)	62	180	48	30
Vermicelli, white, boiled (Australia)	35	180	44	16
PROTEIN FOODS				
Beef	[0]	120	0	0
Cheese	[0]	120	0	0
Eggs	[0]	120	0	0
Fish	[0]	120	0	0
Lamb	[0]	120	0	0
Pork	[0]	120	0	0
Salami	[0]	120	0	0
Shellfish (shrimp, crab, lobster, etc.)	[0]	120	0	0
Tuna	[0]	120	0	0
Veal	[0]	120	0	0
SNACK FOODS AND CANDY				
Burger Rings™ (Smith's, Australia)	90	50	31	28

[0] indicates that the food has so little carbohydrate that the GI value cannot be tested. The GL is therefore 0.

▲ indicates brand not specified

FOOD	GI VALUE GLUCOSE = 100	NOMINAL SERVING SIZE	AVAILABLE CARB PER SERVING	GL PER SERVING
Chocolate, milk, plain				
Chocolate, milk, plain with sucrose (Belgium)	34	50	22	7
Chocolate, milk (Cadbury's, Australia)	49	50	30	14
Chocolate, milk, Dove® (Mars, Australia)	45	50	30	13
Chocolate, milk (Nestlé, Australia)	42	50	31	13
■ *mean of four studies*	43	50	28	12
Chocolate, milk, plain, low-sugar with maltitol (Belgium)	35	50	22	8
Chocolate, white, Milky Bar® (Nestlé, Australia)	44	50	29	13
Fruit bars				
Apricot-filled fruit bar (Mother Earth, New Zealand)	50	50	34	17
Heinz Kidz™ Fruit Fingers, banana (Heinz, Australia)	61	30	20	12
Real Fruit Bars, strawberry (Uncle Toby's, Australia)	90	30	26	23
Roll-Ups® (Uncle Toby's, Australia)	99	30	25	24
Fruity Bitz™, vitamin and mineral enriched dried-fruit snacks				
Fruity Bitz™, apricot (Blackmores, Australia)	42	15	12	5

[0] indicates that the food has so little carbohydrate that the GI value cannot be tested. The GL is therefore 0.

▲ indicates brand not specified

FOOD	GI VALUE GLUCOSE = 100	NOMINAL SERVING SIZE	AVAILABLE CARB PER SERVING	GL PER SERVING
Fruity Bitz™, berry (Blackmores, Australia)	35	15	12	4
Fruity Bitz™, tropical (Blackmores, Australia)	41	15	11	5
■ *mean of three flavors*	39	15	12	4
Jelly beans				
Jelly beans, assorted colors (Australia)	80			
Jelly beans, assorted colors (Australia)	76			
■ *mean of two studies*	78	30	28	22
Kudos Whole Grain Bars, chocolate chip (USA)	62	50	32	20
Life Savers®, peppermint candy (Nestlé, Australia)	70	30	30	21
M & M's®, peanut (Australia)	33	30	17	6
Mars Bar®				
Mars Bar® (Australia)	62	60	40	25
Mars Bar® (USA)	68	60	40	27
■ *mean of two studies*	65	60	40	26
Muesli bar containing dried fruit (Uncle Toby's, Australia)	61	30	21	13
Nougat, Jijona (La Fama, Spain)	32	30	12	4
Nutella®, chocolate hazelnut spread (Australia)	33	20	12	4

[0] indicates that the food has so little carbohydrate that the GI value cannot be tested. The GL is therefore 0.

▲ indicates brand not specified

FOOD	GI VALUE GLUCOSE = 100	NOMINAL SERVING SIZE	AVAILABLE CARB PER SERVING	GL PER SERVING
Nuts				
Cashew nuts, salted (Coles Supermarkets, Australia)	22	50	13	3
Peanuts				
Peanuts, crushed (South Africa)	7	50	4	0
Peanuts (Canada)	13	50	7	1
Peanuts (Mexico)	23	50	7	2
■ *mean of three studies*	14	50	6	1
Popcorn				
Popcorn, plain, cooked in microwave oven (Green's, Australia)	55	20	11	6
Popcorn, plain, cooked in microwave oven (Uncle Toby's, Australia)	89	20	11	10
■ *mean of two studies*	72	20	11	8
Pop Tarts™, double choc (Kellogg's, Australia)	70	50	35	24
Potato chips				
Potato crisps, plain, salted (Arnott's, Australia)	57	50	18	10
Potato crisps, plain, salted (Canada)	51	50	24	12
■ *mean of two studies*	54	50	21	11

[0] indicates that the food has so little carbohydrate that the GI value cannot be tested. The GL is therefore 0.

▲ indicates brand not specified

FOOD	GI VALUE GLUCOSE = 100	NOMINAL SERVING SIZE	AVAILABLE CARB PER SERVING	GL PER SERVING
Pretzels, (Parker's, Australia)	83	30	20	16
Skittles® (Australia)	70	50	45	32
Snack bars				
Snack bar, Apple Cinnamon (Con Agra, USA)	40	50	29	12
Snack bar, Peanut Butter & Choc-Chip (USA)	37	50	27	10
Snickers Bar®				
Snickers Bar® (Australia)	41	60	36	15
Snickers Bar® (USA)	68	60	34	23
■ *mean of two studies*	55	60	35	19
Twisties™ (Smith's, Australia)	74	50	29	22
Twix® Cookie Bar, caramel (USA)	44	60	39	17
Tortilla chips				
Corn chips, plain, salted (Doritos™, Australia)	42	50	25	11
Nachips™ (Old El Paso, Canada)	74	50	29	21
■ *mean of three studies*	63	50	26	17
SPORTS BARS				
PowerBar®				
PowerBar®, chocolate (USA)	58			
PowerBar®, chocolate (USA)	53			

[0] indicates that the food has so little carbohydrate that the GI value cannot be tested. The GL is therefore 0.

▲ indicates brand not specified

FOOD	GI VALUE GLUCOSE = 100	NOMINAL SERVING SIZE	AVAILABLE CARB PER SERVING	GL PER SERVING
■ *mean of two studies*	56	65	42	24
Ironman PR bar®, chocolate (USA)	39	65	26	10
SOUPS				
Black Bean (Wil-Pack, USA)	64	250	27	17
Green Pea, canned (Campbell's, Canada)	66	250	41	27
Lentil, canned (Unico, Canada)	44	250	21	9
Minestrone, Country Ladle™ (Campbell's, Australia)	39	250	18	7
Noodle soup (Turkish soup with stock and noodles)	1	250	9	0
Split Pea (Wil-Pak, USA)	60	250	27	16
Tarhana soup (Turkish soup)	20	–	–	–
Tomato soup (Canada)	38	250	17	6
SUGARS AND SUGAR ALCOHOLS				
Blue Agave cactus nectar, high-fructose				
Organic Agave Cactus Nectar, light, 90% fructose (Western Commerce, USA)	11	10	8	1
Organic Agave Cactus Nectar, light, 97% fructose (Western Commerce, USA)	10	10	8	1
Fructose				
25 g portion (Canada)	11			

[0] indicates that the food has so little carbohydrate that the GI value cannot be tested. The GL is therefore 0.

▲ indicates brand not specified

FOOD	GI VALUE GLUCOSE = 100	NOMINAL SERVING SIZE	AVAILABLE CARB PER SERVING	GL PER SERVING
50 g portion (Canada)	12			
50 g portion	20			
50 g portion	21			
50 g portion (USA)	24			
25 g portion, fed with oats	25			
■ *mean of six studies*	19	10	10	2
Glucose (dextrose)				
■ *mean of 11 studies*	99	10	10	10
GLUCOSE CONSUMED WITH 3 GRAMS AMERICAN GINSENG				
■ *mean in two groups of subjects*	78	10	10	8
GLUCOSE CONSUMED WITH GUM/FIBER				
15 g apple and orange fiber (FITA, Australia)	79	10	8	6
14.5 g guar gum	62	10	10	6
14.5 g oat gum (78% oat ß-glucan)	57	10	10	6
20 g acacia gum	85	10	10	9
Honey				
Locust honey (Romania)	32	25	21	7
Yellow box (Australia)	35	25	18	6
Stringy Bark (Australia)	44	25	21	9
Red Gum (Australia)	46	25	18	8
Iron Bark (Australia)	48	25	15	7
Yapunya (Australia)	52	25	17	9

[0] indicates that the food has so little carbohydrate that the GI value cannot be tested. The GL is therefore 0.

▲ indicates brand not specified

FOOD	GI VALUE GLUCOSE = 100	NOMINAL SERVING SIZE	AVAILABLE CARB PER SERVING	GL PER SERVING
Pure (Capilano, Australia)	58	25	21	12
Commercial Blend (Australia)	62	25	18	11
Salvation Jane (Australia)	64	25	15	10
Commercial Blend (Australia)	72	25	13	9
Honey NS ▲ (Canada)	87	25	21	18
■ *mean of 11 types of honey*	55	25	18	10
Lactose				
■ *mean of three studies*	46	10	10	5
Maltose	105	10	10	11
Sucrose				
■ *mean of 8 studies*	61	10	10	6
Sugar alcohols and alternative sweeteners				
LACTITOL				
■ *mean of two studies*	2	10	10	0
LITESSE				
Litesse II (Danisco, UK)	7	10	10	1
Litesse III (Danisco, UK)	4	10	10	0
MALTITOL-BASED SWEETENERS OR BULKING AGENTS				
Malbit CR (87% maltitol) (Cerestar, Belgium)	30	10	10	3
Maltidex 100 (> 72% maltitol) (Cerestar, Belgium)	44	10	10	4
Malbit CH (99% maltitol) (Cerestar, Belgium)	73	10	10	7

[0] indicates that the food has so little carbohydrate that the GI value cannot be tested. The GL is therefore 0.

▲ indicates brand not specified

FOOD	GI VALUE GLUCOSE = 100	NOMINAL SERVING SIZE	AVAILABLE CARB PER SERVING	GL PER SERVING
Maltidex 200 (50% maltitol) (Cerestar, Belgium)	89	10	10	9
Xylitol				
■ *mean of two studies*	8	10	10	1
VEGETABLES				
Artichokes (Jerusalem)	[0]	80	0	0
Avocado	[0]	80	0	0
Beet (Canada)	64	80	7	5
Bok choy, raw	[0]	80	0	0
Broad beans (Canada)	79	80	11	9
Broccoli, raw	[0]	80	0	0
Cabbage, raw	[0]	80	0	0
Carrots				
Carrots, raw (Romania)	16	80	8	1
Carrots, peeled, boiled (Australia)	32	80	5	1
Carrots, peeled, boiled (Australia)	49	80	5	2
Carrots, NS ▲ (Canada)	92	80	6	5
■ *mean of four studies, raw*	47	80	6	3
Cassava, boiled, with salt (Kenya, Africa)	46	100	27	12
Cauliflower	[0]	80	0	0
Celery	[0]	80	0	0

[0] indicates that the food has so little carbohydrate that the GI value cannot be tested. The GL is therefore 0.

▲ indicates brand not specified

FOOD	GI VALUE GLUCOSE = 100	NOMINAL SERVING SIZE	AVAILABLE CARB PER SERVING	GL PER SERVING
Corn (sweet)				
Sweet corn, "Honey & Pearl" variety (New Zealand)	37	80	16	6
Sweet corn on the cob, boiled (Australia)	48	80	16	8
Sweet corn (Canada)	59	80	18	11
Sweet corn, boiled (USA)	60	80	18	11
Sweet corn (South Africa)	62	80	18	11
■ *mean of five studies*	54	80	17	9
Sweet corn, diet-pack, (USA)	46	80	14	7
Sweet corn, frozen (Canada)	47	80	15	7
Cucumber	[0]	80	0	0
French beans (runner beans), boiled	[0]	80	0	0
Green peas				
Peas, frozen, boiled (Canada)	39	80	7	3
Peas, frozen, boiled (Canada)	51	80	7	4
Peas, green (Pisum sativum) (India)	54	80	7	4
■ *mean of three studies*	48	80	7	3
Leafy vegetables (spinach, rocket, etc.), raw	[0]	80	0	0
Lettuce	[0]	80	0	0
Parsnips	97	80	12	12
Pepper	[0]	80	0	0

[0] indicates that the food has so little carbohydrate that the GI value cannot be tested. The GL is therefore 0.

▲ indicates brand not specified

FOOD	GI VALUE GLUCOSE = 100	NOMINAL SERVING SIZE	AVAILABLE CARB PER SERVING	GL PER SERVING
POTATO				
BAKED POTATO				
Ontario, white, baked in skin (Canada)	60	150	30	18
BAKED, RUSSET BURBANK POTATO				
Russet, baked without fat (Canada)	56			
Russet, baked without fat, 45–60 min (USA)	78			
Russet, baked without fat (USA)	94			
Russet, baked without fat (USA)	111			
■ *mean of four studies*	85	150	30	26
BOILED POTATO				
Desiree (Australia)	101	150	17	17
Nardine (New Zealand)	70	150	25	18
Ontario (Canada)	58	150	27	16
Pontiac (Australia)	88	150	18	16
Prince Edward Island (Canada)	63	150	18	11
Sebago (Australia)	87	150	17	14
Type NS ▲ (Kenya)	24	150	28	7
White (Romania)	41	150	30	12
White (Canada)	54	150	27	15
Type NS ▲ (India)	76	150	34	26

[0] indicates that the food has so little carbohydrate that the GI value cannot be tested. The GL is therefore 0.

▲ indicates brand not specified

FOOD	GI VALUE GLUCOSE = 100	NOMINAL SERVING SIZE	AVAILABLE CARB PER SERVING	GL PER SERVING
Type NS ▲ refrigerated, reheated (India)	23	150	34	8
CANNED POTATO				
Prince Edward Island (Cobi Foods, Canada)	61	150	18	11
New (Edgell's, Australia)	65	150	18	12
■ *mean of two studies*	63	150	18	11
FRENCH FRIES				
French fries, frozen and reheated (Cavendish Farms, Canada)	75	150	29	22
INSTANT MASHED POTATO				
Instant (France)	74			
Instant (Canada)	80			
Instant (Edgell's, Australia)	86			
Instant (Carnation, Canada)	86			
Instant (Canada)	88			
Instant (USA)	97			
■ *mean of six studies*	85	150	20	17
MASHED POTATO				
Type NS ▲ (Canada)	67			
Type NS ▲ (South Africa)	71			
Type NS ▲ (France)	83			
Prince Edward Island (Canada)	73	150	18	13
Pontiac (Australia)	91	150	20	18
■ *mean of five studies*	92	150	20	18

[0] indicates that the food has so little carbohydrate that the GI value cannot be tested. The GL is therefore 0.

▲ indicates brand not specified

FOOD	GI VALUE GLUCOSE = 100	NOMINAL SERVING SIZE	AVAILABLE CARB PER SERVING	GL PER SERVING
MICROWAVED POTATO				
Pontiac, peeled and micro-waved on high for 6–7.5 min (Australia)	79	150	18	14
Type NS ▲, microwaved (USA)	82	150	33	27
NEW POTATO				
New (Canada)	47			
New (Canada)	54			
New (Canada)	70			
New (Australia)	78			
■ *mean of four studies*	62	150	21	13
STEAMED POTATO				
Potato, peeled, steamed (India)	65	150	27	18
Potato dumplings (Italy)	52	150	45	24
SWEET POTATO				
Sweet potato, *Ipomoea batatas* (Australia)	44	150	25	11
Sweet potato, ▲ (Canada)	48	150	34	16
Sweet potato (Canada)	59	150	30	18
Sweet potato, kumara (New Zealand)	77	150	25	19
Sweet potato, kumara (New Zealand)	78	150	25	20
■ *mean of five studies*	61	150	28	17
Pumpkin (South Africa)	75	80	4	3
Rutabaga (Canada)	72	150	10	7

[0] indicates that the food has so little carbohydrate that the GI value cannot be tested. The GL is therefore 0.

▲ indicates brand not specified

FOOD	GI VALUE GLUCOSE = 100	NOMINAL SERVING SIZE	AVAILABLE CARB PER SERVING	GL PER SERVING
Squash, raw	[0]	80	0	0
Tapioca				
Tapioca boiled with milk (General Mills, Canada)	81	250	18	14
Tapioca (*Manihot utilissima*), steamed 1 h (India)	70	250	18	12
Taro				
Taro (*Colocasia esculenta*), boiled (Australia)	54			
Taro, boiled (New Zealand)	56			
■ *mean of two studies*	55	150	8	4
Tomato juice, canned, no added sugar (Berri, Australia)	38	250	9	4
Yam				
Yam, peeled, boiled (New Zealand)	25			
Yam, peeled, boiled (New Zealand)	35			
Yam (Canada)	51			
■ *mean of three studies*	37	150	36	13
INDIGENOUS OR ETHNIC FOODS AFRICAN				
Brown beans (South Africa)	24	50 (dry)	25	6
Cassava, boiled (Kenya)	46	100	27	12
Ga kenkey, prepared from fermented cornmeal (Ghana)	12	150	13	7

[0] indicates that the food has so little carbohydrate that the GI value cannot be tested. The GL is therefore 0.

▲ indicates brand not specified

FOOD	GI VALUE GLUCOSE = 100	NOMINAL SERVING SIZE	AVAILABLE CARB PER SERVING	GL PER SERVING
Gari, roasted cassava dough (*Manihot utilissima*) (Ghana)	56	100	27	15
Gram dhal (South Africa)	5	50 (dry)	29	1
Maize meal porridge (South Africa)	71	50 (dry)	36	25
Maize meal porridge (South Africa)	74	50 (dry)	40	30
Maize meal porridge (Kenya)	109	50 (dry)	38	41
M'fino/Morogo, wild greens (South Africa)	68	120	50	34
Millet flour porridge (Kenya)	107	–	–	–
Unripe plantain (*Musa paradisiaca*) (Ghana)	40	120 (raw)	34	13
Yam (*Dyscoria species*) (Ghana)	66	150	36	23
ARABIC AND TURKISH				
Hummus (chickpea salad dip)	6	30	5	0
Kibbeh saynieh (made with lamb and burghul)	61	120	15	9
Lebanese roll (bread, hummus, falafel, and tabbouleh)	86	120	45	39
Majadra (Syrian, lentils, and rice)	24	250	41	10
Moroccan couscous (stew of semolina, chickpeas, and vegetables)	58	250	29	17

[0] indicates that the food has so little carbohydrate that the GI value cannot be tested. The GL is therefore 0.

▲ indicates brand not specified

FOOD	GI VALUE GLUCOSE = 100	NOMINAL SERVING SIZE	AVAILABLE CARB PER SERVING	GL PER SERVING
Stuffed grapevine leaves (rice and lamb stuffing, tomato sauce)	30	100	15	5
Tarhana soup (wheat flour, yogurt, tomato, green pepper)	20	–	–	–
Turkish bread, white wheat flour	87	30	17	15
Turkish bread, whole wheat	49	30	16	8
Turkish noodle soup	1	250	9	0
ASIAN				
Broken rice, white (Thailand)	86	150	43	37
Butter rice (warm white rice and butter) (Japan)	79	150	51	40
Curry rice (Japan)	67	150	61	41
Curry rice with cheese (Japan)	55	150	49	27
Glutinous rice (Thailand)	98	150	32	31
Glutinous rice (Japan)	86	150	65	55
■ *mean of two studies*	92	150	48	44
Glutinous rice ball with cut glutinous cake (mochi) (Japan)	48	75	28	14
Glutinous rice cake with dried algae (Japan)	83	75	39	32
Glutinous rice flour, instant, with roasted soybean (Japan)	65	100	41	27
Jasmine rice (Thailand)	109	150	42	46

[0] indicates that the food has so little carbohydrate that the GI value cannot be tested. The GL is therefore 0.

▲ indicates brand not specified

FOOD	GI VALUE GLUCOSE = 100	NOMINAL SERVING SIZE	AVAILABLE CARB PER SERVING	GL PER SERVING
Low-protein white rice with dried algae (Japan)	70	150	60	42
Lungkow beanthread (China)	26	180	45	12
Lychee, canned in syrup, drained (China)	79	120	20	16
Mung bean noodles, dried, boiled (China)	39	180	45	18
Non-glutaminous rice flour, as drink (Japan)	68	100	50	34
Rice cracker, plain (Sakada, Japan)	91	30	25	23
Rice gruel with dried algae (Japan)	81	250	19	15
Rice noodles, dried, boiled (Thailand)	61	180	39	23
Rice noodles, fresh, boiled (Australia)	40	180	39	15
Rice vermicelli, Kongmoon (China)	58	180	39	22
Roasted rice ball (Japan)	77	75	27	21
Salted rice ball (Japan)	80	75	26	20
Soba noodles, instant, reheated (Japan)	46	180	49	22
Stir-fried vegetables, chicken and rice (Australia)	73	360	75	55
Sushi, salmon (Australia)	48	100	36	17

[0] indicates that the food has so little carbohydrate that the GI value cannot be tested. The GL is therefore 0.

▲ indicates brand not specified

FOOD	GI VALUE GLUCOSE = 100	NOMINAL SERVING SIZE	AVAILABLE CARB PER SERVING	GL PER SERVING
Sushi, roasted algae, vinegar, and rice (Japan)	55	100	37	20
■ mean of two studies	52	100	37	19
Udon noodles, fresh (Australia)	62	180	48	30
Udon noodles, instant, with sauce and fried bean curd (Japan)	48	180	47	23
■ mean of two studies	55	180	48	26
White rice, dried algae and milk (Japan)	56	300	47	26
White rice with dried fish strip (okaka) (Japan)	79	150	50	40
White rice with fermented soybean (natto) (Japan)	56	150	43	24
White rice with instant miso soup (Japan)	61	150	47	29
White rice with low-fat milk (Japan)	69	300	47	32
White rice and yogurt (Japan)	59	150	32	19
White rice with pickled vinegar and cucumber (Japan)	63	150	43	27
White rice topped with raw egg and soy sauce (Japan)	72	150	36	26
White rice with roasted, ground soybean (Japan)	56	150	51	29
White rice with salted dried plum (umeboshi) (Japan)	80	150	49	39

[0] indicates that the food has so little carbohydrate that the GI value cannot be tested. The GL is therefore 0.

▲ indicates brand not specified

FOOD	GI VALUE GLUCOSE = 100	NOMINAL SERVING SIZE	AVAILABLE CARB PER SERVING	GL PER SERVING
White rice with algae rolled in sheet of toasted algae (Japan)	77	150	51	39
ASIAN INDIAN				
Amaranth, *Amaranthus esculentum*, popped, with milk	97	30	19	18
Bajra (*Penniseteum typhoideum*) as bread	55			
Bajra (*Penniseteum typhoideum*)	49			
Bajra (*Penniseteum typhoideum*)	67			
■ *mean of three studies*	57	75 (dry)	50	29
Banana (*Musa sapientum*), Nendra, unripe, steamed 1 h	70	120	45	31
Barley (*Hordeum vulgare*)	48			
Barley (*Hordeum vulgare*)	37			
■ *mean of two studies*	43	150	37	16
Bengal gram dhal, chickpea	11	150	36	4
Black gram dhal (*Phaseolus mungo*)	43	150	18	8
CHAPATTI				
Chapatti, wheat flour with bottle gourd and tomato curry	66	60	30	20
Chapatti, amaranth flour with bottle gourd and tomato curry	76	60	30	23
Chapatti, baisen	27	–	–	–
Chapatti, bajra	67	–	–	–

[0] indicates that the food has so little carbohydrate that the GI value cannot be tested. The GL is therefore 0.

▲ indicates brand not specified

FOOD	GI VALUE GLUCOSE = 100	NOMINAL SERVING SIZE	AVAILABLE CARB PER SERVING	GL PER SERVING
Chapatti, bajra	49	–	–	–
Chapatti, barley	37	–	–	–
Chapatti, barley	48	–	–	–
Chapatti, maize (*Zea mays*)	64	–	–	–
Chapatti, maize (*Zea mays*)	59	–	–	–
Chapatti, wheat, moth bean and bengal gram	66	60	38	25
Chapatti, popped wheat, moth bean and bengal gram	40	60	36	14
Chapatti, roller dried wheat, moth bean and bengal gram	60	60	38	23
Chapatti, wheat flour, thin, with green gram (*Phaseolus aureus*) dhal	44	200	50	22
Cheela (thin savoury pancake made from legume flour batter)				
Cheela, bengal gram (*Cicer arietinum*)	42	150	28	12
Cheela, bengal gram (*Cicer arietinum*), fermented batter	36	150	28	10
Cheela, green gram (*Phaseolus aureus*)	45	150	26	12
Cheela, green gram (*Phaseolus aureus*), fermented batter	38	150	26	10
Dhokla, leavened, fermented, steamed cake	35			

[0] indicates that the food has so little carbohydrate that the GI value cannot be tested. The GL is therefore 0.

▲ indicates brand not specified

FOOD	GI VALUE GLUCOSE = 100	NOMINAL SERVING SIZE	AVAILABLE CARB PER SERVING	GL PER SERVING
Dhokla, leavened, fermented, steamed cake	31			
■ mean in two groups of subjects	33	100	20	6
Dosai (parboiled rice, fermented and fried)	77	150	39	30
Dosai (parboiled rice, fermented and fried)	55	150	39	22
■ mean in two groups of subjects	66	150	39	26
Green gram (*Phaseolus aureus*)	38	150	17	6
Green gram, with varagu (*Paspalum scorbiculatum*)	57	80 (dry)	50	29
Green gram dhal with varagu (*Paspalum scorbiculatum*)	78	78 (dry)	50	39
Horse gram (Dolichos biflorus)	51	150	29	15
Idli (rice + black dhal)	77	250	52	40
Idli (rice + black dhal)	60	250	52	31
■ mean in two groups of subjects	69	250	52	36
Jowar, bread from Jowar flour (*Sorghum vulgare*)	77	70 (dry)	50	39
Laddu (popped amaranth, foxtail millet, legume flour, fenugreek)	24			

[0] indicates that the food has so little carbohydrate that the GI value cannot be tested. The GL is therefore 0.

▲ indicates brand not specified

FOOD	GI VALUE GLUCOSE = 100	NOMINAL SERVING SIZE	AVAILABLE CARB PER SERVING	GL PER SERVING
Laddu (popped amaranth, foxtail millet, legume flour, fenugreek)	29			
■ *mean in two groups of subjects*	27	50	31	8
Lentil and cauliflower curry with rice (Australia)	60	360	51	31
Millet/Ragi (*Eleucine coracana*), 1 h	68	150	34	23
Millet/Ragi (*Eleucine coracana*)	84	70 (dry)	50	42
Millet/Ragi (*Eleucine coracana*) flour eaten as roasted bread	104	70 (dry)	50	52
■ *mean of two studies*	94	70	50	47
Pongal (rice and roasted green gram dhal)	90			
Pongal (rice and roasted green gram dhal)	45			
■ *mean in two groups of subjects*	68	250	52	35
Poori with potato palya	82			
Poori with potato palya	57			
■ *mean in two groups of subjects*	70	150	41	28
Rajmah, *Phaseolus vulgaris*	19	150	30	6

[0] indicates that the food has so little carbohydrate that the GI value cannot be tested. The GL is therefore 0.

▲ indicates brand not specified

FOOD	GI VALUE GLUCOSE = 100	NOMINAL SERVING SIZE	AVAILABLE CARB PER SERVING	GL PER SERVING
Rice, with bottle gourd and tomato curry	69	150	38	26
SEMOLINA				
Semolina (*Triticum aestivum*), steamed	55	67 (dry)	50	28
Semolina (*Triticum aestivum*), pre-roasted	76	67 (dry)	50	38
Semolina (*Triticum aestivum*) with black gram dhal	46	71 (dry)	50	23
Semolina (*Triticum aestivum*) with green gram dhal	62	71 (dry)	50	31
Semolina (*Triticum aestivum*) with bengal gram dhal	54	71 (dry)	50	27
Tapioca (*Manihot utilissima*), steamed 1h	70	250	18	12
Varagu (*Paspalum scorbiculatum*)	68	76 (dry)	50	34
Upittu (roasted semolina and onions)	67			
Upittu (roasted semolina and onions)	69			
■ *mean in two groups of subjects*	68	150	42	28
Uppuma kedgeree (millet, legumes, fenugreek seeds)	18			
Uppuma kedgeree (millet, legumes, fenugreek seeds)	19			

[0] indicates that the food has so little carbohydrate that the GI value cannot be tested. The GL is therefore 0.

▲ indicates brand not specified

FOOD	GI VALUE GLUCOSE = 100	NOMINAL SERVING SIZE	AVAILABLE CARB PER SERVING	GL PER SERVING
■ *mean in two groups of subjects*	18	150	33	6
AUSTRALIAN ABORIGINAL				
Acacia aneura, mulga seed, roasted, wet ground to paste	8	50	17	1
Acacia coriacea, desert oak, seed bread	46	75	24	11
Araucaria bidwillii, bunya tree nut, baked 10 min	47	50	16	7
Bush honey, sugar bag	43	30	25	11
Castanospermum australe, blackbean seed	8	50	9	1
Dioscorea bulbifera, cheeky yam	34	150	36	12
Macrozamia communis, cycad palm seed	40	50	25	10
PACIFIC ISLANDER				
Breadfruit (*Artocarpus altilis*) (Australia)	68	120	27	18
BANANA/PLANTAIN, GREEN				
Green banana, boiled (New Zealand)	38	120	21	8
SWEET POTATO				
Sweet potato, *Ipomoea batatas* (Australia)	44	150	25	11

[0] indicates that the food has so little carbohydrate that the GI value cannot be tested. The GL is therefore 0.

▲ indicates brand not specified

FOOD	GI VALUE GLUCOSE = 100	NOMINAL SERVING SIZE	AVAILABLE CARB PER SERVING	GL PER SERVING
Sweet potato, kumara (New Zealand)	77	150	25	19
Sweet potato, kumara (New Zealand)	78	150	25	20
■ *mean of three studies*	66	150	25	17
TARO				
Taro (*Colocasia esculenta*) peeled, boiled (Australia)	54			
Taro, peeled, boiled (New Zealand)	56			
■ *mean of two studies*	55	150	8	4
YAM				
Yam, peeled, boiled (New Zealand)	25			
Yam, peeled, boiled (New Zealand)	35			
■ *mean of two groups of subjects*	30	150	36	13
ISRAELI				
Melawach	61			
Melawach	71			
■ *mean of two studies*	66	115	53	35
Melawach + 15 g locust bean (*Ceratonia siliqua*) fiber (soluble)	31	130	53	16
Melawach + 15 g maize cob fiber (insoluble)	59	130	53	31

[0] indicates that the food has so little carbohydrate that the GI value cannot be tested. The GL is therefore 0.

▲ indicates brand not specified

FOOD	GI VALUE GLUCOSE = 100	NOMINAL SERVING SIZE	AVAILABLE CARB PER SERVING	GL PER SERVING
Melawach + 15 g lupin (*Lupinus albus*) fiber	72	130	53	38
PIMA INDIAN				
Acorns, stewed with venison (*Quercus emoryi*)	6	16	100	61
Cactus jam (*Stenocereus thurberi*)	91	30	20	18
Corn hominy (*Zea mays*)	40	150	30	12
Fruit leather (*Stenocereus thurberi*)	70	30	24	17
Lima beans broth (*Phaseolus lunatus*)	36	250	32	12
Mesquite cakes (*Prosopis velutina*)	25	60	4	1
Tortilla (*Zea mays* and *Olneya tesota*)	38	60	25	9
White teparies broth (*Phaseolus acutifolius*)	31	250	32	10
Yellow teparies broth (*Phaseolus acutifolius*)	29	250	26	8
SOUTH AMERICAN				
Arepa, corn bread cake, made with corn flour (Mexico)	72	100	43	31
Arepa, made from ordinary dehulled dent corn flour (25% amylose)	81	100	43	3

[0] indicates that the food has so little carbohydrate that the GI value cannot be tested. The GL is therefore 0.

▲ indicates brand not specified

FOOD	GI VALUE GLUCOSE = 100	NOMINAL SERVING SIZE	AVAILABLE CARB PER SERVING	GL PER SERVING
Arepa, made from dehulled high-amylose (70%) corn flour	44	100	25	11
Black beans	30	150	23	7
Brown beans	38	150	25	9
Corn tortilla (Mexican)	52	50	24	12
Corn tortilla, with pinto beans and tomato sauce (Mexican)	39	100	23	9
Corn tortilla, fried, with mashed potato, tomatos and lettuce (Mexican)	78	100	15	11
Nopal (prickly pear cactus)	7	100	6	0
Pinto beans, boiled in salted water	14	150	25	4
Wheat tortilla (Mexican)	30	50	26	8
Wheat tortilla with pinto beans and tomato sauce (Mexican)	28	100	18	5

[0] indicates that the food has so little carbohydrate that the GI value cannot be tested.
The GL is therefore 0.
▲ indicates brand not specified

Further Reading: Sources and References

Tables of GI Values

Foster-Powell, K., J. C. Brand-Miller, and S. H. A. Holt. 2002. "International table of glycemic index and glycemic load values: 2002." *American Journal of Clinical Nutrition* 76:5–56.

GI Recommendations

American Diabetes Association. 2001. "Nutrition recommendations and principles for people with diabetes mellitus." *Diabetes Care* 24(S1).

The Diabetes and Nutrition Study Group (DNSG) of the European Association for the Study of Diabetes (EASD). 2000. "Recommendations for the nutritional management of patients with diabetes mellitus." European Journal of Clinical Nutrition 54:353–55.

Dietitians Association of Australia review paper. 1997. "Glycaemic index in diabetes management." *Australian Journal of Nutrition and Dietetics* 54(2):57–63.

Food and Agriculture Organisation/World Health Organisation. 1998. "Carbohydrates in Human Nutrition, Report of a Joint FAO/WHO Expert Consultation." Rome, 14–18 April 1997. FAO Food and Nutrition Paper 66.

National Health and Medical Research Council. 1999. "Dietary Guidelines for Older Australians." *Ausinfo*, Canberra.

Position Statement by the Canadian Diabetes Association. 1999. "Guidelines for the nutritional management of diabetes mellitus in the new millenium." *Canadian Journal of Diabetes Care* 23(3):56–69.

The Glycemic Index and Health—General

Frost, G., and A. Dornhorst. 2000. "The relevance of the glycaemic index to our understanding of dietary carbohydrates." *Diabetic Medicine* 17:336–45.

Jenkins, D. J. A., L. S. A. Augustin, C. W. C. Kendall, et al. 2002. "Glycemic index: overview of implications in health and disease." *American Journal of Clinical Nutrition* 76:266S–273S.

Ludwig, D. S. 2002. "The glycemic index. Physiological mechanisms relating to obesity, diabetes, and cardiovascular disease." *Journal of the American Medical Association* 287:2414–2423.

Ludwig, D. S. and R. H. Eckel. 2002. "The glycemic index at 20y." *American Journal of Clinical Nutrition* 76:264S–265S.

Pi-Sunyer, F. X. 2002. "Glycemic index and disease." *American Journal of Clinical Nutrition* 76:290S–298S.

The Glycemic Index and Diabetes

Buyken, A. E., M. Toeller, G. Heitkamp, B. Karamanos, R. Rottiers, M. Muggeo, J. H. Fuller, and the EURODIAB IDDM Complications Study Group. 2001. "Glycemic index in the diet of European outpatients with type 1 diabetes: relations to glycated hemoglobin and serum lipids." *American Journal of Clinical Nutrition* 73:574–81.

Giacco, R., M. Parillo, A. A. Rivellese, G. Lasorella, A. Giacco, L. D'episcopo, and G. Riccardi. 2000. "Long-term dietary treatment with increased amounts of fibre-rich low-glycemic index natural foods improves blood glucose control and reduces the number of hypoglycemic events in type 1 diabetic patients." *Diabetes Care* 23:1461–66.

Gilbertson, H. R., J. C. Brand-Miller, A. W. Thorburn, S. Evans, P. Chondros, and G. A. Werther. 2001. "The effect of flexible low glycemic index dietary advice versus measured carbohydrate exchange diets on glycemic control in children with type 1 diabetes." *Diabetes Care* 24:1137–43.

Salmeron, J., A. Ascherio, E. B. Rimm, et al. 1997. "Dietary fiber, glycemic load, and risk of NIDDM in men." *Diabetes Care* 20:545–50.

Salmeron, J., J. E. Manson, M. F. Stampfer, G. A. Colditz, A. L. Wing, and W. C. Willett. 1997. "Dietary fiber, glycemic load, and risk of non-insulin-dependent diabetes mellitus in women." *Journal of the American Medical Association* 277:472–77.

Willett, W., J. Manson, and S. Liu. 2002. "Glycemic index, glycemic load, and risk of type 2 diabetes." *American Journal of Clinical Nutrition* 76:274S–280S.

The Glycemic Index and Obesity

Agus, M. S. D., J. F. Swain, C. L. Larson, E. A. Eckert, and D. S. Ludwig. 2000. "Dietary composition and physiologic adaptations to energy restriction." *American Journal of Clinical Nutrition* 71:901–7.

Brand-Miller, J. C., S. H. A. Holt, D. B. Pawlak, and J. McMillan. 2002. "Glycemic index and obesity." *American Journal of Clinical Nutrition* 76: 281S–285S.

Ludwig, D. S. 2000. "Dietary glycemic index and obesity." *Journal of Nutrition* 130:280S–83S.

Ludwig, D. S., J. A. Majzoub, A. Al-Zahrani, G. E. Dallal, I. Blanco, and S. B. Roberts. 1999. "High glycemic index foods, overeating, and obesity." *Pediatrics* 103(3).

Spieth, L. E., J. D. Harnish, C. M. Lenders, L. B. Raezer, M. A. Pereira, J. Hangen, and D. S. Ludwig. 2000. "A low-glycemic index diet in the treatment of pediatric obesity." *Archives of Pediatric and Adolescent Medicine* 154:947–51.

The Glycemic Index and Heart Disease

Dumesnil, J. G., J. Turgeon, A. Tremblay, et al. 2001. "Effect of a low-glycaemic index-low-fat-high protein diet on the atherogenic metabolic risk profile of abdominally obese men." *British Journal of Nutrition* 86:557–568.

Ford, E. S., and S. Liu. 2001. "Glycemic index and serum high-density-lipoprotein cholesterol concentration among US adults." *Archives of Internal Medicine* 161:572–6.

Frost, G., A. Leeds, D. Dore, S. Madeiros, S. Brading, and A. Dornhorst. 1999. "Glycaemic index as a determinant of serum HDL-cholesterol concentration." *Lancet* 353:1045–48.

Leeds, A. R. 2002. "Glycemic index and heart disease." *American Journal of Clinical Nutrition* 76:286S–289S.

Liu, S., J. E. Manson, J. E. Buring, M. J. Stampfer, W. C. Willett, and P. M. Ridker. 2002. "Relation between a diet with a high glycemic load and plasma concentrations of high-sensitivity C-reactive protein in middle-aged women." *American Journal of Clinical Nutrition* 75:492–498.

Liu, S., J. E. Manson, M. J. Stampfer, M. D. Holmes, F. B. Hu, S. E. Hankinson, and W. C. Willett. 2001. "Dietary glycemic load assessed by food-frequency questionnaire in relation to plasma high-density-lipoprotein cholesterol and fasting plasma triacylglycerols in postmenopausal women." *American Journal of Clinical Nutrition* 73:560–6.

Liu, S., W. C. Willett, M. J. Stampfer, F. B. Hu, M. Franz, L. Sampson, C. H. Hennekens, and J. E. Manson. 2000. "A prospective study of dietary glycemic load, carbohydrate intake and risk of coronary heart disease in US women." *American Journal of Clinical Nutrition* 71:1455–61.

The Glycemic Index and Colon Cancer

Bruce, W. R., T. M. S. Wolever, and A. Giacca. 2000. "Mechanisms linking diet and colorectal cancer: the possible role of insulin resistance." *Nutrition and Cancer* 37:19–26.

Franceschi, S., L. Dal Maso, L. Augustin, E. Negri, M. Parpinel, P. Boyle, D. J. A. Jenkins, and C. La Vecchia. 2001. "Dietary glycemic load and colorectal cancer risk." *Annals of Oncology* 12:1–6.

Glossary

Alpha-linolenic acid (ALA): The plant form of polyunsaturated omega-3 fat. ALA is found in flaxseed, canola, walnut and soybean oils. There are also small amounts in walnuts, flaxseeds, pecans, soybeans, baked beans, wheat germ, lean meats, and green leafy vegetables.

Antioxidant: Any substance that inhibits the oxidation of another substance. Oxidation is a natural process that occurs in our bodies all the time, but it is implicated specifically in such conditions as cardiovascular disease, cancer and aging. Dietary antioxidants, such as vitamins C and E, are believed to limit these disease processes.

Atherosclerosis: Also known as hardening of the arteries, this condition can lead to heart disease.

Carbohydrates: Carbohydrates are our bodies' preferred fuel source. They consist of glucose, in addition to one or more other compounds containing carbon, hydrogen and oxygen atoms. Because of their chemical composition, it is easiest for our bodies to break down carbohydrate foods into energy.

Docosahexanoic acid (DHA): This essential fatty acid helps to control high blood pressure and is associated with lower risks of rheumatoid arthritis, depression and cancer. Fatty fish, such as shellfish, mackerel, tuna, salmon, bluefish, mullet, sturgeon, anchovy, herring, trout, sardines are all good food sources.

Eicosanoid: A substance in the blood that initiates our body's immune response and the resulting inflammation. Scientists believe that omega-3 fatty acids decrease these reactions.

Eicosapentanoic acid (EPA): This essential fatty acid helps to control high blood pressure and is associated with lower risks of rheumatoid arthritis, depression and cancer. Fatty fish, such as shellfish, mackerel, tuna, salmon, bluefish, mullet, sturgeon, anchovy, herring, trout, sardines are all good food sources.

Flavonoids: These phytochemicals with antioxidant properties help to prevent tumor formation. Flavonoids are especially prevalent in soy foods,

Glycemic index: A numerical ranking of foods based on their immediate effect on our blood sugar levels. Carbohydrate foods that break down quickly during digestion have the highest GI values because the blood sugar response is fast and high. Carbohydrates that break down slowly, releasing glucose gradually into the bloodstream, have low GI values.

Glycemic load: A measure of the degree of blood-glucose and insulin demand produced by a normal serving of food. Glycemic load is calculated by multiplying a food's GI times a nominal serving size, and dividing by 100.

HDL cholesterol: High-density lipoprotein cholesterol, also known as "good" cholesterol because elevated levels of this blood fat protect against heart disease.

High-GI food: A food with a glycemic index greater than 70. High-GI foods raise blood sugar levels the most.

Insulin: A hormone produced by the pancreas, which helps to metabolize carbohydrates and is used to manage and treat diabetes.

LDL cholesterol: Low-density lipoprotein cholesterol, also known as "bad" cholesterol. Elevated levels of this type of blood fat are a risk factor for heart disease.

Lipids: Another term for fats. Cholesterol and triglycerides are all blood lipids.

Low-GI food: A food with a glycemic index less than 55. Low GI foods raise blood sugar levels least.

Macronutrients: The major nutrients that our bodies require, including protein, fat, carbohydrate and water.

Mediterranean diet: A diet consisting primarily of fish, fruits, vegetables, olives and olive oil. People eating this diet tend to have lower rates of heart disease and cancer.

Metabolism: The process by which our bodies use nutrients for energy and to dispose of waste products.

Micronutrients: Nutrients that are present in foods and that our bodies require in relatively small amounts, including vitamins and minerals.

Monounsaturated fats (MUFAs): Oleic acid is one example of a MUFA. These heart-healthy fats are liquid at room temperature.

Omega-3 (linolenic acid): Omega-3 is an essential fatty acid that our bodies cannot produce. Studies show that this fatty acid can reduce arthritis pain and cancer risk and aid in brain development. Good food sources include fats and oils (canola, soybean, walnut, wheat germ and some margarines), nuts and seeds (butternuts, walnuts, soybean kernels) and soybeans.

Omega-6 (linoleic acid): Our bodies can't make linoleic acid, so we must get it from the foods we eat. Omega-6 fatty acids aid in cell membrane integrity, blood pressure regulation, blood clot formation, regulation of blood lipids and immune response to injury and infection. Good food sources include leafy vegetables, seeds, nuts, grains, vegetable oils, including corn, safflower, soybean, cottonseed, sesame and sunflower.

Paleolithic diet: A high-fiber diet that probably consisted of 65 percent animal food and 35 percent plant foods, including fruit, roots, legumes and nuts. Experts speculate that this high-fiber diet would have lowered the incidence of diabetes, colon cancer and anemia.

Phytochemicals: Natural chemicals, found in all plant foods, that can be beneficial to health.

Polyphenols: A group of phytochemicals found in fruits, grains, vegetables, wine, tea, cocoa and chocolate, which is believed to have antioxidant properties.

Polyunsaturated fats (PUFAs): Liquid at room temperature, examples of PUFAs include linoleic acid and linolenic acid. PUFAs are found in all vegetable oils, especially safflower, sunflower, corn, soybean and cottonseed.

Saturated fat: Solid at room temperature (such as butter, for example), saturated fat comes in the form of fatty marbling in meat, the cream in milk and other high fat dairy products, and in some of the tropical oils such as palm oil, widely used as shortening for frying and for making cakes, pies, cookies and crackers. Studies show that saturated fat increases our risk of heart disease, obesity and certain cancers.

Selenium: A mineral often grouped with antioxidants; it may help to prevent cancer.

Sugar: There are six common sugars found in foods: glucose (in all fruits and some vegetables); fructose (in all fruits); galactose (in milk); sucrose (made into table sugar); lactose (in milk); and maltose (malt sugar).

Trans-fatty acids: Produced during the manufacture of margarines, these fats behave like saturated fat both in the product (increasing its firmness) and in our bodies (increasing the risk of heart attack). Foods high in trans fats include fried fast foods, some margarines, crackers, cookies and snack cakes.

Triglycerides: The chemical name for fats stored and circulated throughout our bodies.

Vitamin C: An antioxidant vitamin that helps to keep your immune system, capillaries and gums healthy. It is found in such foods as strawberries, oranges, grapefruit, broccoli and green peppers.

Vitamin E: This antioxidant vitamin plays a role in heart health; good food sources include vegetable oils, nuts and seeds.

Acknowledgments

Many people have contributed to *The New Glucose Revolution*, and we are grateful to them all. Back in 1995, when the first edition of the book (then called *The GI Factor*) was conceived, it was Catherine Saxelby who got us off to a good start. Then Philippa Sandall, our editor at Hodder Headline in Australia and now our literary agent, took over and ensured that our style and content were appropriate to our readers, and in many other ways contributed to the success of all the books.

For their work on the North American editions, we'd like to thank Johanna Burani, our extremely dedicated adapter and a longstanding advocate of the glycemic index; Rick Mendosa, another of our longtime GI advocates, for his careful review of the manuscript; Matthew Lore, our publisher at Marlowe & Company, along with his colleagues Ghadah Alrawi, Peter Jacoby, Sue McCloskey, and Michelle Rosenfield; Donna Stonecipher, for her meticulous proofreading; Pauline Neuwirth, for her book design and typesetting [of the original book]; and Howard Grossman, for his cover design [of the original book].

We are indebted to those who have supported the GI approach and recommended our books, particularly Diabetes

Australia and the Juvenile Diabetes Research Foundation. Many dietitians, doctors, and readers have given us feedback and played a large role in our success, some of whom deserve special mention: Shirley Crossman, Martina Chippendall, Helen O'Connor, Heather Gilbertson, Alan Barclay, Rudi Bartl, Kate Marsh, Toni Irwin, David Jenkins, David Ludwig, Simin Liu, Ted Arnold, Warren Kidson, Bob Moses, Ian Caterson, and Stewart Truswell. Lastly, we thank our long-suffering partners, John Miller, Jonathan Powell, and Ruth Colagiuri, respectively, for all those nights and weekends when we were otherwise occupied.

Subject Index

Boldface page references indicate illustrations and graphs. <u>Underscored</u> references indicate boxed text and tables.

A

Abdominal fat, 319, 363
Acidity, 60, 69–70
ADD, 399
Adrenaline, 316
African food, <u>542–43</u>
Agricultural revolution, 5–6, 338
ALA, 88, 91, 177–178
Alcohol
   athletic performance and, 414–15
   burning, 18
   GI value of, 97–98
   in low-GI diet, 188
Alpha-linolenic acid (ALA), 88,
     91, 177–78
Amaranth, 483
American Diabetes Association,
     205
American Dietetic Association, 30
Amylase, 22
Amylopectin, 59, 64–66, **64**
Amylose, 59, 64–66, **64**
Apple juice, 196, 458, 505
Apples, 184, 196, <u>504–5</u>
Apricots, 196–97, <u>505–6</u>
Arabic food, <u>543–44</u>
Arrhythmia, 90
Arthritis, 91
Artificial sugar, 397, <u>536–37</u>
Asian food, <u>544–47</u>
Asian Indian food, <u>547–52</u>

Atherosclerosis, 371–72
Athletic performance
   alcohol and, 414–15
   bonking and, 407
   carbohydrate loading and,
     416–17
   diet questionnaire and,
     421–24
   glucose and, 407
   glycemic index and, 405–11
   glycogen replenishment and,
     415–16
   high-carb diet and, 406–7,
     417–18
   high-GI diet and, 412–16,
     418–21
   low-GI diet and, 407–12
   portions and, 415
   pre-event meal and, 411
   recovery and, 414
   training diet and, 416–17
Attention deficit disorder (ADD),
     399
Australian Aboriginal food,
     <u>552</u>
Average eaters
   high-carbohydrate diet for,
     39–40
   moderate-carbohydrate diet for,
     41–42
Avocados, 97

Recipe Index

About the Authors

Jennie Brand-Miller, PhD, is one of the world's leading authorities on carbohydrates and the glycemic index. Profesor of Nutrition at the University of Sydney and the President of the Nutrition Society of Australia, she has championed the glycemic index approach to nutrition for over two decades. In 2003 Brand-Miller was awarded Australia's prestigious ATSE Clunies Ross Award, for her commitment to advancing science and technology. She has written more than 200 research papers, including 60 on the glycemic index of foods. She is coauthor of all of the books in the New Glucose Revolution series, including the *New York Times* bestseller *The New Glucose Revolution.*

Thomas M.S. Wolever, MD, PhD, is Professor in the Department of Nutritional Sciences, University of Toronto, and a member of the Division of Endocrinology and Metabolism, St. Michael's Hospital, Toronto. He is a graduate of Oxford University (BA, MA, MB, BCh, MSc, and DM) in the United Kingdom. He received his PhD at the University of Toronto. Since 1980 his research has focused on the glycemic index of foods and the prevention of type 2 diabetes.

The co-author of most books in the Glucose Revolution series, he lives in Toronto, Canada.

Kaye Foster-Powell, BSc, MNutr & Diet, is an accredited dietitian-nutritionist in both public and private practice. A graduate of the University of Sydney, she has extensive experience in diabetes management and has researched practical applications of the glycemic index over the last ten years. With Jennie Brand-Miller, Foster-Powell is coauthor of all of the books in the New Glucose Revolution series, including the *New York Times* bestseller *The New Glucose Revolution*.

Stephen Colagiuri, MD, is the Director of the Diabetes Centre and Head of the Department of Endocrinology, Metabolism, and Diabetes at the Prince of Wales Hospital in Randwick, New South Wales. He graduated from the University of Sydney in 1970 and received his Fellowship of the Royal Australasian College of Physicians in 1977. He has a joint academic appointment at the University of New South Wales. He has more than 100 scientific papers to his name, many concerned with the importance of carbohydrates in the diet of people with diabetes, and is the co-author of most books in the Glucose Revolution series.